EXECUTIVE EXCELLENCE

Combine Leadership and Management
to Create and Deliver Value

NICOS TIMOTHEOU
KORALIA TIMOTHEOU

Foreword by Professor
ANDREW KAKABADSE

RETHINK PRESS

First published in Great Britain 2019
by Rethink Press Limited (www.rethinkpress.com)

This book may be purchased at volume discount for educational use. For information please email Rethink Press Ltd or the authors.

Cover image © Adobe Stock / Sashkin

Printed and bound by CPI Group (UK) Ltd, Croydon, CR0 4YY

PRAISE FOR *EXECUTIVE EXCELLENCE*

'In an ever so complex, demanding and highly competitive environment, such as that of executives in the twenty-first century, this book is very useful, as it presents valuable insights on topics such as management and leadership in a simple and understandable way. The reader–executives who wish to further develop their competences in the management as well as in the leadership field, will greatly appreciate it.

There's only a handful of books that dive into this specific subject matter giving applicable practices and advice on the development of organisational, management and leadership skills. The long experience of the authors renders this book an exceptionally interesting guide, a source of knowledge worth reading. After all, there's always room for improvement no matter what position one holds.'

Constantinos Petrides, Minister of the Interior, Republic of Cyprus

'The book remains true to its title: it's a guide for executive excellence. It is thoughtful and visionary but also useful! It should be required reading for all executives.'

Professor CL Max Nikias, President Emeritus, University of Southern California

'The writing of this book brings together the insights from successful practical experience in managing a complex organisation facing major challenges and a deep understanding of the findings of rigorous academic research, to address afresh the important question of why organisations succeed or fail. The analysis centres around the absolute necessity for the simultaneous presence of sound management techniques and strong leadership qualities. The result is an easily readable and well-documented narrative that should be extremely valuable to both practising and aspiring executives. At the personal level, the usefulness and practical relevance of this book comes as no surprise as I have benefitted from conversations with Nicos over many years, collaborated closely with him when we were both in office, and knew of the respect his telecommunications work commanded internationally.'

Dr Michael Sarris, Former World Bank Department Director,
Former Cyprus Finance Minister

'The essence of a Mini-MBA in Executive Excellence in just one volume!'

Nicos Peristianis, PhD, Founding President, University of Nicosia

'Nicos and Koralia Timotheou have written a comprehensive book on what it means to be a leader and a manager in a contemporary organisation. They argue that a good executive must be both and they offer a rich array of perspectives to guide executives on their road to success. In the choppy ocean of business literature, this book stands out as a trusty companion that outlines the multi-dimensional aspects and complementarity of these two key roles, from the cerebral high-level strategy, systems and organisational modelling to the hands-on operational processes that create value through people and their tools. It's the kind of book you want to have next to you for a very long time because you know you will often come back to it in your professional life.'

Dimis Michaelides, Speaking and Workshops on Leadership, Creativity and Innovation

'Nicos and Koralia's book provides an excellent read, at both theoretical and practical levels. It is divided into three parts, each one providing ample information on the role of leadership and management at the organisational level. In their own words, its purpose is to "enlighten our reader on what we consider to be the successful executive's world and job", its mission is to "deliver value to our readers so that they can develop further their competences and competencies in both management and leadership" and its vision is to "help our fellow executives and aspiring executives maximise the value the organisations create and deliver". They succeed: this is a complete, holistic aid for the modern executive to be able to lead and manage their organisation to success.'

Professor George Boustras, Dean of the School of Business Administration European University Cyprus

'Nicos Timotheou and Koralia Timotheou, besides being seasoned and experienced executives and consultants, retain the benefit of kinship and therefore absolute alignment of approach. Their experiences are contained in a book that is the outcome of exposure to complex and demanding strategic challenges at a high international level. The hot issue of leadership vs management, seen and analysed in a practical and expert way, addresses the major contemporary problem of the 'structure' of multi-functional, multi-skilled, forward-looking leaders. I found the book very usable and helpful, providing useful insights to contemporary leadership/management concerns. I believe you will enjoy it, too.'

Antonios Spanos, EFQM Excellence Ambassador, EU-approved Management and CSR Expert

'The book by Nicos and Koralia Timotheou tries and, I believe, succeeds in answering the key questions: what do successful executives do, how do they do it, and which skills do they develop and employ to do it? It is different in the sense that it merges what the authors were taught by experts and academics or found in their meta-research and, most importantly, what they have learnt in the real business world. It serves as a guide, or more like a reference book, and as a checklist of dos and don'ts. It is a book that the reader will need to keep handy and return to from time to time.'

Demetris Georgiades, BSc (Econ) LSE, ACA ICAEW,
Chairman of the Fiscal Council of the Republic of Cyprus

'The existing bibliography and current thinking have brought us before a false dilemma, management vs leadership, as if these two roles are mutually exclusive or even contradictory. And yet, in the excellent book by Nicos and Koralia Timotheou, *Executive Excellence – Combine Management and Leadership to Create and Deliver Value*, a great truth is clarified: that an executive, to be effective and efficient, should be skilled in both management and leadership. I consider this book an excellent guide that gives, in a practical and highly explanatory way, the directions for the processes, skills, talents, methods and practices that an executive is required to follow in order to excel at both roles.'

Odysseas Michaelides, PhD,
Auditor General, Republic of Cyprus

'The business world is growing ever more complicated and disruptive. Understanding it in-depth and keeping up with developments, comprehending your organisation, its environment, its people, strengths and weaknesses, following internal and external pressures, improving its productivity, enhancing its innovation capability, improving its culture and executing its mission and vision puts a tremendous strain on its executives at all levels – especially those who strive for management, leadership and business excellence. They can now draw unparalleled guidance from the present comprehensive all-embracing executive's bible which Timotheou and Timotheou offer us, drawing from their widely acclaimed successful careers and meta-research.'

Angelos Gregoriades, Chairman KPMG (Cyprus) Ltd

'Reviewing this book was both a challenge and a pleasure. I found it in-depth yet simple and analytical yet practical. The authors, drawing from their many years of experience, mentor through the pages of the book the aspiring executive on how to develop and improve.

At the same time, they help the seasoned executive refocus on the important aspects of making an organisation better. They describe in an in-depth yet simple way, how to manage the organisation's value chain developing value for the customer and how to lead its people delivering better results. They analyse and explain in detail each business subprocess without losing focus on the big picture. The book achieves the distinction of being a comprehensive 'manual' on how the new executive can become a great leader, and how a seasoned leader can maintain and even improve their edge at the helm of the organisation.'

Christopher Christodoulides, Director of Administration and Finance, Open University of Cyprus

'I have had the privilege to collaborate with Nicos Timotheou firstly as my client in 2004 and subsequently as an industry expert and a mentor. Nicos is clearly one of the most influential and visionary leaders and CEOs in Cyprus. During his tenure in Cyprus Telecoms (firstly as the CIO and subsequently as the CEO), he truly re-engineered and reformed the organisation with great vision and passion. The book contains the gist of the practice and experience he acquired during his long and successful career. It is a very useful and comprehensive resource for the young, the seasoned, and the aspiring executive aiming for executive excellence. Enjoy!'

Nikos Angelopoulos, BSc, MSc, MBA, Group CIO, MTN, Johannesburg, SA

'This book provides a comprehensive look at the world of a successful business executive. The authors meticulously synthesise a great magnitude of existing literature and skilfully complement that knowledge with their own personal experience. Their effort is a fresh perspective in the never-ending debate of managers versus leaders where they posit that a successful executive must perform both management and leadership activities in a complementary fashion. The book can act as a primer for current executives and as a guide for aspiring ones and I would definitely recommend it as a reading in my strategic management courses.'

**Dr Paris Cleanthous, Director of MBA and MPSM programmes,
Associate Professor of Marketing and Strategy,
Cyprus International Institute of Management (CIIM)**

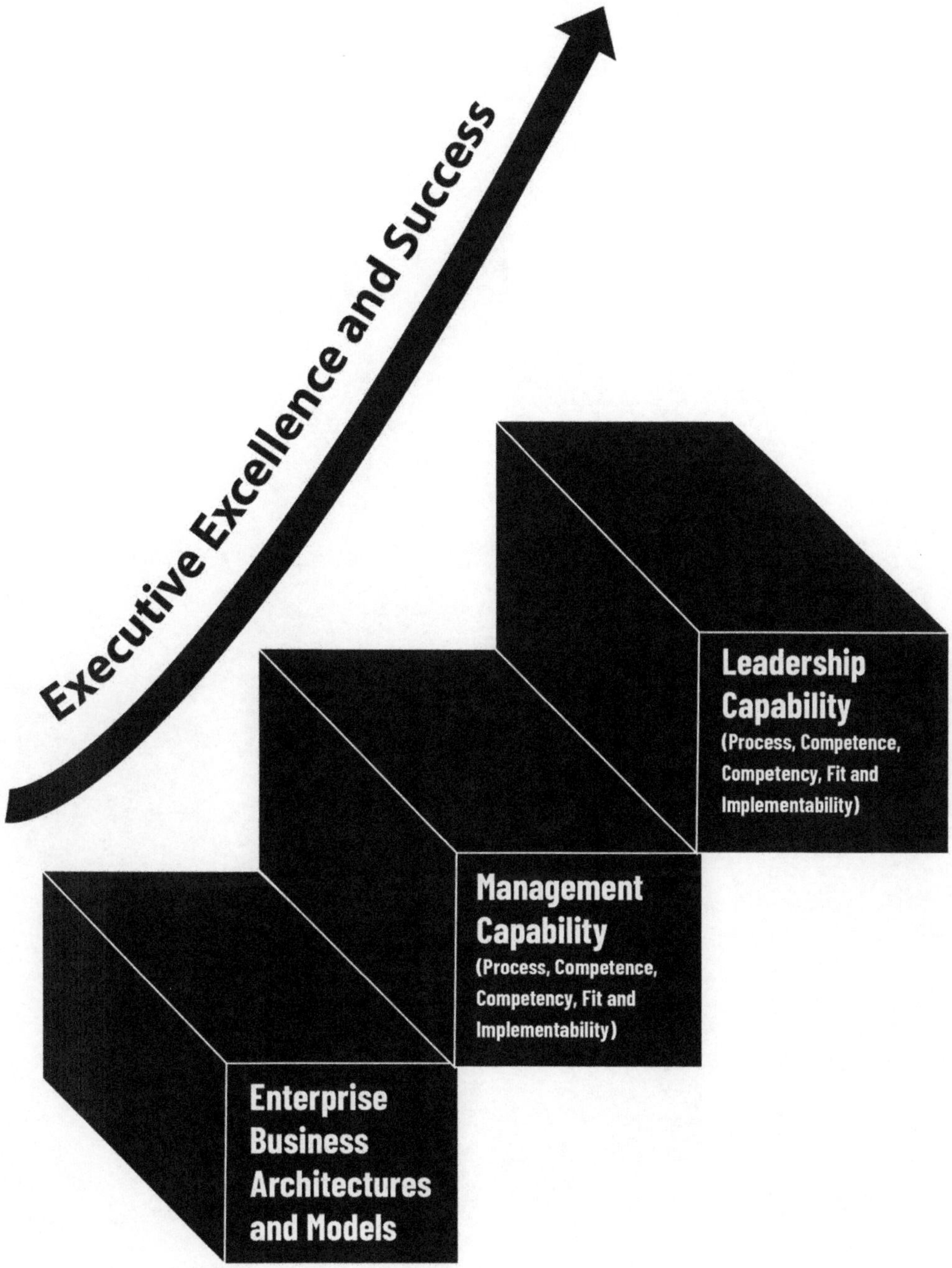

Executive Excellence and Success
Leadership Capability
(Process, Competence, Competency, Fit and Implementability)
Management Capability
(Process, Competence, Competency, Fit and Implementability)
Enterprise Business Architectures and Models

Dedicated to Despina, Eleftheria and Irini, three young ladies who aspire to change the world.

CONTENTS

LIST OF FIGURES AND TABLES

FOREWORD

Some of the best business books are the result of the authors' experience. Why? Because what is captured is real and the lessons learnt strike such a clear chord. This book is no exception.

The authors, Nicos and Koralia Timotheou, are father and daughter, and both engineers; Nicos an electrical and mechanical engineer and Koralia a civil and environmental engineer. Both are extraordinarily successful, with Nicos having been the CEO of Cyprus Telecom and Koralia an international management consultant.

Both have channelled their experiences and conclusions into this most remarkable text which, unusually, explains how to deliver value through both large systems thinking and the application of digital technology. Few publications can boast such an accomplishment.

Two core questions are at the heart of this book:

- Why is there such a high rate of executive failure?
- Why do so many organisations, private, public and state-owned companies, governments, and NGOs fail to the detriment of their stakeholders, owners, investors, creditors, employees, partners, suppliers, communities and the economy at large?

Nicos and Koralia's long experience with numerous entities, corroborated by their extensive meta-research, has led them to conclude that, for an executive to be successful, they must satisfy all of the following criteria:

- In-depth comprehension of how an organisation is, or must be, designed and constructed and how it operates as a 'holarchical' system – ie as a system of semi-autonomous subsystems
- Know what the management process comprises and have knowledge of, and possess, competence needed to execute it productively (effectively, efficiently and competitively)
- Be realistic about the leadership process and have the capability and competency, personal traits, qualities and characteristics needed to exercise it productively (effectively, efficiently and competitively)
- Have the capability and willingness to deliver the best possible value to shareholders and stakeholders through a realistic and down to earth ethical and philosophical approach
- Both as manager and as leader, continue to learn and develop

This truly is an outstanding book because it achieves what few others have: it conceives, in a holistic way, the contemporary executive's world; identifies and comprehends all 'executive' processes and how they are executed; identifies and develops the successful executive's capabilities and competencies; and brings all this together in a manner that makes eminent sense.

Nicos and Koralia strongly argue that a successful executive is one who practises both management and leadership in a complementary way, within a well-structured organisational system. They equally emphasise that the successful executive can learn the necessary management and leadership processes.

Let us take a look at this text in more detail.

Part I presents a high-level holistic picture of what a modern organisation is and how it operates.

Chapter One outlines contemporary complex organisational systems: their diverse enablers, assets, resources, stakeholders and results; their environments; their operation; and their dynamics.

In Chapter Two, the key theme is that business success is equal to the delivery of value. Nicos and Koralia emphasise the building of meaningful business models, managing value streams and effectively executing the processes which make up the various value streams.

Chapter Three outlines the various enterprise business architectures, as a dynamic coherent system.

In Chapter Four, Nicos and Koralia present the most common and significant generic business subprocesses, from culture and governance to risk, and from business continuity to performance and process management.

That is the organisation. Next, Part II highlights how successful executives manage their enterprise effectively and efficiently by leading their people to create and deliver extraordinary value in a holarchical and sustainable way.

Chapter Five exposes, in detail, the management process and the contemporary management and leadership philosophies that differentiate the successful executive.

Chapter Six highlights how leadership is exercised, emphasising an emergent best practice based on extensive research from thousands of organisations and executives.

Chapter Seven brings together the essential ideas of all previous chapters by comparing the executive to an orchestra director/conductor, in a lucid simile.

Lastly, in Part III, Chapter Eight, the authors pinpoint the competencies of successful executives.

What is particularly helpful for the reader is that each chapter finishes with key questions concerning performance and practice. This book is all-encompassing, comprehensive yet detailed to the point of being applicable and distinctly practical. What can one say, other than this is a 'must-read' book. This is the book for 2019.

DR ANDREW KAKABADSE

Professor of Governance and Strategic Leadership, Henley Business School and Emeritus Professor, Cranfield School of Management, UK

Andrew holds a number of international Visiting Professorships and Fellowships and has published 40 books (the most recent being *The Success Formula: How Smart Leaders Deliver Outstanding Value* (2015)), over 230 articles, and 18 monographs.

Andrew has been ranked in the 2011 and 2013 Thinkers50, the list of the world's top fifty business thinkers.

www.kakabadse.com

INTRODUCTION

Successful executives comprehend profoundly their business sector, their organisation and human nature. They execute effectively and efficiently, in a seamless complementary way, the management and the leadership processes and the organisation's plans and projects, creating and delivering value to the satisfaction of all stakeholders.

Organisational success

Extensive international research[1] and our own experiences have shown that success in for-profit, not-for-profit, and state-owned organisations or government services is equal to the creation and delivery of value to their stakeholders – *all* of their stakeholders, at least in the long run. Failure of an organisation means that it has not succeeded in satisfying some or all of its stakeholders, even if it was able to create some value and tried (unsuccessfully) to deliver it in a sustainable way. Failure will inevitably lead to the demise of the organisation. In many cases, it even causes the destruction of value for some or all of its stakeholders.

The causes of failure are diverse, though they usually have the same origin. Many organisations do not succeed because their executives fail on both the personal and collective levels.

Research carried out by distinguished academics and specialised institutions[2] shows that many boards of directors, executive committees, board members and executives at all hierarchical levels exhibit serious weaknesses.

Our own meta-research and experience show that the majority of executives are judged as good enough managers and not good enough leaders, or as good enough

1 Kakabadse A. (2015) *The Success Formula – How Smart Leaders Deliver Outstanding Value.*

2 www.heidrick.com/Knowledge-Center/Publication/European-Corporate-Governance-Report-2014-Towards-Dynamic-Governance

leaders and not good enough managers. The likelihood of either type being deemed successful executives, especially in the long run, is minimal. Even worse, quite a few are evaluated as neither good enough managers nor good enough leaders.

It is a sad reality that there are many and severe problems in the upper echelons of a significant percentage of organisations of all kinds, all over the world. This is so even though the incumbents of board and executive positions attend academic and professional courses and seminars on administration, management and leadership offered by thousands of academic and professional institutions, and study specialised books on management and leadership authored by renowned academics and executives.

Like many other academic and professional researchers, we have been puzzled, for a long time, by the legitimate question of the reasons for this widespread problem, which results in the destruction of collective and personal value to the detriment of wealth, health and happiness.

To address this issue, one can break it down to a few basic questions:

- Who are the contemporary executives?
- Which executives are considered successful?
- Are successful executives good managers?
- Are successful executives good leaders?
- What are the activities of the successful executive?
- What competencies (personal qualities, traits and personality characteristics) and competences (knowhow and implementable knowledge) do successful executives possess?
- Are successful executives born, or can they be developed?
- What is the philosophy of the forward-looking executive?

Based on our long experience and having carried out extensive meta-research, we concluded that while there is a large body of literature dealing with each of the above questions in isolation, to our knowledge there is none that holistically addresses all of them. We are, therefore, offering our own humble contribution by writing the present guide.

The executive and the executive process

We considered the above fundamental questions, and grouped and paraphrased them into the following key questions that we strive to answer in this book:

1. What do contemporary executives face? What is their organisational world?
2. What process (ie activities and tasks) do executives perform for the productive operation of the organisation, or any value stream, project or team they head?
3. What are the competences and the competencies of the successful executive?
4. Can the executive process be broken down into a management process and a leadership process?
5. Are leadership and management two faces of the same coin? Are they completely different in essence and nature? Do they overlap?
6. In other words, is the successful executive a leader, a manager, or both?

Leader versus manager

We have reached four main conclusions:

1. Management and leadership are different, though intertwined.
2. Certain leadership activities and certain management activities are so different and distinct that they are executed separately. Others, however, are similar and complementary and can be executed either independently or in combination, while certain others are inseparable by nature.
3. All executives perform management and leadership activities to some extent at certain times. What determines whether they are successful in this is whether:
   - they understand the organisation and its people
   - they have a deep understanding of what the management and the leadership processes entail
   - they have the competences and competencies required for the optimum execution of each management and leadership activity
   - they know when and how to execute them
   - they are willing and capable of managing and leading in the specific environment of the organisation they have been mandated to head
4. Successful executives perform management and leadership activities in a complementary manner, within the appropriate context, at the right time, to achieve the best result in creating and delivering value to all of the organisation's stakeholders.

We have also observed that the more competencies and competences executives possess and put to good use in executing the activities of both their managerial and leadership roles, and the more management and leadership activities they comprehend and exercise productively within their respective context, the higher the likelihood that they will succeed in the business world and beyond. We have further concluded that executive success can only be maintained when executives continue to develop their management and leadership competences and competencies through study, training, coaching, mentoring and especially by putting them to productive use.

> **Successful executives continue developing their management and leadership competences and competencies indefinitely.**

Our purpose, mission and vision

This book is not concerned with the academic or philosophical study of leadership versus management. We leave this near-impossible task to academics and other researchers.

Our purpose is to enlighten our reader on what we consider to be the world and job of successful executives, how they carry their role out successfully, and which competences and competencies they possess and develop.

Our mission is to deliver value to our readers so that they can develop further their own competences and competencies in both management and leadership and become (more) successful executives.

Our vision is to help our fellow executives and aspiring executives maximise the value created and delivered by the organisations they head, to achieve a higher level of happiness while making better use of our planet's resources and striving for sustainability.

Why write the book? What does it cover?

One might ask why we decided to devote time, effort, grey matter, energy and money to carrying out extensive meta-research and writing a book that must compete with hundreds of others addressing a similar, if not the same, subject, written by eponymous academic and professional authors.

Whereas management books teach how to be a good manager and leadership books how to become a good leader, our aim is to communicate to our readers how to be and become successful executives. So, our answer to the above question is twofold:

1. There are few books aiming at helping today's aspiring, young, and seasoned executives that:
    - › Conceive, holistically, the contemporary executive's world
    - › Identify and comprehend all 'executive' processes
    - › Identify and develop their executive competences and competencies
2. In this book, we prove that:
    - › It is impossible to be a successful executive if one is either a good leader and a bad manager, or a good manager and a bad leader.
    - › A successful executive is one who executes successfully the activities of both management and leadership in a complementary way, with a contemporary forward-looking philosophical approach, within a well-structured organisational system.
    - › Both the management and leadership processes of the successful executive can be learnt.
    - › The competences and competencies demanded for the optimum execution of the activities that make up the management and the leadership processes can be acquired and continuously developed.

Based on our conclusions and beliefs, this book is an exposition of the management and leadership processes, competences, competencies, and personal development process, presented in a way that the average executive can, we hope, understand, adopt and then implement. In doing so they will be able to create and deliver extraordinary value, delighting their organisation's stakeholders; continuously develop their own and their people's competencies and competences; and, improve their executive capability.

In this book we first present a high-level holistic picture of what a modern organisation is and how it operates. We then elaborate on how successful executives manage the organisation effectively and efficiently, and how they lead its people in creating and delivering extraordinary value in a 'holarchical' and sustainable way. Lastly, we identify the competencies of successful executives and outline the most important competences, besides the knowledge offered in this book.

We shall be using the term 'executive' to refer to the incumbent of any hierarchical post with the mandate of creating and delivering value by ensuring that the mission and vision of an organisation, or any permanent or temporary organisational entity, are achieved. We shall be using, in a qualitative manner, the term 'manager' to refer to the executive who performs the management process, and the term 'leader' to the executive who performs the leadership process. An executive may hold a hierarchical post, or head a project or team.

In light of our observation that the definitions of management and leadership are debated and lack unanimity, this book progresses based on the following assumptions:

- The two terms are distinct from each other but complementary in the sense that they both define processes that executives must perform productively (effectively, efficiently and to the prespecified quality of outcome and performance) to fulfil their mandate of realising the organisation's mission of creating and delivering value and, thus, satisfying stakeholders' needs.
- The term 'management' encompasses, in general terms, the planning, organisation, direction, coordination and control of the use of non-human resources (such as infrastructure, fixed assets, raw materials and consumables), processes, data, information and knowledge, and the execution of the activities of the human workforce – where 'direction' has the narrow meaning of issuing instructions and orders.
- The term 'leadership' defines, in broad terms, the navigation of people through their professional lives, their development, their growth, their performance, their motivation to work towards the success of the organisation and of themselves, and the production and delivery of value.

Besides striving to answer the above fundamental **what** questions, we endeavour also to answer the question of **how** successful executives execute their management and leadership processes and develop their competences and competencies.

To do this, we walk our reader through the corridors of what an organisation comprises and how it operates – or, rather, how it should be designed and function. We define and explain the key components of organisations and their interdependencies, and what management and leadership mean in terms of processes, ie activities and tasks, states of mind and skill-sets. We discuss how executives, in their roles as leaders and managers, can optimally allocate their time and effort to executing the appropriate (at any given time) management and leadership tasks, to be successful.

What we expose in this book is the sum of our long experience and meta-research. Throughout our business lives, we have attended hundreds of conferences, short courses and seminars, and studied extensive literature and research papers on management and leadership, comparing their findings and conclusions with our own experiences and observations, reaching our own conclusions that we share in this book. We believe in the power of sharing – sharing of experiences, practices and knowledge. Sharing is what drives individuals, organisations, societies and civilisations forward.

Structure of the book

The book is organised as eight chapters grouped into three parts and an epilogue, as shown in Figure 0.1.

As the necessary background and an essential aspect of an executive's competence, we present in **Part I** a high-level holistic picture of what a modern organisation is and how it operates: its complex organisational systems, business models, value streams, processes and other enablers. We then elaborate on the various enterprise business architectures and present the most common and significant generic business subprocesses, from culture and governance to risk and business continuity, performance and process management.

We then elaborate, in **Part II**, on how successful executives manage their organisation effectively and efficiently and lead its people in creating and delivering extraordinary value in a holarchical and sustainable way.

Lastly, in **Part III**, we present, in detail, the competencies of successful executives and outline certain essential competences in addition to the knowledge offered in the first two parts of the book.

We recommend that you, our reader, work through the chapters in succession as they are laid out. You can, however, read each part and each chapter in isolation. This is made possible for two reasons. On the one hand, you may have attended management courses or other studies or seminars and wish to dive directly into certain subjects that interest you without reading the previous chapters. On the other hand, once you have read the whole book, you may later like to return to certain subjects again.

Since each chapter has been written to stand, more or less, on its own, there is a certain level of repetition, linking the subject matter with concepts presented previously. We beg your forgiveness for the repetition and hope that it will contribute to a deeper understanding.

We hope that this book will serve as a guide to which you will repeatedly revert to remind yourself what executives do to be successful. Furthermore, we invite you to challenge what we expose and compare it with what your own experience reveals and what other authors describe. We provide an extensive bibliography, noting that not all authors agree fully with our views and recommendations.

To help you acquire a detailed overview of what we cover in this guide, we have included, at the end of the book, an extensive index.

Our wish

Our wish is that our guide will help you identify and fill any gaps you may have in the knowledge that you draw on in performing your dual executive role, in gradually developing your organisational, management and leadership competences and competencies, and in becoming a successful executive: that is, a good manager and a good leader, or a good leader and a good manager, depending on where you start from.

Carry on developing your executive competencies and competences.

Be successful. Create and deliver value. Delight your stakeholders.

Be happy!

Nicos Timotheou and Koralia Timotheou

January 2019

<table>
<tr><td colspan="5">Epilogue</td></tr>
<tr><td>PART III</td><td colspan="4">Chapter Eight – The Successful Executive's Competencies And Competences</td></tr>
<tr><td rowspan="3">PART II</td><td colspan="4">Chapter Seven – The Executive: Manager Or Leader?</td></tr>
<tr><td colspan="4">Chapter Six – Leading The Organisation In Creating And Delivering Value</td></tr>
<tr><td colspan="4">Chapter Five – Managing The Organisation In Executing Its Mission And Vision</td></tr>
<tr><td rowspan="11">PART I</td><td colspan="4">Chapter Four – Generic Business Subprocesses</td></tr>
<tr><td colspan="4">Chapter Three – Organisational Architectures And Business Process Management</td></tr>
<tr><td rowspan="7">The Organisation's Structures</td><td>People architectures</td><td rowspan="7">The Organisation's Enablers</td><td>Partners, suppliers, sellers</td></tr>
<tr><td>Automation architectures</td><td>Organisation's people</td></tr>
<tr><td>Infrastructure architectures</td><td>Non-human assets</td></tr>
<tr><td>Process–data architectures</td><td>Processes, data, information and knowledge</td></tr>
<tr><td>Value streams</td><td>Value streams</td></tr>
<tr><td>Value cycle</td><td>Values, governance and culture</td></tr>
<tr><td>Purpose–values–mission</td><td>Leadership</td></tr>
<tr><td colspan="4">Chapter Two – The Business Model</td></tr>
<tr><td colspan="4">Chapter One – The Executive's World</td></tr>
<tr><td colspan="5">Introduction</td></tr>
</table>

Figure 0.1: The book structure

PART I
THE ORGANISATION

CHAPTER ONE

THE EXECUTIVE'S WORLD

Twenty-first-century organisations are complex. Successful executives devote time and energy to acquiring a profound understanding of their organisation, its purpose, mission, vision, enablers, stakeholders, and the value that is expected to be provided. They manage its enablers and lead its people in creating and delivering the right value to the right stakeholders.

The executive's world in the twenty-first century is vast, unbelievably complex, highly competitive and, as a result, extremely demanding.

Contemporary executives are called upon to act as heads of organisations that must operate as holistically structured systems made up of holarchical enablers, with the sole purpose of creating and delivering diverse value to a broad spectrum of stakeholders.

Their job is complex, with elements such as:

- Identifying the various groups of stakeholders and the value that they demand, envision, expect, or are willing to receive and pay for, directly or directly
- Identifying the value streams that can create and deliver value to the satisfaction of stakeholders
- Identifying conflicts of interest between the various groups of stakeholders, or even within a specific group of stakeholders, and provide solutions that can satisfy all
- Identifying which enablers – values, governance rules, policies, assets, people, partners, suppliers, processes, information, knowledge, etc – make up the various value streams to create and deliver the specified value to the stakeholders, and which capacity they can put to productive work

- Organising the various enablers in a system that can create and deliver the specified value in an optimal way
- Identifying the competition the organisation will face and their capabilities
- Designing the organisation by considering parameters such as:
  - The quantity of value that stakeholders can consume
  - The golden mean of potentially contradicting value that will satisfy all different stakeholder groups within the existing or potential competitive environment
  - The available assets for creating and delivering the specified value within the legal, financial, demographic and geographic environment the organisation operates/will operate in
- Planning and building the organisation
- Translating the specified value to be created and delivered in the short term to the organisation's mission and designing its execution in detail
- Translating the value the various stakeholder groups wish to receive in the foreseeable future into the organisation's vision and designing the strategic projects that will realise it
- Recognising that executives, operatives (employees), customers, partners, suppliers, sellers and competitors are human beings with biases, different attitudes, preferences and priorities; that they are not 'econs'[1] and should not be treated as such; remembering that one size does not fit all when it comes to human interactions, needs and desires
- Envisaging, at an early stage, the future effects of new technology on all aspects of the organisation and its sector and taking all necessary action at the right time (neither too early nor too late)
- Recognising the resource limitations of the organisation, assessing the impact of changes in the external environment over the medium to long term, planning ahead, and being able to address effectively all possible contingencies
- Formulating, in detail, the short-term plans and budgets that will be used to execute the mission and the short-term strategic projects

---

1 Thaler R. H. and Sunstein Cass R. (2008) *Nudge: Improving Decisions About Health, Wealth, and Happiness.* The authors differentiate 'Econs' from 'Humans'. The former are the efficient calculators imagined in economic theory, able to weigh multiple options, forecast all the consequences of each and choose rationally. The latter are ordinary people, who fall well short of *homo economicus*. Humans operate according to rules of thumb that often lead them astray. They are too prone to generalise, biased in favour of the status quo, and more focused on avoiding loss than making gains, among other shortcomings. Therefore, they often fail to manage their personal affairs to the best advantage.

- Executing the plans, monitoring the actual results, identifying deviations, analysing their causes, taking corrective actions, and modifying plans and budgets as dictated by evolving internal and external parameters

Executives carry out their job both through their own work and through their people. They need to have the competences (knowhow) and competencies (personal qualities) to both carry out, themselves, numerous diverse activities and ensure that their people perform various similar and different activities. They need to manage themselves and manage and lead all other enablers of the organisation in creating and delivering value to its stakeholders.

We present the executive's world in **Part I**, which commences with the current chapter, before guiding our readers, in detail, in **Part II**, through the executive's management and leadership processes and, lastly, exposing them, in **Part III**, to the competencies and competences required to successfully execute these processes.

Stakeholders: their needs, value creation and delivery

What matters in life, be that our private or our professional life?

Most people will reply spontaneously: 'results'.

As individuals, we understand results in our private life in various ways. It could be the fulfilment of aspirations and dreams. Or simply happiness, whatever that means to the individual. Or, in a broader sense, the happiness of our people, meaning our family, friends, tribe members, compatriots, and fellow citizens of the world, as well as ourselves.

As executives of our organisations, we understand results to mean performance, ie as the outcome of our work, which should satisfy the stakeholders involved. We are their agents and, consequently, the stewards of their stake – their interest – in the organisation.

Being responsible professionals, incumbent executives think, or should think, that what matters is the satisfaction of the stakeholders or, in other words, the satisfaction of the stakeholders' needs. Being stakeholders themselves, this includes the executives' own satisfaction, ideally, to the level of self-actualisation.

Who are these stakeholders? What are their needs?

Executives of all kinds of organisations are asked to define their stakeholders and those stakeholders' needs, and then exert their best efforts to satisfying them. To do so, executives need not only to identify the various stakeholders' needs but also how these needs relate to each other, whether they are complementary or contradictory, and where the golden mean lies. In business terms, executives need to determine what value must be created and delivered to satisfy the identified needs.

Thus, executives are deemed successful when they create and deliver value to all stakeholder groups: shareholders, owners, investors, lenders, employees, suppliers, partners, customers, students, patients and the communities that are, directly or indirectly, associated with the organisation. Value needs to be delivered to the stakelolders' satisfaction, as they themselves perceive and express it, and not as it is perceived by the executives alone.

Where the different stakeholders' needs are in conflict, executives are obliged to convince all affected groups that what they strive to achieve is in the best interests of everybody – in the short or, at least, the medium term, and certainly in the long term.

Research shows that the only way they can achieve this almost impossible goal is to act based on a consistent set of values, a code of business ethics adopted by the majority – though ideally all – of the organisation's stakeholders.

We distinguish two distinct types of value: the value produced and delivered by the organisation to its stakeholders, usually incremental improvement on the stakeholders' assets, work, quality of life, or happiness; and the value(s) lived by, in other words the principles (mostly ethical) that the organisation's people as individuals, and the organisation as a communal entity, abide by.

Organisational or business modelling

To satisfy stakeholder needs, value needs to be created and delivered through the operations of an organisation. The same principles apply to the individual professional. The organisation can be any kind of legal entity: a private company, a public corporation, a state-owned entity, a non-governmental organisation, a partnership, an association, a government department, agency, or even a professional practice.

We shall be using the term 'organisation' to refer to any (legal) structure aiming at creating and delivering value.

The organisation

It is important to note that any organisation is a living and dynamic structure with a purpose to its existence, with people, resources, assets, consumables and structured activities organised in value streams[2] to create and deliver value to all its stakeholders. It may depend on the supply of raw and semi-finished goods, data, information, knowledge and services, as well as marketing, sales and customer support services. Being dynamic, its constituent parts may change at any time.

The purpose

An organisation is established for a specific purpose: its *raison d'être*, its reason for existence. This can be anything and may range from preventing and alleviating human suffering in the face of emergencies by mobilising the power of volunteers and the generosity of donors (for example, International Federation of Red Cross), to meeting people's everyday needs for nutrition, hygiene and personal care via brands that help people feel good, look good and get more out of life (for example, Unilever). Its purpose may be to meet the needs of other organisations and professionals to help them realise their own purpose, such as consultancy firms; or, to maximise the return on invested or saved capital, such as investment advisors.

The organisation's purpose specifies the value to be created and delivered and may define the founding stakeholders as well as other related groups of stakeholders. It may specify the value that is offered in a unique way or in a general one, to be revised from time to time depending on legal, market, technological and other conditions.

The mission

The owners and/or the executive management of the organisation define, from time to time, how the organisation will realise its purpose by formulating the organisation's mission.

EXAMPLES

- A world-class university: 'Imperial College embodies and delivers world-class scholarship, education and research in science, engineering, medicine and business, with usually articular regard to their application in industry, commerce and healthcare. We foster multidisciplinary working internally and collaborate widely externally.'[3]

2 Martin J. (2006) *The Meaning of the 21st Century: A Vital Blueprint for Ensuring Our Future.*
3 www.imperial.ac.uk/strategy/developing-this-strategy/strategy2014/mission

- Furniture maker, Natuzzi: 'Natuzzi combines design, function, materials and colours to create harmony in spaces.'[4]
- Stora Enso, probably the oldest existing company in the world: '"Do Good for the People and the Planet" is the purpose that guides us in all that we do: producing and selling our renewable products, buying trees from local forest owners, selling electricity generated at our mills or managing our logistics on a global scale.'[5]
- Our boutique consultancy firm NAN Strategic Change Consultants: 'We help our customers improve their operations, their strategy, their productivity, their quality, their profitability and their sustainability by offering value-for-money effective consultancy and related services always respecting our and their values.'[6]

The organisation's mission dictates its operation and, partially or wholly, the value to be created and delivered to the stakeholders. Once the value that is required to satisfy the stakeholders' needs has been defined, in terms of tangible and intangible goods, services with their specific characteristics, information, knowledge or assets, executives must ensure that it is created and delivered to the respective stakeholders at the specified quality.

The business model

To formulate business plans, executives need to fully understand the **business model** that will create and deliver the value. In the case of a start-up, the executives must formulate, define and fully understand the business model. In this way, they will be able to explain it clearly to the various groups of stakeholders.

To realise the organisation's mission, executives formulate short to medium-term development and operation plans and execute them by **leading** the organisation's people and **managing** the necessary and available assets, resources and partnerships.

They begin by estimating the volume of stakeholders' needs, including the market demand, and the volume of the products, services and money that the organisation will create and deliver over time depending on the available assets and enablers, and the competition.

4 www.natuzzigroup.com
5 www.storaenso.com/en/about-stora-enso/our-purpose-and-values; www.storaenso.com/en/newsroom/news/2015/12/business-with-a-purpose
6 http://strategic-change-consultants.com/index.php/who-we-are/our-mission

The executive needs to depict, in detail, the business model as **a value-adding model**, ie as value streams, or value-adding process chains, with the related assets and resources.

Further, the executive will describe the business model as a **workflow** that shows the core business processes, which will be using various resources and assets to turn raw and semi-finished materials and services, as well as information and knowledge, into finished goods, assets, services, information or knowledge, to deliver them to the various stakeholders and to service the customers and other recipients of value. In parallel, all necessary **support, staff, and executive processes** must be defined.

The **business processes** comprise the business mechanism that creates and delivers value to the stakeholders. To operate optimally, this mechanism must be thoroughly defined and understood. This can only be possible if all business processes and their interdependencies are fully defined and catalogued in a **process map**.

Processes utilise materials, services, information and knowledge, described by **business data**. The output of each process serves either as the input to another process or, finally, as the finished product, asset, service, information or knowledge to be delivered to stakeholders, also described by data. Hence, to describe thoroughly the business mechanism, the executive must have all business process-related data wholly defined and catalogued.

Each business process is governed by **rules and regulations**, imposed either internally by the organisation or externally by the legal and market environment. These rules and regulations also need to be defined in business terms and catalogued.

In addition, to be able to plan and monitor the operation of each and every process and the organisation as a whole, suitable indicators are required for each process, which again need to be fully and clearly defined and catalogued. These indicators describe the various quantitative and qualitative characteristics of the enablers, the inputs, and the outputs. Those indicating the productivity (ie effectiveness, efficiency and quality) of the enablers are usually called performance indicators, the most significant of which are known as **key performance indicators (KPIs)**.

The business information is organised in an **entity relationship diagram (ERD)**. The interaction between business processes and information is the foundation for automating the business processes so that they can be optimally executed by machines (computers, dedicated machines and robots) and/or by human beings, the people of the organisation and its partners, suppliers or sellers.

Furthermore, in defining each business process to be executed by people, executives need to specify the **competences** and **competencies** that will enable its optimal execution, ie the ideal person to play the role(s) required for the optimal performance of each process. Here, competences refer to relevant knowhow, dexterity and experience, while competencies comprise the required personality traits, personal qualities or characteristics.

By completing the above, successful executives build a comprehensive blueprint of the business model of the organisation they are appointed to head, enabling it to create and deliver the value expected – and demanded –by the organisation's stakeholders.

In addition, executives need to create a blueprint for the various non-human enablers required by each process. Lastly, they must also define and catalogue the information and processes related to the organisation's suppliers, partners, sellers and customers, formulating a blueprint for what is called the **extended enterprise**, since the livelihood of the organisation depends on the performance of these parties.

Successful executives recognise that the necessity of outsourcing non-core business processes renders the need for a blueprint of the extended enterprise of paramount importance for the successful operation of the organisation.

Business planning for success

Having a thorough view of the business mechanism, the executive can proceed with planning its construction and operation in terms of the quantity, quality, location, layout, interrelations and other characteristics of the assets and resources that will be required for creating and delivering the specified value to the stakeholders.

In doing so, the executive must formulate and maintain a detailed business plan specifying capital expenditures, operational expenses and revenue, required assets in terms of money, land, buildings and other enablers, the input resources and partnerships needed and, above all, the required staff – the organisation's people.

With regard to non-human assets and resources, one could claim that planning, budgeting and monitoring are mechanistic/algorithmic management activities and can, at least in theory, be executed by artificial intelligence (ie software and machines).

> **When it comes to people, however, things are quite different. Humans are complex and often unpredictable.**
>
> **They have competences and competencies that are required for the execution of the processes they are assigned, but they also have personal needs, peculiarities, circumstances, motivators and demotivators. They have feelings.**
>
> **Humans need to be led, in any social structure, to enable them to contribute to the realisation of any common mission.**
>
> **Leading people is very different from managing people in the sense of executing the management processes, as we will go on to explain.**

Vision, strategic planning, and visioning

The purpose of an organisation is, as a rule, perpetual, or at least long-lasting. Therefore, in executing the organisation's mission, executives must ensure that the mission and, in turn, the value created and delivered, remain current. To this end, they must formulate a **vision** for the mid to long-term future: where they envision the organisation to be at a specified future point in time.

To realise the organisation's vision, executives carry out a process of **strategic planning**. They formulate strategic projects aimed at modifying, or even replacing, the created and delivered value to satisfy changing stakeholder needs in view of market, technological, geopolitical, and cultural changes. In this way, the organisation's mission evolves. In rare cases, it may even be replaced by a completely different mission. Strategic planning may aim at modifying or replacing enablers or business models while continuing to produce and deliver the same value. This process needs to be carried out continually and be adjusted or even replaced to keep the mission current and in line with the ever-changing internal and external environments.

Striving for continuous improvement and innovation, executives inspire the organisation's people through **visioning**. As we will see in Chapter Six, the activities involved in conceiving the organisation's vision and then realising it via strategic planning are only parts of the larger process of visioning.

Strategic planning is usually carried out by a small group of the organisation's executives and specialists, and strategic projects are executed by a small percentage of the organisation's people, or even by third parties. Stategic planning may be deemed a subprocess belonging to both the leadership process (in leading the people to innovate and conceive a bold vision and specific strategic projects that will realise it) and the management process (in managing the projects using suitable planning techniques and tools). Visioning, however, is a leadership activity and is organisation-wide, since it should lead to both short and long-term innovation and improvements that encompass the whole organisation.

EXAMPLE

Through its vision statement, Google aspires 'To develop a perfect search engine,' whereas BMW wants 'To become the most successful premium manufacturer in the car industry.'

Visioning and formulating – revising and realising the organisation's vision and updating, in essence, its mission – aims at achieving sustainability.

EXAMPLE

Stora Enso: 'Sustainability[7] at Stora Enso is divided into nine focus areas, with human rights integrated in all of them. Stakeholder relations and materiality guide our sustainability work. Our aim is to ensure a positive total contribution to society.'

The organisational structure

Having defined the business processes and data and formulated the business plan for the mid-term horizon, it is possible to estimate the workload required by the various roles that will execute the business processes or parts thereof, be those production, delivery and servicing, support, staff, or executive processes.

At this point, all the necessary information is available for defining the organisational posts required for the optimal execution of the business processes, and for estimating the required number of people for each post.

7 www.storaenso.com/en/sustainability/;
www.storaenso.com/en/sustainability/sustainability-strategy-and-governance

Depending on these numbers, the nature and complexity of the processes, and the geographical dispersion of production, delivery and customer servicing, the number of executive (or managerial) posts needed can be estimated and an organisational chart drawn.

Executive posts are those required for:

- **Managing** the processes and the non-human assets and resources for organising, directing, coordinating and controlling the workforce, and for formulating business plans

and

- **Leading** the people in executing processes, plans and projects

It should be noted that, in the past, executive or managerial posts demanded that the incumbents had solely managerial and leadership duties, as we discuss and describe later in this book. This is no longer true. Nowadays, practically all such posts demand the execution of production, support or staff activities in addition to leadership and management.

Execution

Once the business plan has been formulated, executives proceed with implementation. In doing so, they manage and lead. Management and leadership activities may be executed simultaneously, ie concurrently, or separately, as needed and depending on their nature. They may be understood by the executive as distinct processes, or they may not. In any case, in presenting and discussing them in this book, we consider them separately, though cross-references are made where needed.

Let us now look briefly at what we understand so far about how the best executives create and deliver outstanding value.

Managing: the management process

In practice, all organisations comprise both human and non-human assets. They process non-human materials, assets, services, data, information and knowledge to produce goods, assets, services, information and knowledge, which are delivered to stakeholders with the aim of adding value, ie satisfying their needs. In a similar way, some organisations process humans to produce 'enhanced' humans in the sense of enriching their competences and/or competencies, for example schools, universities, training centres, etc, or in the sense of curing or rehabilitating them, for example hospitals and treatment centres, or even in the sense of correcting them, for example, prisons. Other organisations create and deliver abstract services, such as security and public safety (for example the police, the security services, and the army).

In an ideally designed and constructed organisation with well-designed and highly automated processes, one could claim that what is needed to create and deliver the specified and expected value is to manage the organisation's assets and resources in such a way that optimal performance is achieved, and that this management process could be automated, or even relegated to machines with artificial intelligence.

In scientific management theory and practice, the management process is decomposed into planning, organising, staffing, direction, coordination, reporting, and budgeting: POSDCORB.[8] Subsequent research has shown that management is inadequate for achieving extraordinary success and, in particular, sustainability. It must be complemented with leadership. The differences between the two will be made clear in Part II, Chapters Five, Six and Seven.

Leading: the leadership process

Creating value for all stakeholders and achieving outstanding results cannot be accomplished solely by applying the elements of scientific management.

> **Successful executives achieve outstanding success by leading the people of their organisation in devoting their best selves, exerting their best efforts, putting to productive use their competences and competencies, and continuously improving themselves with the aim of realising the organisation's mission and vision.**

They employ the best elements of leadership and execute effectively many, if not all, of the leadership activities presented briefly in the next paragraphs, and more extensively in Chapter Six.

8 This is what Nicos was taught in the early 1970s when studying Production Management at the National Technical University of Athens, Greece (1970/71) and, later, on a postgraduate course leading to a Scientific Industrial Management Diploma, Nicosia, Cyprus (1973/75). Refer to Afterword (pp. 373–375).

Perspectives on management and leadership

As we have mentioned above, the fundamental elements of management are planning, organising, staffing, direction, coordination, reporting and budgeting.

One could claim that leadership is the interpretation of the direction and coordination elements of management and, hence, that leadership is merely an aspect of management. As we shall see, however, leadership is much broader and stands on its own, though it has elements that are closely associated with, or even overlapping with, elements of management. We should note that in this book, direction and coordination have very narrow meanings and are understood as the issuing of written and oral instructions, orders and guidelines for the execution of plans.

Leadership can be considered from various perspectives, according to Matthew and Gilbert Fairholm,[9] at least in terms of how it has been researched, described and understood over time. In addition, leadership can be analysed into a number of subprocesses, or elements, according to the research of Andrew Kakabadse.[10]

Let us first take a brief look at the different perspectives.

Scientific Management

The first perspective on what many academics and researchers understand to be management is called Scientific Management or Taylorism, after its founder, Frederick Winslow Taylor. According to this perspective, the main elements of management are to:

- Ensure efficient use of resources so that group activity is controlled and predictable
- Ensure verifiably optimal productivity and resource allocation
- Measure, appraise and reward individual performance
- Organise (including such activities as budgeting and staffing)
- Plan, coordinate, monitor and report
- Incentivise
- Direct, monitor, and control

9 Fairholm M. and G. (2009) *Understanding Leadership Perspectives: Theoretical and Practical Approaches.*
10 Kakabadse A. (2015) *The Success Formula – How Smart Leaders Deliver Outstanding Value.*

These remain valid today. When applied to non-human enablers, they can be considered as mechanistic, or even, algorithmic. They are still the basic elements of the job of executives; in other words, they are basic managerial tasks, activities or subprocesses. Today, they may be considered to represent the bulk of the managerial competences (knowhow) expected from a young and inexperienced executive and they are taught at most management schools and MBA courses.

Excellence Management

The Scientific Management movement caught on quickly and significantly increased organisational productivity, mainly in the United States and in Japan. Progressive executives and management gurus differentiated themselves by emphasising quality and excellence. They preached that the elements of Scientific Management could be enhanced through a continued focus on improvement of process performance, and on systematic problem-solving, with elements such as:

- Cultivating a continuous process improvement environment for increased productivity and service levels
- Encouraging the design and production of high-quality products, excellent services, and continuous innovation by transforming the environment and perceptions of the staff
- Encouraging continuous process improvement
- Engaging the organisation's people in defining and solving problems, introducing quality circles

What began as Quality Management led to the development of Excellence Management, which includes leadership elements such as:

- Listening actively
- Being accessible
- Managing by walking around
- Motivating staff and rewarding improvement and innovation

This new movement of managing quality and excellence introduced, for the first time, a cultural model based on values such as quality, excellence, cooperation in problem-solving, continuous improvement and rewarding proposals for improvement.

Values Leadership

The Excellence Management movement demonstrated to forward-looking executives and management teachers, trainers and consultants that basing people management on specific values yields better results and leads to improved performance. Thus, Values Leadership was born, with elements such as:

- Visioning
- Prioritising values
- Formulating and enforcing a value set
- Focusing communication around the vision
- Encouraging high organisational performance
- Encouraging the organisation's people to become self-led value and innovation creators working to shared values
- Empowering the individual employee to own the agreed goals and strive to accomplish them
- Training, coaching and mentoring
- Being authentic – acknowledging that people recognise the executive who means what they say, who lives the values and does not pretend

> **Leadership is based on values. Leadership can be thought of like a pyramid with successive levels of distinct activities, each one based on higher values. Our own experiences and meta-research show that effectively leading people belonging to a social structure requires a suitable glue. At its worst, this glue can be a force, as in forcefully applied direction. Living under such force makes people unhappy, reactionary and unwilling to exert their best efforts. At its best, the glue comprises common, shared values inspiring people to devote their best selves and exert their best efforts towards the common purpose. These are the human values postulated in the fourth century BC by Aristotle, and others later added and widely accepted, related to human rights and business excellence.**

EXAMPLES

Apple's[11] values:

- 'Accessibility, education, environment, inclusion and diversity, privacy, supplier responsibility.'

The UK National Health Service's[12] values include:

- 'Working together for patients; respect and dignity; commitment to quality of care; compassion; improving lives; everyone counts.'

Stora Enso[13] states:

- 'Our Values, "Lead" and "Do What's Right", are a natural part of our purpose. Our value "Lead" does not particularly refer to our top management or division management. It is more about setting the example, to lead in every aspect of our business and responsibility.'

Culture Leadership

Values Leadership showed that leading people based on a coherent value set could significantly improve performance; this led to a stronger leadership model based on systematically managing culture, focusing on trust rather than authority and hierarchy.

We remind the reader here that culture, in its scientific essence, comprises behaviour patterns shared by members of a community that rely on socially transmitted information.

Culture Leadership, also known as Tribal Leadership[14], involves elements such as:

- Creating and maintaining an organisational culture through visioning
- Prioritising common shared values and, consequently, common organisational behaviour
- Cultivating a shared culture based on trust by sharing governance and team-building
- Ensuring that the organisation's culture is conducive to mutual trust and unified collective action
- Measuring, appraising and rewarding performance

11 www.apple.com
12 www.hee.nhs.uk/about/our-values
13 www.storaenso.com/en/about-stora-enso/our-purpose-and-values
14 Logan D., King J. and Fischer-Wright H. (2008) *Tribal Leadership – Leveraging Natural Groups to Build a Thriving Organisation.*

> **Experience proves that 'culture-based leadership' can work wonders and that the level of its success depends on the set of common shared values and the quality of the relationships between individuals. The best results are accomplished when spiritual rapport is achieved between individuals who are liberated in the sense of continuous improvement through activities such as formulating and fostering a code of ethics based on common shared moral values; cultivating wholeness in a team context; inspiring subordinates through a stewardship and a service delivery paradigm and encouraging them to do and promote the same; and building a knowledge-based organisation encouraging continuous improvement of self, culture, service delivery, and innovation.**

Culture Leadership enhanced with spiritual rapport and direction can be seen as the ultimate perspective: Spiritual Leadership.

The leadership process analysed

Renowned leaders have practised the leadership process over aeons. These leaders have had inherent leadership capabilities as a personality competency. They learnt by studying the leaders under whom they served as apprentices or deputies, or were taught by wise philosophers (as Alexander the Great was by Aristotle). In the past, leadership was taught as a military skill and, circumstantially, as a political competency.

Until the last century, leadership had never been systematically analysed and synthesised so that it could be taught and then applied widely across various fields, from the military to politics, and in the running of state services or private and public organisations. Since the Industrial Revolution, and especially from the mid-nineteenth century, academics and consultants have carried out extensive research in the context of thousands of organisations and with tens of thousands of executives. They have not only extensively analysed both leadership and management but have also synthesised the two to identify learnable processes, competences and competencies, as we have seen briefly above and will explore in more depth later.

In his seminal book *The Success Formula – How Smart Leaders Deliver Outstanding Value*, the product of extensive international research, Andrew Kakabadse presents the leadership process in a wonderful way, as successive subprocesses. Our personal experiences and our own meta-research mirror his findings.

In brief, Kakabadse breaks the leadership process down into several elements:

- Maintaining diversity of mind among the organisation's people and, especially, the executive team
- Achieving a deep common understanding of purpose, mission and, later, vision
- Cultivating a climate of open, unhindered dialogue where problems, concerns and doubts are openly put forward and discussed
- Achieving (near) consensus in decision-making
- Aligning people with corporate values, purpose and mission
- Engaging people in executing decisions and plans
- Solving political and power-related problems
- Being authentic and leading by example
- Striving to achieve wisdom

In addition, Dave Logan and colleagues, in their book *Tribal Leadership: Leveraging Natural Groups to Build a Thriving Organisation*,[15] state that successful executives create and nurture a tribe based on shared values.

Considering the conclusions of both works, the successful executive's leadership process can be analysed as consisting of the following subprocesses:

- Communicating to the organisation's people its purpose and mission
- Formulating with their close team the organisation's code of ethics, selecting those values that represent the essence of the organisation's purpose and the values of the owners and executives
- Presenting the code to the organisation's stakeholder community and fine-tuning it based on their feedback so that it is ultimately adopted by the great majority
- Cultivating a climate of open dialogue, ensuring diversity of thought and open discussion until everybody has an in-depth understanding of the organisation's purpose, values, mission, goals and plans
- Maintaining a climate of open dialogue, ensuring diversity of thought and unhindered expression of genuine dispute until conclusions are reached and decisions are made with broad consensus

15 Logan D., King J. and Fischer-Wright H. (2008) *Tribal Leadership – Leveraging Natural Groups to Build a Thriving Organisation.*

- Being able to evaluate conflicting opinions, suggestions and comments made by members of the executive team and make decisions based solely on true data and arguments, and explaining these decisions convincingly to discourage future disputes
- Cultivating a culture of trust based on the organisation's code of ethics and ensuring that it is cascaded downwards throughout the organisation
- Aligning the organisation's people around the purpose, values, mission and decisions
- Achieving widespread engagement and commitment by living, preaching and demonstrating the organisation's values and ensuring that their people do the same
- Ensuring the productive execution of the organisation's plans by developing, motivating and rewarding its people
- Maintaining a climate of continuous creativity and innovation through visioning
- Formulating the organisation's vision for the mid/long term through sincere and open dialogue based on the evolving organisational and individual competences and competencies, discoveries and inventions, and environmental developments, be those societal, financial, technological, geopolitical or other
- Ensuring the effective and efficient execution of the strategic projects that aim to realise the organisation's vision
- Ensuring that the purpose, the code of ethics, the governance codes and the mission of the organisation continually evolve so that they remain current, thus ensuring sustainability

As we shall see later, the need to systematically execute the leadership subprocesses leads us to develop suitable tools to identify the required leadership competences and competencies and to draw a roadmap for their development.

Modelling the executive's world

In this book, we present the successful executive's world and job as a structure built up of successive layers, as depicted in Figure 1.1 (reading from the bottom–up):

The Executive's Personal Characteristics	
The Management Competencies (Planning, organising, directing, coordinating, reviewing human and machine activities)	**The Leadership Competencies** (Leading individuals and teams, comprehending, conceptualising, informing, dialoguing, visioning, inspiring, aligning, delegating, empowering, engaging, committing, leading execution, assessing, rewarding humans)
The Management Competences (Understanding the organisational system, its components and its dynamics)	**The Leadership Competences** (Understanding individual and societal human nature and dynamics)
The Management Process	**The Leadership Process**
The Organisation as a Human Society	
The Organisation as a System of Holarchical Interdependent Architectures, Structures and Enablers	
Values, Governance, Policies and Compliance	
Management and Leadership Philosophy	

Figure 1.1: The successful executive's world

1. Each executive, as a manager-cum-leader, has **a philosophical foundation** – even when he or she does not recognise it. The particular philosophy of the successful executive reflects the most advanced contemporary trends in management and leadership. We present it briefly in Chapter Five.
2. **A cohesive set of ethical values, governance rules and cultural traits** presented by successful organisations, as reflected in the beliefs and behaviour of the successful executive(s) heading them – the *glue* holding together the organisation in terms of (business ethical) values, governance rules and policies, and compliance with them.
3. **The organisation as a system** of interdependent abstract architectures and physical and abstract structures of assets and enablers.
4. **The organisation as a human society.**
5. **The management process.**
6. **The leadership process.**
7. **The management competences** (as knowhow) required for the optimum execution of the management process.
8. **The leadership competences** (as knowhow) required for the optimum execution of the leadership process.
9. **The management competencies** (as personal qualities) required for the optimum execution of the management process.
10. **The leadership competencies** leadership (as personal qualities) required for the optimum execution of the leadership process.
11. **The executive's personal characteristics.**

In summary

Successful executives have a deep understanding of contemporary organisational systems: their diverse enablers, assets, resources, stakeholders and results; their environments; their operation; and, their dynamics. They have the competence to manage these systems so that they operate optimally, and the competence and competency to lead their main enabler, their people, to executing productively their processes and projects, creating and delivering value that satisfies – ideally delights – the organisation's stakeholders in the short, mid and long term.

CHAPTER TWO

THE BUSINESS MODEL

Successful executives conceptualise their organisation's business model, thinking about how it can create and deliver value to satisfy its consumer and other stakeholder's needs and translate this into value propositions, value streams, enablers and plans. They continually evolve the business model through innovation.

Purpose – creating and delivering value

What is the primary reason for the existence of an organisation?

An organisation exists for a specific purpose; this is the reason for its existence – its *raison d'être*. The purpose defines the value to be created and delivered to one or more groups of stakeholders – the people who have, or will have, some interest in the organisation.

EXAMPLES

For an ordinary for-profit organisation, the stakeholders include, as a rule, its owners or shareholders. These are named in the organisation's founding document and its constitution.

For social and other not-for-profit organisations, they include its founders and may include its sponsors, as well as its beneficiaries, ie the recipients of the goods, services, information or knowledge to be produced.

The same is true for utilities, services and other non-governmental organisations.

Modern organisational theory and practice consider stakeholders to be all individuals and groups who have a direct, or even indirect, interest in the organisation. These people have a vested interest in the organisation. For some, this interest may be vital, for others important, and for others still it may be of only minor importance. Reversing the statement, all these stakeholders are, to various degrees, significant for the livelihood and longevity of the organisation.

The various groups of stakeholders have different needs:

- Owners, shareholders, investors or sponsors expect a competitive return on and market value increase in their investment, or the satisfaction of any beneficiaries.
- Lenders expect to be paid interest and capital according to the terms of an agreement.
- The people of the organisation (ie its employees) expect competitive salaries, a positive work environment, fair pension, competitive perks and experiences.
- Executives (at various hierarchical levels), who often have their own personal agendas and objectives, may expect power or status in addition to what other employees may expect or demand.
- Customers, clients, consumers, patients, members, students, and citizens expect value for money, and the promised or implied quality or functionality, reliability, durability, and aesthetics.
- Suppliers, partners and associates expect the prompt settlement of their invoices, and productive and reliable cooperation.
- Regulators expect compliance with all applicable legislation, regulation and permit terms.
- The community in which the organisation operates, and even any communities indirectly impacted by the organisation, expect that they will not suffer adverse effects, but, on the contrary, will benefit through high-quality employment, fair prices for their services, raw or semi-final products or natural resources, social responsibility projects, and so on.

Many of these needs are not clearly or formally defined and, in many cases, may even be contradictory.

Successful executives, in periodic consultation with the various stakeholder groups:

- **Strive to identify their different and varying needs**
- **Identify a golden mean of the value to be produced and delivered to each group and convince them that this is fair to all**
- **Submit a proposal (business plan and budget) to the organisation's deciding body (such as the owner[s], the board of directors, the general assembly, the supervisory council or a public authority) and ensure an approved plan and budget**

[continued]

- Execute the plan, and create and deliver value in as close accordance with the approved plan as possible
- Monitor the level of satisfaction of the various stakeholder groups
- Revise the plan to keep it as realistically ambitious as possible

Executives strive to accomplish the above through an open dialogue with representatives of the various stakeholder groups, aiming at achieving the greatest possible consensus. In doing so, they try to reconcile the organisation's capability in the production, promotion and delivery of value to the respective stakeholder groups in comparison to its competition with regard to product, service, labour and capital demand and supply, technological and process capability and knowhow. In this way, they achieve optimal productivity and sustainability.

EXAMPLES

Stora Enso's[16] purpose and values: 'Our Purpose is: Do good for people and the planet. Replace fossil-based materials with renewable solutions. The purpose underpins our belief that everything that can be made with fossil-based materials today can be made from a tree tomorrow, and highlights Stora Enso's opportunity to contribute to a greener economy.

With our Values, 'Lead' and 'Do What's Right' we endeavour to set the example and to lead in all aspects of our business as well as sustainability. We dare to take the initiative and continuously ask ourselves what more can we do, what can we do better...'

IKEA's[17] purpose 'is to create a better everyday life for many people. This is achieved by supplying to the market a large variety of furniture and home utilities at affordable prices.'

The purpose of Kellogg's[18] is: 'Nourishing families so they can flourish and thrive.'

---

16 www.storaenso.com/en/about-stora-enso/our-purpose-and-values
17 www.ikea.com/ms/en_SG/about_ikea/our_business_idea/index.html
18 www.kelloggcompany.com/en_US/our-vision-purpose.html

Modelling the organisation

To be able to realise its purpose, an organisation needs to have a business model that describes how it will create and deliver value to its stakeholders for as long as possible or, in rare cases, for a set period of time. It must serve as the foundation of a common understanding, among the various stakeholders, of the multiple concepts inherent to the operation of the organisation.

The business model describes the various components of the organisation, their interrelations or interdependencies, and how the organisation operates:

- **Customers** (ie the targets of the organisation's primary purpose, who could be clients, consumers, patients, students, members, etc, or groups of the same)
- **Value propositions** (the value to be produced and delivered to the customers, which could be goods, assets, services, information or knowledge)
- **Other stakeholders** (owners, shareholders, investors, creditors, employees, partners, suppliers, sellers, regulators, the community, etc)
- **Channels** linking the organisation with its customers and the other stakeholder groups for communication, promotion, proposition, delivery and support
- **Stakeholder relationships** (for example, customer relationships)
- **Value streams** and the **organisational architectures** of each
- **Enablers** (knowledge, executives, values, policies, rules, people – employees and partners – fixed and movable assets, money, processes, data, etc) **for the production and delivery of value to stakeholders**
- **Resources** required for the production and delivery of value
- **Cost structure**
- **Revenue streams**
- **Leadership** (culture, leadership and management processes, and executives' competency and competence)
- **Planning process** (short, mid and long-term plan content, and planning, monitoring, reviewing and revising methodologies)

A comprehensive business model offering a high probability of success must answer clearly these fundamental questions:

- **What?**
  - What is the purpose of the organisation?
  - What is/will be the value created and delivered by the organisation to its stakeholders?
  - What is the ethical foundation of the organisation, upon which its culture and leadership style is/will be built?
- **Who?**
  - Who are/will be the customers (clients, consumers, patients, students, members, etc) of the organisation?
  - Who is founding the organisation?
  - Who is funding the organisation?
  - To whom will the value to be produced be proposed, offered and delivered?
  - Who are/will be the executives managing and leading the organisation?
  - Who are/will be carrying out the organisation's activities?
  - Who are/will be the organisation's other stakeholders (suppliers, partners, sellers, regulators, etc)?
  - Who are its competitors, and what is the level of competition?
- **How?**
  - How will the proposed value be produced and delivered to the various stakeholder groups? In other words, what are/will be the value streams of the organisation, and how will they be realised?
  - How will the organisation be financed?
- **Why?**
  - Why is the organisation being established?
  - Why will the business model be viable and able to realise the organisation's purpose? In other words, why will it make/does it make the organisation profitable or sustainable?
- **Where?**
  - Where does/will the organisation operate?
  - Where will/do its input resources (assets, materials, services, information and knowledge) come from?
  - Where will/is its main value being delivered?

- **When?**
  - What is the seasonality of the various events and activities of the organisation?
- **Under which rules and conditions?**
  - Which laws and regulations govern the operation of the organisation?
  - Which rules and conditions govern the organisation?
- **Probable consequences?**
  - Are/will there be any direct or indirect adverse consequences due to the organisation's operations on any of its stakeholders or the environment, and how can these be mitigated and insured/compensated?
  - Are/will there be any direct or indirect positive consequences due to the organisation's operations on any of its stakeholders or the environment, and how can they be enhanced and exploited?

Successful executives build their organisation's business model so that it is simple and relevant enough, without oversimplification.

A successful business model:

- **Is univocally comprehensible**
- **Provides clear communication between the various stakeholders**
- **Helps achieve comprehension, alignment and engagement**
- **Is aligned with the organisation's management and leadership concept**
- **Acts as the foundation for the organisation's planning, visioning and innovation processes**
- **Helps achieve financial viability and sustainability**
- **Evolves through innovation**

In the next sections, the business model components are briefly highlighted, and those relating to the successful executive's management and leadership processes, competencies and competences are developed in detail in the subsequent chapters.

Business ethics – values

What is the best foundation on which an organisation's executives can build the necessary alignment, engagement, commitment and trust to reconcile potentially contradictory stakeholder needs and convince the various stakeholder groups to devote their best selves to the realisation of the organisation's purpose, and to continuous improvement and innovation?

Experience has shown that the only realistic foundation for the above is the adoption, by both the individual executives and the wider organisation, of a code of business ethics (usually referred to simply as a code of ethics), comprising a set of business-related ethical values that can be adopted by the vast majority of the organisation's people, in the sense of abiding by them in all their actions and behaviours.

These values need to be adopted at all levels, from the board of directors and the CEO to the operational staff on the floor, and in all corporate processes and activities, official and unofficial documents, and oral, written and electronic communication and promotional materials. They must be seen not only to be adopted but taught, demonstrated and lived by. Posting the code of ethics on the organisation's walls or websites is not enough. Neither is having people reciting the values or an acronym.

Successful executives ensure that their organisation, its operatives, the non-executive members of the board and even external stakeholder groups (such as sellers, after-sales service providers, partners and suppliers) can not only recall the organisation's values but apply them spontaneously in their day-to-day behaviour, in their interactions with each other and with any external parties, ie in their everyday communications, dialogues, debates, disputes and dilemmas, as well as in their written and electronic correspondence.

To ensure real-life embodiment, successful executives employ the organisation's ethical values as KPIs for as many processes as possible, and hence in all related work or post descriptions and plans; in setting targets, and monitoring and evaluating actual performance; in rewarding overperformance and penalising intentional underperformance; and in developing their people's competencies and competences via training, coaching and mentoring.

Many organisations do not elaborate on how their values can/will be applied in practice, while others do, as we can see in a few typical examples:

EXAMPLES

Aristotle's values, such as virtue of character, wellbeing, happiness, wisdom, potentiality and actuality, prudence, temperance, courage, justice, nobility.

Starbucks' values:[19]
'Creating a culture of warmth and belonging, where everyone is welcome.
Acting with courage, challenging the status quo and finding new ways to grow our company and each other.
Being present, connecting with transparency, dignity and respect.
Delivering our very best in all we do, holding ourselves accountable for results.
We are performance driven, through the lens of humanity.'

Procter & Gamble's[20] **values:**

'Integrity
- We always try to do the right thing.
- We are honest and straightforward with each other.
- We operate within the letter and spirit of the law.
- We uphold the values and principles of P&G in every action and decision.
- We are data-based and intellectually honest in advocating proposals, including recognising risks.

Leadership
- We are all leaders in our area of responsibility, with a deep commitment to delivering leadership results.
- We have a clear vision of where we are going. We focus our resources on achieving leadership objectives and strategies.
- We develop the capability to deliver our strategies and eliminate organisational barriers.

Ownership
- We accept personal accountability to meet our business needs, improve our systems and help others improve their effectiveness.
- We all act like owners, treating the Company's assets as our own and behaving with the Company's long-term success in mind.

Passion for Winning
- We are determined to be the best at doing what matters most.
- We have a healthy dissatisfaction with the status quo.
- We have a compelling desire to improve and to win in the marketplace.

19 https://news.starbucks.com/views/starbucks-mission-and-values
20 www.pg.co.uk/who_we_are/our_approach/purpose_values_principles

Trust

- We respect our P&G colleagues, customers and consumers, and treat them as we want to be treated.
- We have confidence in each other's capabilities and intentions.
- We believe that people work best when there is a foundation of trust.'

Mission and success

Mission

How is the organisation's purpose realised? How is business success achieved?

The purpose of an organisation is expressed in its mission. The mission of an organisation is to deliver specific value to its stakeholders. An extensive body of international research has proved that the sole sustainable way of creating value, and thus wealth, is through delivered value. Leaders who focus on realising an organisational mission of delivering the value required by their stakeholders have a much higher probability of succeeding in comparison to leaders who seek to create the value they themselves perceive as needed. The latter will try to build on a mission that is detached from reality.

Delivered or perceived value is different from the Aristotelian or ethical value described previously. The former is the benefit offered by the organisation to a stakeholder, while the latter is the ethos by which a person lives.

Success

What is success? How can we measure or quantify it?

The definition of success for an organisation, be it an enterprising entity (a for-profit company), a not-for-profit organisation, or any other type, such as a government department, a non-governmental organisation, a regulatory body, a security agency or an association, has been the subject of hundreds of academic and professional books, articles, conferences and symposia, and the object of research for many outstanding minds.

Despite the volume of time, energy and grey matter devoted to this fundamental issue, there has been no unanimous answer until now, either in theoretical or in practical terms. The truth can be revealed by empirically observing and studying successful organisations – successful in the sense of realising their purpose and, hence, their mission, by creating and delivering value in a sustainable way, as judged by the stakeholders.

A vital question thus emerges: do all the stakeholders of the average organisation have a clear understanding of its mission?

In reality, and as we have already seen, the meaning of value is different among stakeholder groups and evolves over time. As a result, they have different levels of understanding of the organisation's mission.

In many cases, external stakeholders have little, if any, knowledge of the organisation's purpose and mission. Often, internal stakeholders (executives and operatives) and non-executive directors can recite the mission statement but rarely can they explain it in plain and simple terms. It does not resonate with them. The same is true for many partners, suppliers and sellers.

A clearly defined mission, widely and univocally understood by the organisation's stakeholders, is a prerequisite for business success.

> **Successful executives ensure that the organisation's people and its other stakeholders comprehend thoroughly the organisation's purpose and mission.**

EXAMPLE

Procter & Gamble's mission statement:

'We will provide branded products and services of superior quality and value that improve the lives of the world's consumers, now and for generations to come. As a result, consumers will reward us with leadership sales, profit and value creation, allowing our people, our shareholders and the communities in which we live and work to prosper.'[21]

Value streams

A value stream is an end-to-end collection of activities that create a specific result for a particular recipient, who may be the ultimate customer (consumer, client, student, patient, member, student, etc) or an internal end user of the value stream. The value stream has a clear goal: to satisfy or, better, to delight the recipient.

21 www.pg.com/translations/pvp_pdf/english_PVP.pdf

Value streams are more than simple value-adding chains of processes, because of the way they are designed, derived and inter-connected via the value each one produces and feeds into the next one, and the strict methodology followed for their presentation and specification. Value streams reflect customer-centric end-to-end flows through the organisation and explicitly capture dependencies and relationships between processes in terms of their various components: inputs, outputs, enablers, assets, resources and rules. Modern methodologies, notation standards (such as BPMN 2.0) and software tools for designing and presenting information systems around processes capture most of the value stream architecture.

Organisations have grown up and out from an Industrial Age functional architecture to an Information Age data-centric architecture and are now moving to the Knowledge Age customer-centric – or, more broadly put, stakeholder-centric – value stream, end-to-end process thinking and architecture. This architecture enables the top–down presentation and understanding of the organisation at interlinked levels of abstraction and in practical terms.

Successful executives use customer-centric and process-centric integrated value streams as their basis for architecting their organisation and communicating with the various stakeholders in a significantly more effective and efficient way than the older function-centric and data-centric approaches which didn't enable easy and practical integration of the various components of the organisation with a well-defined and purposeful principle.

In doing so, successful executives apply certain principles. They look at the organisation from various perspectives.

From the outside in:

- From the perspective of the recipients of the organisation's purposive value: customers, clients, consumers, students, colleagues, internal departments, patients, members, etc
- From the perspective of all other external stakeholder groups – owners, investors and creditors, partners and suppliers, regulators and communities – in terms of the value characteristics each group expects

From the inside out:

- From the value stream and the process perspective: how value is created and delivered to stakeholders
- From the perspective of the organisation's people: their competences, competencies, working environment, personal growth, performance assessment, reward and work–life balance expectations

They formulate the organisation's operational and strategic plans so that they are tightly integrated with both the stakeholders' expectations and the organisation's value streams and processes. They communicate the organisation's mission and operational plans and its vision and strategic plans to achieve clarity and alignment from top to bottom, and to inspire and achieve engagement, commitment and ownership.

They plan action around processes engaging all relevant people in:

- Analysing the current situation, identifying opportunities, threats and weaknesses
- Setting targets using external KPIs (representing stakeholder expectations) and internal KPIs (representing process and people performance, critical success factors and potential inhibitors)
- Visioning the future
- Formulating actions and projects for accomplishing critical success factors, surpassing inhibitors, effecting improvement, and achieving innovation

They ensure that the organisational architectures are holarchically harmonised to enable optimal process and project execution, by doing what we outline in later chapters.

Successful executives present their organisation as a top-level value-stream architecture, which is expanded top–down in various coherent architectures, enabling the effective and efficient management and leadership of the organisation.

The organisation as a dynamic system

Successful executives see their organisation as a dynamic system, in which the various entities of the organisation interact in workflows activated by events, for example, a customer order or a stock replenishment order/signal; where workflows are decomposed into activity and action flows, which transform inputs into desirable outputs; and, where activity flows depict the most elementary collaboration between humans, between humans and machines (computers, robots, etc), and between machines.

These workflows are, in essence, value chains using enabling resources (non-human assets and human expertise and labour) to transform input resources into value and deliver it to interested stakeholders. Hence, they are called value streams.

Our experience shows that an organisation has between sixteen and twenty-four value streams.

EXAMPLE

A manufacturing company may have the following value streams, as defined in the 1990s by James Martin, the father of Information Engineering, in his book *The Great Transition: Using the Seven Disciplines of Enterprise Engineering:*[22]

- Prospect-to-Customer (customer engagement)
- Order-to-Cash (order fulfilment)
- Manufacturing-to-Distribution (operations and logistics)
- Request-to-Service (customer service)
- Insight-to-Strategy (strategic planning)
- Mission/Vision-to-Enterprise Management (visioning, enterprise management/leadership)
- Concept-to-Development (R&D, product/service evolution)
- Initiative-to-Results (implementation, execution)
- Relationship-to-Partnership (strategic partnering and outsourcing)
- Forecast-to-Plan (business planning and budgeting)

22 Martin J. (1995) *The Great Transition: Using the Seven Disciplines of Enterprise Engineering.*

- Requisition-to-Payables (supply chain, procurement/vendor management)
- Resource Availability-to-Consumption (resource management)
- Acquisition-to-Obsolescence (fixed asset management)
- Financial Close-to-Reporting (finance and accounting)
- Recruitment-to-Retirement (human resource management)
- Awareness-to-Prevention (quality and safety management)

Value streams are best formulated as process dependency flows and as major data entity lifecycles. They result in the creation and delivery of finished or intermediary products, services, assets, information and knowledge.

Value streams are a vital component of the enterprise business architectures. They can serve as the foundation for architecting the organisation's diverse facets hierarchically to form a compelling, comprehensive and holarchical picture of all its entities and operations. Of vital importance is the business process-mapping, which can help executives streamline the organisational structure so that it becomes process-centric and enhances optimal end-to-end process management, significantly raising productivity.

This in turn makes the formulation of value streams much easier on a per business unit basis, which is helpful – necessary, even – in large and complex organisations.

Successful executives use the value stream architecture to help themselves, the organisation's operatives, and other stakeholders comprehend the organisation, and lead and manage it to optimise performance and achieve the organisation's objectives.

They use value streams as a powerful communication tool for achieving common understanding within the organisation, on which they then build alignment, engagement, commitment and successful value creation and delivery, resulting ultimately in satisfied stakeholders and organisational sustainability.

The enterprise architecture is the foundation for automating and managing the organisation's processes. Unfortunately, most organisations do not build an enterprise business architecture and, of the few that do, even fewer maintain it. Without knowledge of the current architecture, any plan the executives formulate for improving its operations and for exploiting the latest technology is doomed to fail. They will miss opportunities to successfully exploit the digital technology, robotics and software tools that would enable the organisation to achieve and maintain a competitive edge. Their digital transformation, even if attempted, will not reap optimal results and, in many cases, will cause disruption and frustration, at a high cost, being equivalent to navigating a ship in open sea without a map.

The modern concept of an enterprise business architecture is drastically different to what it was in the recent past. Maintaining a contemporary enterprise business architecture for an organisation proves to be crucial to the ability of its executives to transform and prepare it for the future.

Understanding the organisation's 'as-is architecture' and visioning the 'to-be architecture' is critical for its continuous evolution and its ad hoc reengineering whenever disruptive changes make this necessary.

In the following sections and chapters, we explore the various components of an enterprise business architecture.

Processes

The organisation's mission describes the value the organisation must create and deliver. The mission is reflected in the various value streams and realised through the execution of processes, the activities of the organisation's people (executives and operatives) in conjunction with its other enablers (assets, such as capital, buildings, machinery and tools, software, information and knowledge) and resources (raw materials, semi-finished products, energy and services), complemented by processes executed by external partners and suppliers.

These processes can be categorised as:

- **Core business processes** – those of the primary value stream (traditionally referred to as the value chain), which produce the core value outlined in the mission. These are the processes that an organisation, as a rule, does not outsource. Core processes might be purchasing, manufacturing and selling for a manufacturing company, or teaching and research for a university.

- **Support processes** – those that are necessary for the operation of the organisation, though they do not belong in the value chain. Examples include advertising, ICT management, personnel administration, training, accounting and auditing.
- **Generic subprocesses** – those that are embedded in all others to achieve compliance with legislation, rules, regulations, and codes of ethics and governance, environmental management, quality management, risk management, competitive intelligence, and so on.
- **Management processes** – those carried out by executives at all levels in planning, budgeting, organising, staffing, directing, coordinating and monitoring the execution of the core, support and staff processes.
- **Leadership processes** – those carried out by executives of all levels for achieving comprehension of the organisation's purpose, mission, plans and decisions; for aligning, engaging and committing the organisation's people around its purpose, mission, plans and decisions; for visioning the organisation's continuous improvement and innovation; for the continuous development of the people's competences and competencies; and for leading execution of plans.
- **Staff processes –** those that support all staff in carrying out their processes, and the organisation's executives in carrying out their management and leadership processes in an effective and efficient way. These include advising on designing, automating, introducing, managing and improving processes, on performance management, on the implementation of and compliance with legislation, rules, regulations, codes and mandatory and adopted standards, and guiding the introduction and maintenance of models of excellence, such the EFQM Business Excellence Model.

EXAMPLE

A university's top-level processes could include:

Core processes

- Create scientists through learning
- Create new knowledge through research
- Improve society through interventions
- Offer library services
- Manage education courses
- Manage student studies
- Offer student care services

Support processes

- Manage the university's people affairs
- Manage information and communication systems
- Manage infrastructure
- Manage supply chains for materials, equipment and services
- Manage finances
- Manage publications, public relations and events
- Manage archives
- Manage secretarial services
- Manage legal affairs
- Support graduates' careers
- Manage consultancy services
- Internal auditing

Staff processes

- Operational and strategic planning
- Execute strategic projects
- Business architectures management

Management processes

- Direct, coordinate, monitor and review the execution of the business plans and budgets
- Manage the university's relations with its stakeholders
- Manage the university's generic business subprocesses (risk, continuity, health and safety, etc), business excellence and sustainability

Leadership processes

- Lead the university's staff in creating and delivering outstanding value to its stakeholders
- Lead the university's people in continuously innovating its products, services, processes and business model

All of the processes are presented in a process architecture, which describes:

- The inputs and outputs of each process
- The workflow decomposition of each process into subprocesses, activities and tasks
- The rules governing each process
- The events triggering or created by subprocesses, activities or tasks
- The data created, read, updated or deleted at the various stages of the workflow
- The operatives or equipment executing atomic activities (those that cannot be further decomposed) and making decisions at relevant execution milestones
- The interdependencies between processes
- The various characteristics and attributes of each process (or subprocess), such as its seasonality, its specific material, service and time consumption as a quantity per execution instance, its specific output, the expertise (ie the competences and competencies) required for its optimum execution performance, and the KPIs measuring its effectiveness, efficiency and the quality of its execution and outputs

Successful executives use the process architecture for various useful purposes:

- **For building subordinate architectures, such as the decision-making architecture; the data architecture, usually in an ERD (entity relationship data) model; the competence and competency model; and the KPI architecture, as a bottom-up Business Intelligence (BI) composition model**
- **For designing and building the automation system of each process and, ideally, of each value stream or end-to-end process**
- **For establishing a univocal language in the organisation and as a tool for precise and efficient communication at all levels**
- **For formulating the organisation's operational plans and budgets**
- **For monitoring the performance of processes and projects, and the execution of plans**

EXAMPLE FROM NICOS' PERSONAL EXPERIENCE

In the beginning of the 1980s, I was asked to 'computerise' the budget formulation and the budgetary control processes of the entire organisation. Until then, I had been working in one of many technical departments and had had the chance to become acquainted with only a couple of others. I quickly found out that the organisation was structured as tens of fenced silos, which communicated with each other solely in formal writing, meaning that the people working in each had no idea what was going on in any other department. It took me quite a few months to find out what each department was doing and how each formulated its budget. I also found out that no department carried out actual expenses follow-up and budgetary control, besides 'post-mortem' yearly aggregation accounting.

I managed to design a common architecture for detailed budget preparation, analytical actual expenses follow-up, and budgetary control. I implemented the system in batch mode – online systems were beginning to appear in 1983–84 and the organisation had a single mainframe computer, used for customer invoicing, payment collections, inventory management and payroll. In parallel, I computerised all closely associated processes, such as purchasing and ordering, inventory management, labour allocation and costing, and project financial management. The batch system produced reports monthly and ad hoc when required.

In essence, I had managed to computerise process and project financial lifecycles without ever mentioning these terms. We achieved the direct benefits for which the project had been conceived: accurate and timely budget preparation, presentation and approval; follow-up of actual, analytical expenses; computation and analysis of deviations at various aggregation levels. At the same time, we achieved better correlation of the interdependent processes. Another benefit – unexpected at the time – was that, for the first time, the people of the various departments recognised and understood the value streams of the organisation, the interdependencies in their activities, and the impact of errors at handovers – the 'fault lines' – between departments.

Without recognising it, we had laid the architectural and psychological foundation for subsequent reengineering and online computerisation – as we found out a few years later.

KPIs, actual results and deviation analysis

> **Successful executives realise the mission of their organisation by defining key performance indicators (KPIs) describing the level of the effectiveness, the efficiency, and the quality of every process and its outcome, and using these to set targets and monitor performance; and by effectively managing all of the organisation's processes and leading its people in executing its processes, strategic projects, and plans.**

Depending on the nature of the process and its outcome, the KPIs can be objective, measured by well-designed and indisputable measurement methods, or subjective, expressing the impression or opinion of the recipient stakeholders, measured statistically using sampling methods.

EXAMPLE

Cash flow, return on investment, company turnover, and budgetary controls are objective, measurable KPIs. On the other hand, customer satisfaction, employee loyalty, and market trust are subjective KPIs that reflect the point of view of the respective stakeholder group.

In the computerisation project described above, we introduced for the first time a few objective KPIs: tolerance brackets for budgetary control deviations, eg 3% for material unit prices, 5% for material quantities, 3% for labour unit costs, 10% for services by third parties, and 7% for overall project cost. Whenever the actual deviation sat outside of the respective tolerance level, a jeopardy flag was raised in interim and final statements, the cause was scrutinised, and improvement sought to avoid similar deviations in the future. We had introduced Kaizen for the first time.

> **Successful executives build an architecture of KPIs beginning from the bottom up, ie from raw data up to a few organisation-wide compound KPIs, such as EBIDTA.**

Executives use these KPIs for:

- Setting targets
- Monitoring performance
- Analysing deviations
- Communicating at various levels within the organisation and with external stakeholders
- Achieving alignment, engagement, commitment and ownership of targets and actions
- Modelling decision-making and delegating authority for achieving balanced RAEW (see below)
- Specifying and demanding responsibility
- Setting performance-based rewards for the organisation's people

Inputs

The organisation creates and delivers value by transforming inputs into produced and delivered value. These inputs can be:

- Raw materials and semi-finished goods
- Services by third parties
- Energy and other resources
- Information and knowledge generated internally or supplied by third parties

> **Successful executives map the various inputs in the value stream and the end-to-end process architectures together with their respective specifications, suppliers and partners.**

The organisation might even go to the extent of specifying the rules and standards they expect their suppliers and partners to abide by to conform to the organisation's codes of ethics and governance.

Non-human assets

An organisation uses various kinds of non-human assets as enablers for transforming inputs into value.

These can include: capital; land, buildings, roads; immovable and movable machinery, robots, computers, software and vehicles; tools; and data, information, knowledge, intellectual property rights (IPRs), and patents.

> **Successful executives map the organisation's non-human assets in its value stream and process architectures, and in various other ways, such as in blueprints and fixed asset registers (FARs) and ensure that they and their lifecycle are managed systematically using KPIs.**

Examples of services, information and knowledge provided by third parties could be: support processes, such as information and communication technology (ICT), automation, accounting, human resource management, advertising, marketing, legal, and training services; staff processes, such as competitive intelligence; and consultancy services. These are mapped in the various architectures of the extended organisation, which include the supply, sales, and after-sales chains.

The purchase, utilisation or consumption of assets, resources and services, and the use of information and knowledge provided by third parties, are managed in the context of the execution of business plans for the development of infrastructure and the production and delivery of goods, services, information and knowledge. In other words, they are managed as inputs consumed or used in the execution of processes for the creation and delivery of value.

People and related architectures

The heart and soul of the organisation are its people, who are employed in various forms: semi-permanent employment; on a contract basis; on a per-project basis; on loan; or as services provided by third parties.

The organisation's people can act either as operatives executing core, support and/or staff activities, but not management and leadership ones; or, as executives performing management and leadership activities. In doing so, executives administer, manage and lead the people reporting to them in executing the activities and projects entrusted to them; develop themselves; and innovate continuously. Executives undertake specific operational – core, support or staff – activities, in addition to the above.

The internal affairs of the organisation's people are administered as subprocesses within the human resource management or personnel administration process. These cover: posting each person on the organisation's chart; salaries; sick leave and health care; annual leave; social insurance and pension contributions; interim (pay-as-you-earn) taxation; personal and group development plans and formal training, coaching and mentoring; health and safety at work guidelines and training; and even support for people facing personal problems.

The bulk of these activities are allocated to the centralised Human Resource Management function, while specific tasks, such as periodic appraisal for development, are decentralised by assigning them to executives or operatives of the various organisational entities.

Managing the organisation's people is the responsibility of executives, and involves planning, organising, staffing, direction, coordination, reporting, budgeting (POSDCORB) activities as part of the *mechanistic* execution of the organisation's core, support, staff and even lower-level management processes and projects. These are classic Scientific Management subprocesses, such as:

- Planning, in terms of time scheduling, asset utilisation and resources, and consumption of third-party services
- Coordinating the execution of various interdependent processes
- Monitoring the execution of processes
- Ensuring health and safety at work

Leading the organisation's people is the objective of subprocesses or elements of the leadership process followed by the organisation's executives at all levels, such as:

- Ensuring that everybody understands clearly the organisation's values, purpose, mission, architectures, their own (sub)processes or activities and those related to them
- Aligning everybody so that they execute their activities productively
- Inspiring and engaging everybody so that they devote their best selves to carrying out their atomic activities and cooperating effectively
- Ensuring that everybody's competences and competencies are developed systematically so that they optimally execute their processes and devote time and energy to continuous improvement and innovation

People-related architectures

> **Successful executives architect the employment of people so that those architectures are in harmony with the architectures of the rest of the organisation.**

The organisation's people execute processes and projects. People occupy (work) posts positioned within a hierarchy and play (work) roles that utilise their competences and competencies. They execute business plans and are managed and led by their colleagues who hold executive posts. They are evaluated for placement, development and reward through specialised activities and are rewarded based on the post they occupy and their performance within it.

Roles

Depending on the design, the automation level, and its complication, each process can be executed entirely by one person or it can be decomposed into subprocesses executed by more than one person, in roles. A role may comprise a whole process or a part of a process, usually a group of subprocesses or atomic activities.

A role is defined by:

- The atomic activities (belonging to the same process or subprocess) allocated to it
- The periodicity, seasonality and workload of the allocated activities
- The competences and competencies demanded for the optimal execution of its atomic activities
- The authority required for its optimal execution with due consideration to containing risks that may arise by/from exercising discretional power and to embedding/specifying/defining all necessary process internal audit checks and controls
- The expected responsibility in light of the allocated authority and the significance of the role to the success of the organisation

EXAMPLE

While the primary role of school teachers is to teach, once or twice a year they carry out student registrations, acting as registrars or doing secretarial work.

Posts

Depending on the workload of each role, its periodicity and seasonality, and the complexity of the competences and competencies demanded by its atomic activities, one or more roles are allocated to a work post. Hence, the role or roles allocated to a single person make up an organisational post. Depending on the workload of each post, it may be executed by one or many persons.

Each post is described in detail by specifying:

- The role(s), ie the (sub)processes or atomic activities to be executed. A post may be allocated only main roles, ie roles exclusively assigned to the post (or to a group of similar posts, depending on the role workload). In addition, it may be allocated complementary roles, to be undertaken by the post incumbent to supplement the work of other posts, depending on workload, periodicity and seasonality, or extraordinary circumstances.
- The competences and competencies demanded by the role(s).
- KPIs related to the activities and to the competence and competency capacity of the incumbent, their personal development progress, the cultural fit, and the degree of competence and competency implementation.
- The authority delegated to the post and the responsibility expected of the incumbent.
- The position of the post within the organisational chart.
- The applicable reward schemes.

RAEW

For every post, a Responsibility, Authority, Expertise and Work (RAEW) allocation is specified so that these are well balanced, and the incumbent may execute their roles optimally, ie effectively, efficiently and at the required quality.

The RAEW is based on:

- The complexity of the roles allocated to the post
- The requisite expertise, ie competence and competency
- The estimated workload
- The span of leadership of other people (where applicable)
- The level of discretion and the impact of the required decision-making
- The risks involved in executing the post's roles
- The targets specified for a given time period

Depending on the level of the executive or operative post, the RAEW model should contain a balanced degree of responsibility, authority, expertise and workload.

> **Successful executives build and maintain two architectures as two-dimensional matrices derived from the process architecture: roles versus processes or subprocesses, or even atomic activities; and posts versus roles.**

These specify the level of expertise required, of the allocated workload, of the delegated authority, and of the expected responsibility in a RAEW matrix.

Executive posts and post hierarchy

In building the activity, role, post and RAEW architectures, management and leadership roles are allocated to executive posts at various levels of the organisational hierarchy. These are executive posts which, besides being allocated core, support or staff activities, also head groups of other posts; in other words, they carry out management and leadership processes.

RAEW matrices are also allocated to these posts, so that an optimal balance is achieved for both managing and leading, taking into consideration the complexity and significance of the processes, subprocesses or activities of the grouped posts; their geographic dispersion; the span of leadership of each executive post; and the workload of any additional core, support or staff role allocated to the executive post.

In this way, the post hierarchy of the organisation is determined.

Ideal organisational chart

The organisational chart is derived from the post hierarchy built in the RAEW matrix as an ideal organisational structure.

Realistic organisational chart – staffing the organisation

The various posts are staffed by matching as closely as possible the competences and competencies of candidates with those specified in each post description. At the same time, candidates should be evaluated for cultural fit and, for specific posts in which collaboration is essential, for team fit.

Yet, reality seldom coincides with theoretical constructs, and gaps of various sizes are always identified when staffing an organisation. Executives try to bridge these gaps through targeted development of incumbents by building and executing personal development plans for training, coaching and mentoring.

> **Successful executives adapt the organisational chart to fit the capabilities of the available people and to minimise the gaps in satisfying the process requirements for competence and competency, acknowledging that it is the people who execute the processes, manage enablers and assets, and lead other people to create and deliver value, and that organisational structures and technologies are nothing more than tools in the hands of people.**

Value cycle

> **Successful executives describe their organisation by answering the fundamental questions identified at the start of this chapter in various contexts, to build its business model and its value cycle, ie its financial sustainability model.**

Value cycle for for-profit organisations

The organisation translates the value to be created and delivered to its stakeholders (customers and others) as its value proposition, creating supply. The market responds, creating demand, and purchases the created value. The delivered value then creates revenue. The organisation activates its processes to produce and deliver goods, services, information or knowledge, incurring cost. The organisation makes a profit or loss, as the difference between revenue and cost (see Figure 2.1).

The organisation continues being operational for as long as it has positive cash flow. When cash flow becomes negative, the organisation is bankrupt. The value expected by the owners, shareholders and investors is the operating profit of the organisation. Any loss of the organisation's market share is, as a rule, equivalent to value destruction for its stakeholders.

For-profit organisations strive to increase their capacity for value creation and delivery until their incremental revenue becomes equal to their incremental cost, or until any of the necessary enablers (such as an asset or resource) become unavailable, or the market demand is fully satisfied.

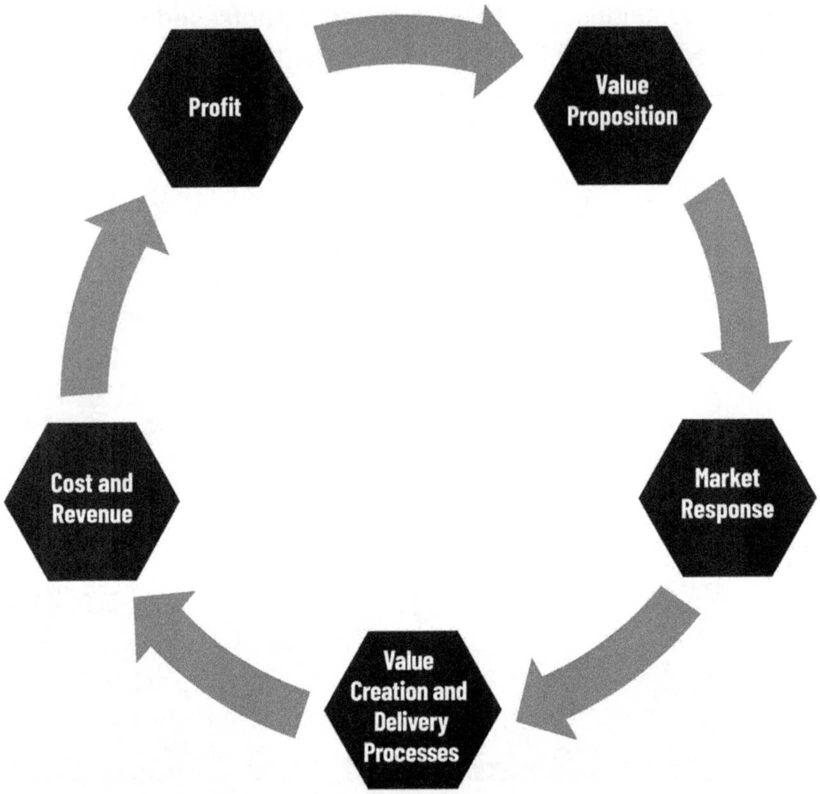

Figure 2.1: For-profit organisation's value cycle

Profit margin = revenue - cost

Profit maximisation is attained when the incremental revenue increase is equal to the incremental cost increase.

Value cycle for not-for-profit organisations

A not-for-profit organisation, such as a public hospital, translates the value to be created and delivered to its consumers (or beneficiaries, ie the primary stakeholders for whose benefit the organisation was established) as its value proposition, creating supply. The targeted stakeholder group creates the demand, either *a priori* (eg ill people, for a public hospital) or *a posteriori* (eg talented young people, for a specialised school), and applies for the delivered value, indirectly creating revenue, which is paid by the sponsors of the organisation, either as a fixed amount or in proportion to the value delivered. Sponsors can be philanthropists, the state, charity institutions, or for-profit-organisations within their corporate social responsibility

(CSR) framework. The organisation activates its processes to produce and deliver goods, services, information or knowledge, incurring cost. The organisation has a surplus or deficit, being the difference between revenue and cost (see Figure 2.2). It is operational for as long as it has positive cash flow.

When cash flow becomes negative, the organisation is bankrupt. The value expected by the sponsors or owners is the value delivered and consumed by the customers (the beneficiaries) of the organisation and not the operating surplus of the organisation. They usually expect that the organisation will break even, ie end its financial year without any surplus or loss.

For state-owned organisations, an operational loss is illegal. Expenses cannot exceed the approved budget. Any operational surplus created in a fiscal period – usually a year – is, as a rule, lost (or written off) and cannot be transferred to the next year's budget. As a result, many of these organisations strive to use all of their approved budget so that the sponsor is not tempted to shrink the next year's budget.

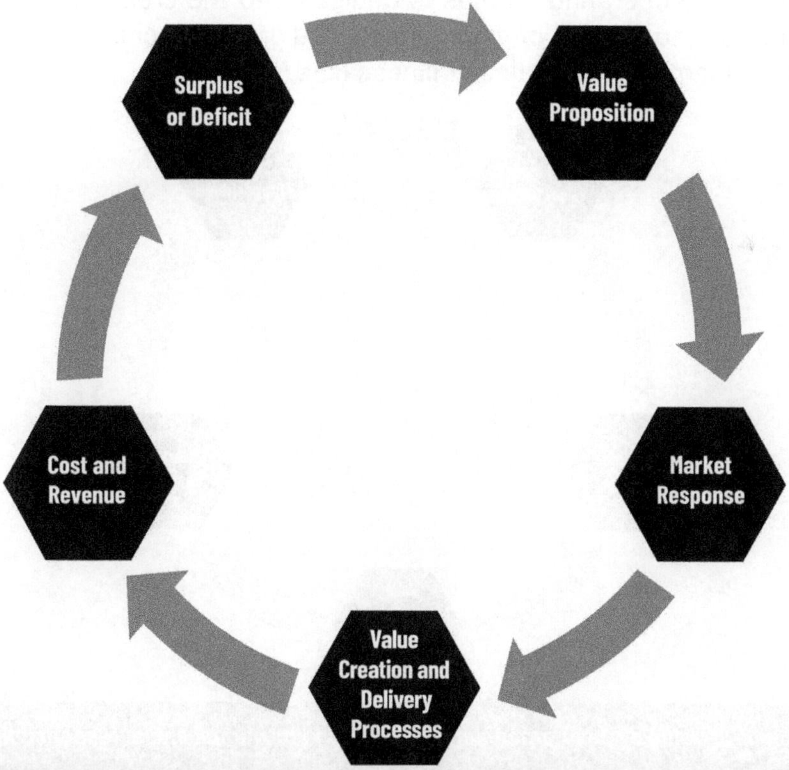

Figure 2.2: Not-for-profit organisation's value cycle

Surplus margin = revenue - cost

Maximisation of value is achieved either when more value is produced and delivered for the maximum approved budget expenditure, or when the incremental revenue increase (including any grants and subsidies) equals the incremental cost increase, if approved budget cost is not a limiting factor.

Value cycle for organisations with an institutional social responsibility

The mission of these organisations, in addition to the primary purpose for which they are established, includes, as a corollary, the mandate to contribute to an improvement of wider society. This is customary for state-owned universities, for example, the purposes of which state that, besides teaching/learning and research, they should educate and improve the society at large. The same is true for certain medical institutions, which, besides their primary purpose of providing medical services, strive for the improvement of the health of the population, and/or conduct research from which no direct financial benefit is expected.

In these cases, any operating surplus is dedicated to the creation and delivery of institutional value[23] to society, or to various related groups of citizens, for example, a group that is vulnerable to a particular illness (see Figure 2.3).

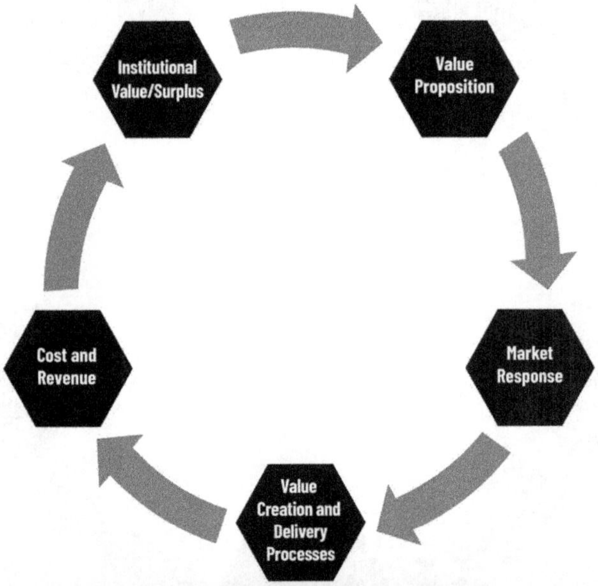

Figure 2.3: Value cycle of organisations with an institutional social responsibility

Surplus margin = revenue - cost > = institutional value

23 Massy W.F. (2016) *Reengineering the University: How to be Mission Centered, Market Smart and Margin Conscious.*

Maximisation of value is achieved when the cost of creating and delivering the value that satisfies the consumers' needs is minimised and any surplus is able to be turned into and delivered as institutional value.

Mission, sustainability and vision

The purpose of an organisation nearly always mandates, explicitly or implicitly, that it must achieve sustainability, in the sense that it must remain successful indefinitely. In other words, a for-profit organisation should continue to create a profit indefinitely, while a not-for-profit one must forever continue to satisfy its stakeholders' needs, ensuring that the total revenue plus any grants and subsidies, plus financing from its sponsor(s), is not less than its expenses. The exceptions are those organisations established with a single purpose that has a finite lifespan, eg to extract natural resources from a specific field, or to build just one project, such as a bridge.

To achieve sustainability, the organisation must include in its mission elements that aim at continuous improvement and innovation so that its value propositions remain current and competitive in regard to changing stakeholder needs, ie market demand, competitor value propositions, technological evolution, and societal and environmental changes.

These elements comprise the organisation's vision, the visualisation of where it aspires to be in the medium to long term.

EXAMPLE

Procter & Gamble's vision statement: 'Be, and be recognised as, the best consumer products and services company in the world.'

Compare this vision statement to its mission statement (given earlier in this chapter).

Successful executives, to avoid confusion, define their organisation's mission distinctly as the creation and delivery of value at the present time, and its vision as its future mission, ie an aspirational mission for a targeted time horizon.

They realise their mission through the execution of the current value streams and the respective processes, creating and delivering value that satisfies the current stakeholder needs. In parallel, they achieve their vision through the execution of strategic projects aimed at creating new value – goods, assets, services, information or knowledge (such as patents or research announcements); improving current processes and creating new processes; improving people's competences and competencies and creating new ones; and improving the current business model(s) or, ideally, conceiving and implementing new ones.

Thus, they reflect, in the organisation's business plans, the realisation of both their mission and their vision, and devote the necessary assets, resources, and management/leadership time and effort (in competence and competency) to the optimal realisation of both the mission and vision, as we shall see.

They update the mission regularly and, whenever needed, replace it with a new one to keep it contemporary at all times.

Successful executives maintain a contemporary holarchical* enterprise business architecture linking the various subordinate architectures so that each can be managed as a semi-autonomous whole (Greek ὅλον, Romanised as *holon*), while functioning as components of a larger whole (*holon*), as we shall see in the next chapter.

*Koestler A. (1976) *The Ghost in the Machine.*

Business model innovation

Successful executives build their organisation's business model so that it allows for additional innovation on top of product and process innovation.

Most organisations try to innovate by improving their products, services, processes and value models, and by inventing new ones. The organisations that succeed in this achieve sustainability. The few that manage to evolve innovative business models in addition to innovative products and processes, create extraordinary value and success.

Innovating in regard to the business model is significantly different from product and process innovation because it affects at least two of the fundamental questions that are answered in the business model (the what, the who, the how and the why), aiming at significantly increasing the created and delivered value.

> **Successful executives strive to create and maintain temporary monopolies or a dominant market position through innovation. Being innovative in regard to their organisation's business model enables them to maintain a long-term temporary monopoly which cannot be easily imitated.**

To achieve this, they establish a culture of:

- Visioning and thinking outside of the box.
- Thinking in business model terms and not in terms of isolated technology, product or process, and overcoming the common myths surrounding business model inception, such as:
  - Being a pioneer. On the contrary, being fast second increases the probability of success significantly.
  - Being lucky. On the contrary, business model design needs hard work and experimentation.
  - Having genius. On the contrary, teams of people with diverse expertise, backgrounds and competencies are far more innovative than isolated geniuses.
  - Inventing new technology. Research shows that what matters is the application of technology, not necessarily the invention of it.
  - Being big. Experience shows that size does not determine business model innovation capability.
- Thinking outside of the traditional economy and technology sector of the organisation.
- Using appropriate methodologies and tools.
- Including business model innovation as a subprocess of the organisation's innovation process and managing it systematically.

EXAMPLES

Apple:[24] selling music.

Amazon:[25] selling millions of items without a single retail shop and, in many cases, without warehousing the items sold.

Skype:[26] providing voice, message and video communications without owning a network.

Coffee Island:[27] selling coffee out of hundreds of franchised shops without owning any.

Red Hydrogen LLC[28] (an offshoot of the successful cinematic camera manufacturer Red Digital Cinema[29]): selling 'the world's first 4-View Media Machine' exhibiting 'a 4-view lightfield display that creates an experience that goes beyond 3D – with no glasses required' and 'proprietary A3D sound... that surrounds and stuns the senses.' In essence, a mobile, cellular phone/communicator/media machine with holographic display and enhanced sound capability.

In summary

Successful executives acknowledge that success for their organisation is equal to:

- The competitive execution of its mission to create and deliver value to the delight of its stakeholders
- The continual contemporisation of its mission through continuous innovation of products, processes and business models, and the realisation of its vision by successfully executing its strategic projects
- The productive execution of its processes, recognising the prerequisite for high productivity being the holarchical design and construction of its various architectures in a harmonious whole
- The optimal design and build of the various components of the architectures, such as the processes, the organisational structure, the work posts and the respective competence, competency, tools (including mechanisation and automation) and KPIs, with balanced RAEW

24 www.apple.com/lae
25 www.aboutamazon.com
26 www.skype.com/en
27 www.coffeeisland.gr/en/pages/company/history
28 www.h4v.com
29 www.red.com

- Its optimal staffing with people whose competences, competencies and personal values match as closely as possible the organisation's culture and productivity needs, the realistic adaptation of its organisation chart to their capabilities, and their continuous development
- The productive (effective, efficient and quality) management of its value streams, its non-human enablers and resources, and its plan-act-monitor-revise cycle
- The productive (effective and efficient) leadership of its people in a collaborative and innovative culture based on its codes of ethics and governance, achieving excellent communication, shared understanding, alignment, engagement, commitment, extreme ownership and devoted action

They devote themselves to realising this success, and accomplish it.

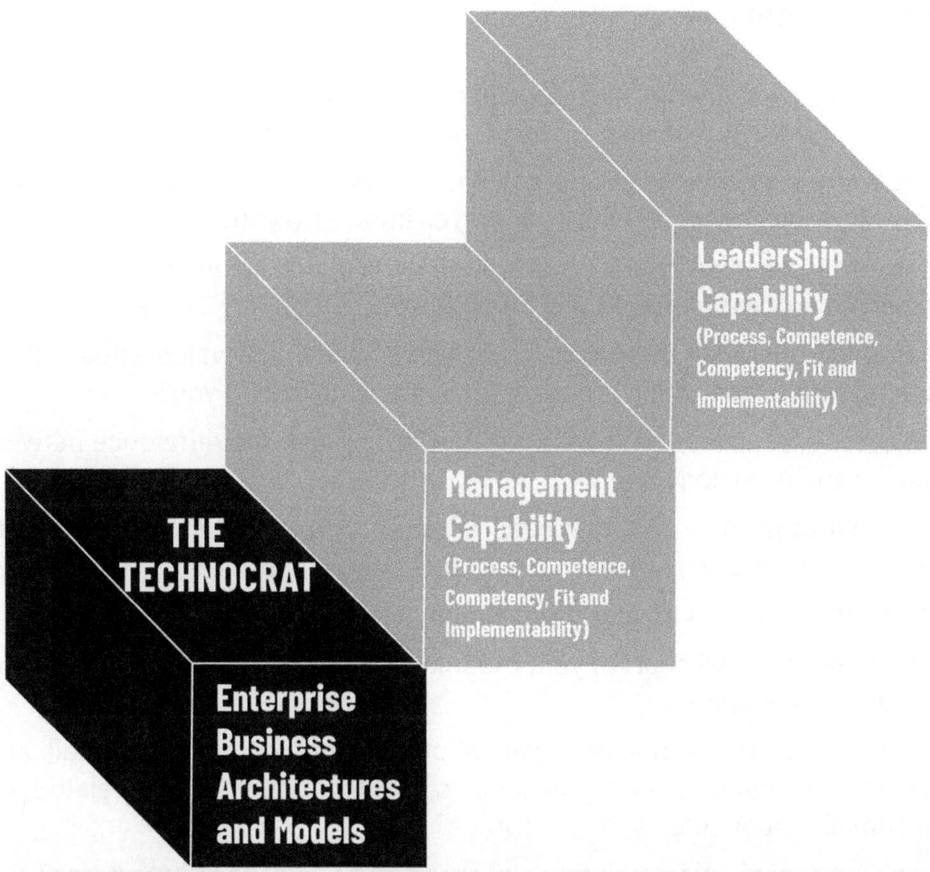

Figure 2.4: The executive as technocrat

Successful executives use the comprehensive business model they build and maintain for their organisation not only for managing and leading it but also as an excellence model for assessing its performance and for continuous learning, improvement and innovation. In this sense, they hold and perform the role of the technocrat (Figure 2.4) who architects, designs, plans and leads construction and maintenance of the organisation and its operation (see next chapter) striving for excellence.

Vital questions

1. Does every executive in your organisation know the purpose of its existence and its mission? Do the operatives know this? Do you?
2. Does every executive in your organisation know who its stakeholders are and what value they expect? Do the operatives know? Do you?
3. Does every executive in your organisation know which are its main value streams, and which processes make up each of these? Do you?
4. Does each operative in your organisation know which value stream they are working within, and which processes it is made up of? Do you?
5. Can every executive in your organisation distinguish the difference between its mission and its vision?
6. Does your organisation have a code of ethics or a formal set of ethical values? If yes, does everybody know what they are and abide by them?
7. Are the ethical values of your organisation reflected in its KPIs?
8. Is the organisational chart of your organisation clearly documented and communicated to its people?
9. Are the various posts in your organisation defined clearly and in detail, and are they communicated to the organisation's people together with all related personnel administration rules and procedures?
10. Does your organisation maintain any enterprise business architectures?
11. Are the business model and the business cycle of your organisation well understood by the organisation's executives? By its operatives?

CHAPTER THREE

ORGANISATIONAL ARCHITECTURES AND PROCESS MANAGEMENT

Successful executives conceive and comprehend their organisation as a coherent system of holarchical semi-autonomous components. They present them as architectures and models; they build the necessary structures that create and deliver value to stakeholders in an optimal manner; and they manage them systematically.

- What is an organisational or enterprise business architecture?
- Why should an organisation maintain a holarchical enterprise business architecture (EBA)?
- Which architectures does an EBA comprise?
- What is business process management?
- Why should an organisation manage its processes and its other enablers?
- Why should an organisation not only manage but lead its people?
- How do successful executives use EBAs to enhance productivity, competitiveness and innovation in their organisations?

An organisation is a factory, or mechanism, creating and delivering value to its stakeholders. Depending on its purpose and mission, it produces services, goods, assets, information or knowledge that it delivers to its various stakeholder groups to satisfy their needs. It utilises assets, resources, people, partnerships, information and knowledge to create and deliver value, by executing specific processes along with various value streams.

A value stream is an end-to-end collection of activities that create a result for a customer, who may be the ultimate external or internal consumer, or an end user of the produced value. The value stream has a clear goal: to satisfy, ideally to delight, the customer.

By decomposing it into value streams, executives can more easily gain a holistic view of the organisation. Each value stream focuses on measurement criteria that are important, first, to the external and internal customers and, second, to all other stakeholders, including the executives themselves. Each value stream is connected to the appropriate external entities, as well as other enterprise value streams. Each value stream focuses on a result, output, or deliverable.

The customer is interested only in the output. He or she is indifferent to which organisational entity performs a particular activity. With value streams, executives gain a focus and alignment that cannot be achieved by looking at the organisational chart, or even the process model. The value stream's contribution to success is measurable through KPIs linked to organisational goals.

The focus of each value stream is its outputs: products, assets, services, information, knowledge – its deliverables. This enables the measurement of results and, through a proper feedback mechanism, comparison of actual results with targets, analysis of deviations, and adjustment of the various value stream components for the next cycle of operations.

Successful executives achieve synergy in a customer-centric focus on the whole organisation by modelling it based on value streams seen from a customer perspective. They build an organisation-wide architecture, which enables them to understand how each value stream impacts others, by identifying interdependencies between the various streams.

They then build a series of other organisational architectures based on the value stream architecture, which serve to:

- Achieve excellence in productivity, ie operational effectiveness, efficiency and quality
- Accomplish excellence in value creation and delivery
- Achieve continuous innovation
- Manage and lead successfully the organisation and its people
- Delight the customer and other stakeholders
- Achieve success
- Achieve sustainability

The architecture of a system:

- **Is defined as the synthesis of its various components, their relationships and the principles and guidelines governing their design and relationships**
- **Describes how it operates – for an operating system – or its usefulness**
- **Defines how the system may evolve over time – for an entity that must remain contemporary**
- **Has the format of blueprints, models, specifications and descriptions**
- **Refers to a holarchically organised set of elements with clear relationships with one another, which together form a whole defined by its finality**
- **Prescribes the style and the methodology for the design of its component architectures**
- **Defines a culture for its construction, operation and evolution**

EXAMPLE

Think about your house, a hospital, a museum, or another simple or complex, modern or old building you have visited, a school or college you have attended, or an organisation you have worked in. Consider the various drawings the architects and civil, electrical, mechanical, information, communications and other engineers/experts built before construction began. The various architectures (drawings and specifications) had to be aligned and harmonised for the building to function effectively and efficiently and enable high-quality usage for its intended purpose.

For an organisation, the various architectures need to be well defined and reasonably well understood by all concerned:

- Executives at all levels
- Operatives of the various processes
- Staff experts who assist in value creation and delivery
- Process management and automation (such as ICT and robotics) professionals, who are mandated with designing, improving or reengineering and automating the organisation's processes

- Various other professionals who will design, build and maintain, expand or renovate its fixed and movable assets
- People management experts, who are mandated with staffing the organisation's work posts, the continuous development of the people's competences and competencies, their assessment and their rewards
- Shareholders, investors, financiers and creditors
- Regulators and other authorities

Successful executives ensure that the architectures of their organisation present it in a unified, holarchical form by bringing all semi-autonomous parts (*holons*) together to create a harmonised whole.

They use these architectures to achieve a common language, clarity of communication, and alignment around purpose, mission, value streams, end-to-end processes, goals, targets, plans and actions.

They exploit the various architectures, as outlined below, to achieve clarity of comprehension on:

- The organisation's purpose and mission
- Customer expectations
- Other stakeholders' expectations
- Value streams, processes, workflows, automation systems: ICT, machinery, robotics, instruments, tools, etc
- Data, information and knowledge
- Assets and resources
- Relationships with external stakeholders: suppliers, partners, sellers, regulators, the community, etc
- Work roles and post descriptions with their requisite competences and competencies, KPIs, delegated authority, and expected responsibility
- Organisational structures (chart)
- People (employed executives and operatives)
- Events
- Planning, monitoring, review and revision standards, methodologies and guidelines
- Plans
- The relationships between the various enablers, resources and plans

The organisational architectures enable a unified top-down understanding of the organisation from purpose, ethical values and mission to customer and other stakeholder value expectations; to value streams, processes, workflows, assets, data, information and knowledge; to competences, competencies and workloads; to authority and responsibility; to work posts, hierarchies and organisational charts; to people, their performance assessment and rewards; to external relations; to management approach and leadership culture; to plans, actions, results and accountability.

In the next sections, we analyse the various architectures and how they are used.

Organisational architectures and blueprints

To construct and operate a modern building, a number of interrelated architectures, blueprints and specifications need to be created, such as:

- Floor layouts, elevations, sections, finishing details, etc by architects
- Static designs by civil engineers
- Mechanical networks and installations (plumbing, sewage, heating, ventilation, and air-conditioning) by mechanical engineers
- Electrical networks and installations by electrical engineers
- Communication networks and data rooms by information and communications engineers
- Security and surveillance systems by security specialists
- Furnishings by interior decorators

Similarly, to construct a vessel, an airplane, a satellite, or a factory, a number of interrelated and harmonised architectures and blueprints must be created by various specialists.

Likewise, successful executives ensure that their organisation is thoroughly and clearly described by maintaining all the necessary architectures and blueprints.

They acknowledge that it is necessary to:

- Depict the organisation's value streams as value-adding chains
- Specify the final services and products, and the required input resources, raw materials, semi-final products, services, information, knowledge and patents
- Architect, map, define and describe various architectures and blueprints of the organisation's core, support, staff, management and leadership processes (and hence activities, procedures and tasks) required for the creation and delivery of value to the various stakeholder groups
- Architect, define and describe all other enablers required for the creation and delivery of value, such as:
    - The competences and competencies needed for the optimum execution of each process, ie the highest possible productivity (effectiveness and efficiency at the prescribed quality), as measured by the respective performance measures (or KPIs)
    - The roles and posts required to execute the processes in a way that balances required expertise (competences and competencies), allocated workload, delegated authority and expected responsibility (RAEW)
    - The organisational structure of posts, including the managerial ones
    - The applicable mandatory or preferred legislation, regulation, rules, standards, methodologies and measurement methods
- Define the business planning, monitoring, review and revision process, techniques and deliverables

> **Successful executives acknowledge that defining and managing the corporate architectures and processes is a prerequisite for effectively managing and leading the organisation.**

The organisation's architectures can be modelled in many ways, which can serve different purposes, as we outline at various points in this book.

> **In pursuing excellence, successful executives introduce in their organisation an excellence model, such as the Excellence Model of the European Foundation for Quality Management (EFQM),* to manage the various enablers and lead the people of the organisation productively.**
>
> * *www.efqm.org/index.php/efqm-model-2013*

According to this model, the organisation has **enablers** that turn raw inputs into products and services, which are then delivered to interested stakeholders adding value to them:

- The **people** of the organisation
- The **resources** and the **partners** (and **suppliers**) of the organisation
- The **strategy** (policies, rules and regulations, and methods) and **plans** of the organisation
- The **processes, products** and **services** of the organisation
- The **leadership** (and management) of the organisation

We describe the successful organisation using as a base our own slightly expanded model (Figure 3.1).

<table>
<tr><td rowspan="3">RESULTS</td><td colspan="5">Organisational Results (Value Created and Delivered: Financial, Social, etc)</td><td rowspan="3">KPIs, Actual Results vs Targets</td></tr>
<tr><td>Shareholders/ Investors</td><td>Organisation's People</td><td>Customers</td><td>Others</td><td>Society</td></tr>
<tr><td colspan="5">Stakeholder (Needs) Satisfaction Results</td></tr>
<tr><td rowspan="5">ENABLERS</td><td>Non-Human Assets (Capital, Land, Buildings, Machinery, Robotics, Movable Equipment)</td><td colspan="2">People (Competences, Competencies, RAEW, Cultural Fit and Implementability)</td><td colspan="2">Partners, Suppliers, Sellers</td><td rowspan="5">Learning, Improvement Creativity, Innovation</td></tr>
<tr><td colspan="5">Processes, Data, Information and Knowledge</td></tr>
<tr><td colspan="5">Value Creation and Delivery Streams</td></tr>
<tr><td colspan="5">Ethics, Governance and Culture</td></tr>
<tr><td colspan="5">Leadership</td></tr>
</table>

Figure 3.1: Organisational model – enablers, results, learning and innovation

Successful executives, to realise their organisation's mission and achieve sustainability, manage systematically all necessary enablers and lead the people, in an optimal (excellent) way to create and deliver the prescribed (again, excellent) value, as measured by a number of suitable result criteria and evaluated against prescribed targets – the result criteria being business and stakeholder-related (staff, customer, society, etc) KPIs.

Process architectures and blueprints

Processes are the activities to be carried out by the organisation (ie its people) as dictated by the value streams, to create and deliver value to its stakeholders.

Certain academics and practitioners distinguish processes from operations. We do not: all operations and projects are realised by executing processes.

A process is made up of activities, tasks and procedures. Its activation results in turning ideas and inputs into final services, goods, assets, information and knowledge, which then realise the value dictated by the organisation's purpose, accomplishing its mission.

Processes are executed by people and machines. They are governed by legislation, rules and guidelines that ensure compliance with external and internal policies and constraints so that specific technical characteristics, quality standards, limits and tolerances are met.

Processes, their inputs (raw or semi-finished materials, services, information and knowledge), their enablers (ie their resources), their constituent subprocesses and atomic activities, the rules that govern each one, their characteristics (such as duration, valid values, authorised operatives and approvers), their outputs (ie their products) and their execution are described by information. Ideally, this is in a standard notation, such as BPMN 2.0[30] or the Enterprise Business Architecture – Modelling Language (EBA-ML).[31]

Furthermore, the human competences and competencies required for executing all processes optimally, at the highest possible productivity, need to be defined and described. A process is 'of high productivity/highly productive' when it is effective, efficient, and both its execution and its products are of high quality. Process performance is measured by defining appropriate KPIs.

Processes have interdependencies in the sense that the product of one is the input for another, and in the sense that one cannot be executed unless one or more other processes have previously been performed.

Each process is characterised by various qualifiers, such as its:

- Periodicity
- Seasonality
- Specific manpower consumption (eg per unit of output, or per unit of time)

30 www.omg.org/spec/BPMN/2.0

31 Whittle R. and Myrick C. (2005) *Enterprise Business Architecture.*

- Specific resource consumption, such as raw or semi-finished materials, services, energy and natural resources (eg per unit of output, or per unit of time)
- Specific output (eg per unit of time, or per unit of input resources)

A process may be decomposed into subprocesses, activities and tasks, down to unitary actions, which cannot be meaningfully broken down further, or down to atomic activities, which must be executed by the same person to achieve optimal productivity.

Depending on various parameters, a process, or a part of it (subprocesses or atomic activities), is allocated to an organisational post as a role to be executed by the post incumbent. A post may have a single or many roles.

To decide whether, and to what extent, a process (or subprocesses thereof) can and should be automated, it is necessary to describe it in detail with all relevant business information: business data.

To execute optimally the organisation's mission, executives must manage the business processes to make them as productive as possible. To fully understand, communicate, teach, plan the execution and monitor the performance of each process, appropriate KPIs are defined, targets are set and actual results monitored, creating more business data.

To raise process productivity, executives strive to automate the execution of each process in an attempt to achieve value for money, by reaching a golden mean between people's input and equipment utilisation. They acknowledge that automating the execution and management of each process necessitates its comprehensive description by business data.

Successful executives ensure that the organisation's processes and all related information are comprehensively mapped, described and managed, in the sense of productive execution, continuous improvement and occasional reengineering.

Similarly to blueprinting the process architecture, all other enablers are architected as well as their various interdependencies. All of these architectures make up the enterprise architecture of the organisation.

Successful executives ensure that a thorough enterprise architecture of the organisation is built, continually updated and used in operating and managing it and in leading its people.

They use it to:

- Keep themselves and all related people fully informed about all aspects of their extended organisation and its enablers, including all interfaces with the various enablers
- Select suitable KPIs for setting targets and monitoring the actual capacity and productivity of the various enablers, and the production and quality of their outputs
- Achieve effective and efficient communication between the organisation's people, and between them and the rest of its stakeholders: suppliers, partners, sellers, customers, regulators, etc, as needed
- Manage the organisation effectively and efficiently
- Lead the organisation's people effectively
- Manage the organisation's performance
- Achieve continuous improvement and innovation

In summary, a process is a sequence of activities that adds value by producing required outputs utilising a variety of inputs and enablers. So, all organisations use processes to manage their enablers and lead their people. Processes include: purchasing materials and services, producing products and services, selling services, and supporting customers, but also formulating plans, coordinating their execution, monitoring process output, promoting, selling, delivering and supporting products and services, improving processes, designing products and services, and so on. The inputs are usually the outputs of other processes. Throughout transformation, value is added and resources are consumed. The output can be an object, an asset, information, data, knowledge or a decision. The process customer may be either external or internal to the organisation.

Any representation of a process should include all of the inputs, activities, outputs, and resources required, as well as the rules that govern it.

Each process can be decomposed into steps, for each of which specific basic questions must be posed and answered:

- Who are the customers (people or processes)?
- What are the outputs?
- Which enablers are involved in executing the process?
- Who are the suppliers?
- What rules govern the process?

- What are the output acceptance criteria?
- Which performance indicators describe how well the process is performing and the characteristics of its outputs?
- What are the necessary control loops to ensure the enforcement of the rules and the productivity – effectiveness, efficiency and quality – of the process and its enablers, resources and outputs?

To identify the organisation's processes and analyse and describe each one, executives and specialised associates or consultants begin by identifying the organisation's various stakeholder groups and the value to be created and delivered to each.

They then follow the value stream for the creation and delivery of value, thus identifying the core production and delivery processes of the organisation and decomposing each one into its subprocesses, atomic activities, and then steps or tasks, answering the above questions.

EXAMPLES OF CORE PROCESSES

- For a house structure, the creation of a set of drawings
- For a bakery, the preparation, baking and packing of bread
- For a travel agent, the booking of an itinerary

They then identify which support processes are required to execute the core processes and ensure they are productive.

EXAMPLES OF SUPPORT PROCESSES

- The book-keeping in any organisation
- The archiving of documents in a legal office
- The repairs and maintenance of IT equipment in an office
- The cleaning of a retail outlet

Next, they identify which are the executive, management and leadership, processes carried out by the line management, including themselves, at all levels of the hierarchy, as part of planning, coordinating and monitoring the execution of the core, support and staff processes, and of projects.

EXAMPLES OF MANAGEMENT PROCESSES

- The identification of suitable KPIs for the processes of a telecommunications operator, the setting of annual targets, the formulation of the annual business plan and budget
- The building of the EBA of the organisation

Successful executives ask themselves which are the leadership processes carried out by the line management, including themselves, at all levels of the hierarchy for achieving comprehension of the organisation's purpose, mission, plans and decisions; for aligning, engaging and committing all executives and operatives around the purpose, mission, plans and decisions; for visioning the organisation's continuous improvement and innovation, and the continuous development of the people's competences and competencies; for decision-making; and for executing the decisions and plans.

EXAMPLES OF LEADERSHIP PROCESSES

- The heading of a team meeting for exchanging information, discussing outstanding issues, reaching unanimous conclusions, making decisions, aligning all team members around decisions, targets and action plans, and achieving ownership of delegated tasks, projects and targets
- The continuous evaluation of subordinates: honouring extraordinary results, pointing out weaknesses and mistakes, keeping a critical incidents diary, carrying out formal periodic evaluations for development, and agreeing with each assessed subordinate a personal development plan (PDP) and organising its realisation
- The heading, by a newly appointed CEO, of the executive team of a hospital in selecting an appropriate set of ethical values, formulating a code of ethics, and setting out to create a new values-based culture

In identifying the management and the leadership processes, they also identify the staff processes that support the organisation's people in carrying out their processes efficiently and effectively, including the organisation's executives in their management and leadership processes.

EXAMPLES OF STAFF PROCESSES

Advising on designing, automating, introducing, managing and improving processes; on performance management; on the implementation of and compliance with legislation, rules, regulations, codes, and mandatory and adopted standards; and guiding the introduction and maintenance of excellence models, such the EFQM Business Excellence Model.

While analysing each of the above types of process, successful executives ask themselves which supplementary generic subprocesses need to be embedded within it to achieve compliance with legislation, rules, regulations and ethical and governance codes, environmental management, quality management, risk management, competitive intelligence, and so on.

The organisation's executives may need to identify and analyse specific supplier and partner processes, depending on the nature of the organisation and their significance to realising its mission, to ensure that whatever resources and services they deliver to the organisation satisfy its needs and that their delivery processes integrate productively with its own processes, guaranteeing value for money.

Similarly, they may need to identify and analyse certain of their customer processes, depending on the kind of products and services delivered to them, so that they are optimised to the customers' needs. In this way, executives can ensure that they deliver optimal value, satisfying those needs. In certain cases, they may even advise and try to convince customers to improve their own processes, to gain most benefit from the products and services delivered to them by the organisation.

Successful executives identify the core end-to-end processes that realise the organisation's value streams and describe them thoroughly to be able to manage them productively and lead their people in executing them optimally, thus creating and delivering value to the satisfaction (ideally the delight) of the organisation's stakeholders.

By identifying the interdependencies of the processes, information is collected for mapping the organisation – ideally the extended organisation – with regard to processes.

The identification and decomposition of the processes is achieved by interviewing key stakeholders, brainstorming with groups of people who are carrying out, affected by, or having an impact on the processes discussing the organisation's activities, analysing them, identifying possible weaknesses or deficiencies, and proposing solutions and improvements.

In many cases, the organisation does not have internal people with the knowhow and experience to carry out the process identification, decomposition and mapping, so it uses external consultants.

The organisation's information defined

A process needs information as input; it then processes that information and produces outputs, also described by information. Similarly, its execution, enablers and resources are described by information, as are its dependencies and interactions with other processes and enablers, and the rules governing it.

While analysing processes, all of their interdependencies and related information is identified and defined using standard notations.

All of this information is described by data in a way that is useful for mapping both itself as well as its interaction with the processes.

Successful executives use the resulting data definitions and maps to automate their organisation's processes.

EXAMPLES OF INFORMATION

Work post:

- Title
- Hierarchical position on the organisation's chart
- Activities (processes or subprocesses) allocated to post
- Competences and competencies required of the incumbent for the optimum execution of the allocated activities
- Authorities delegated to the post
- Responsibilities for achieving results as evaluated via specific KPIs and deliverables
- Reward scheme

Employee:

- First name
- Surname
- Date of birth
- Social insurance/identity number
- Competences and competencies

Employee placement:

- Date of placement beginning
- Date of placement termination
- Reason for placement termination

Competences and competencies for optimal process execution

Executing each process requires specific competences and competencies. Complex processes are decomposed into subprocesses, which may need different competences and competencies. Depending on the nature of the required competences and competencies, whole processes, subprocesses or atomic activities are allocated to different roles (see below) and hence to different persons.

EXAMPLE

- A corporate internal auditor needs to be methodical, analytic, able to combine information and arrive at conclusions, respectful but also firm, fair and consistent.
- Information systems management is a complex process. In medium and large organisations, it is decomposed into subprocesses and atomic activities that are allocated to different roles, and ultimately posts, such as information systems (IS) development, IS operations, and information technology (IT) management.

Competences cover the knowhow and the performance level, ie academic, vocational and professional knowledge and qualifications; dexterities, where required; and experience in having carried out the process.

EXAMPLE

Primary school teachers must:

- Have an academic degree in their subject
- Have a diploma in teaching
- Be able to formulate and implement effective teaching plans
- Be able to manage the various activities of their classes
- Be able to assess the progress of each student

Competencies cover personality traits, personal qualities and personal characteristics.

EXAMPLE

Primary school teachers must:

- Be effective and inspirational speakers
- Be good listeners
- Be patient with children and parents
- Love teaching young children
- Lead their students in learning, and in developing specific competences and competencies, such as critical judgement and an ethical character

Successful executives, in their efforts to achieve optimal mission realisation, identify the level of the specific competences and competencies required for the optimal execution of each process, subprocess or activity, and use them to staff the organisation and to evaluate and develop its people.

They observe how the most productive (ie the most effective and efficient) persons in a reasonably large group or population execute the (sub)process/activities and identify the competences and competencies of those persons. Or, they use benchmarking databases populated with data collected from organisations with mature, fully designed, implemented and productively managed processes.

Roles, posts and organisation charts

Roles

Taking into consideration the complexity and other characteristics (such as periodicity, seasonality, specific consumption of manpower, etc) of each process or its subprocesses, and the required competences and competencies, work roles are specified.

Each work role is specified by defining its atomic activities (belonging to a process or subprocess) and through this, the respective:

- Activity characteristics
- Competences and competencies
- Authority for its optimal execution
- Affinity with other work roles

Workload

The workload of each process, subprocess or activity is estimated periodically based on the planned production and delivery of goods, services, information or knowledge. In this way, the workload of each role is estimated.

EXAMPLES

- The registration of first-year students at a university requires fifteen person-days over two five-day weeks: three persons during the first week of September, and the last week of January. The registration activity is part of the role of executing the process of managing student studies, and is seasonal. This role is allocated to the Officer of Student Studies and Manager of Student Studies posts as a primary role, and as a complementary (secondary) role to the post of Officer of Student Affairs.
- The allocation of first-year students to classes at a high school needs thirty person-days over two days during the first week of September, and the finalisation of the allocation needs fifteen person-days during the second week of September. This is allocated as a primary role to the post of Headmaster and as a supplementary role to the post of High School Teacher.

Based on the characteristics of the various productive roles, such as their workload, periodicity, seasonality, the geographic location of their execution and the affinity to their atomic activities, the work posts required for the execution of the processes are specified so that the planned production and delivery of value can be achieved. A work post may be allocated one or more roles. These roles may have activities belonging to one or more kinds of process: core, support, executive (managerial and leadership), or staff.

Successful executives ensure that each work post is allocated one or more roles in such a way that the incumbent person can execute it optimally, by achieving a balance of the required expertise (competences and competencies), the allocated workload, the delegated authority, and the expected responsibility – a balanced RAEW.

As a rule, posts can be either purely productive (operative), strictly executive, or executive with operating in addition to management and leadership roles.

Posts

Productive posts are assigned roles with activities belonging to core, support and staff processes, but not to executive (management, or supervisory, and leadership) ones.

EXAMPLES

- Accountant
- Maintenance technician
- Contact centre agent

Based on their workload, affinity, and the geographical location of their activities, productive posts are grouped together so that they can be managed and led effectively by an executive post, into sections or small departments under junior executives; sections are then grouped into departments under senior executives; departments are grouped into divisions under divisional executives, and so on up to the CEO. Executive posts are obviously allocated management and leadership activities.

Contemporary management and leadership theory and practice dictate that executive posts, as a rule, execute productive roles in parallel with their managerial and leadership roles.

These productive roles can be of any type. At the lower levels, executives and supervisory posts include roles executing core processes, while at the higher levels they usually include staff processes, such as business planning and budgeting, and support processes, such as management accounting.

> **Successful executives ensure that the executive posts in their organisations are also allocated core, support or staff activities that complement their management and leadership roles.**

EXAMPLES

- The post of Financial Manager in a small organisation is allocated the human resource management process in addition to the finance management and accounting processes.
- The post of Human Resource Manager in a small company is assigned the quality management and personnel management processes.

Depending on the affinity and complexity of the productive posts to be managed as a group, the number of executive posts is determined.

> **Successful executives ensure that iterations of the role and post definition exercise are carried out and repeated periodically, or whenever process reengineering is carried out or processes are automated.**

Organisation chart

By specifying the type, number and hierarchical relation of managerial and purely productive posts, the organisation chart is designed, taking into consideration geographical requirements for production and delivery.

> **Successful executives design the theoretically ideal organisational chart, but they do not forget that reality is not ideal and seldom coincides with theory. They therefore adapt the organisational chart to the capabilities of the persons appointed to the executive posts without sacrificing the organisational and managerial responsibility for end-to-end processes.**

EXAMPLE

In a medium-sized organisation, the design of a process-centric organisational structure – during business reengineering – indicates that the Information Systems Manager post should be allocated the process management process in addition to the IS management process.

At a later stage, during personnel competence and competency evaluation (by a specialised assessment centre) it becomes apparent that the HR Manager is far more competent than the IS Manager in process management and in business analysis, while the IS Manager is excellent at systems development and systems operations.

The CEO then modifies the description of the respective posts so that the process management process is removed from the post of IS Manager and added to the HR Manager post.

Architecting and blueprinting the organisation

In executing the above business analysis and design process, the organisation is mapped and described in various ways, which serve different purposes besides organisational charting.

Process mapping

Processes are analysed, described and mapped in various ways using:

- Process descriptions
- Decomposition tables
- Dependency diagrams
- Workflow diagrams

Information mapping – ERD

Information data is also analysed, described and mapped in various ways, as:

- Information data entity descriptions
- Entity decomposition into attributes, valid values, and other relevant characteristics
- Entity relationship diagrams (ERDs)

Process – data interaction mapping

As we have already mentioned, processes interact with information.

Every time a process, or subprocess, or atomic activity is executed, it affects data in one or more of the following ways:

- Creates data values of one or more instances of data entity fields
- Reads data values
- Updates data, ie it modifies values
- Deletes data values

Mapping the process–data interaction is done in a CRUD matrix. CRUD is an acronym for the above four interaction types (Create, Read, Update or Delete).

The CRUD matrix is the foundation for building the information systems architecture of the organisation, ie an automation systems architecture, as well as policy rules, and for designing the information systems that automate the processes and their interfaces, not only within the organisation but also with suppliers, partners, authorities, sellers and customers, as required.

Information systems mapping

Based on the affinity in the process–data interaction and especially the Create and Update actions, the information systems architecture is built, and its realisation is prioritised as automation roadmapping. The prioritisation criteria may include cost–benefit, competitive advantages, implementability, customer service improvement, and minimisation of time-to-market.

Automation roadmapping

The automation architecture and roadmapping resulting from the process–data interaction affinity analysis is complemented by and enriched with appropriate information systems, satisfying other needs with the objective of maximising productivity. These systems can include:

- Automating support processes, such as financial management
- Automating staff processes, such as scenario planning and competitive intelligence (CI)

- Satisfying managerial needs, such as monitoring actual results and statistical analysis, analysing deviations between actual results and planned targets, and business intelligence (BI)
- Satisfying regulatory and other compliance obligations
- Automating personal and collaboration tasks, such as emailing, word processing, authoring, calendaring, task management and social networking
- Satisfying management and leadership needs, such as planning, executing and monitoring, culture management, supporting, coaching and mentoring, brainstorming, and visioning

RAEW mapping

One of the most significant usages of business process analysis is RAEW analysis. This is done by mapping processes against roles and then roles against posts and, at the crosspoints, specifying:

- The expertise (E), ie the level or degree of the competences and competencies required for optimal productivity, which any incumbent should have and put to productive use
- The workload (W) expected from the incumbent
- The authority (A) vested in the post
- The responsibility (R) the post is burdened with

The name of the method is again an acronym, representing the four qualifications of each post in executing the respective process or subprocess.

The purpose of RAEW mapping is to achieve a reasonable balance between:

- Specified and demanded expertise (E) application, and expected workload (W) throughput
- Expected workload (W) throughput, and delegated authority (A)
- Delegated authority (A), and expected responsibility (R)
- Specified and demanded expertise (E), delegated authority (A), and expected responsibility (R)

Figure 3.2 presents an example of the RAEW matrix.

Activity title / Post title	Activity 1		Activity 2		Activity 3	
Post 1	R	A	r	a	-	-
	E	W	e	w	-	-
Post 2	r	-	-	-	R	A
	e	w	-	-	E	W
Post 3	-	-	R	A	-	-
	-	-	E	-	-	-
Post 4	-	-	r	-	-	-
	-	-	e	W	-	-

Figure 3.2: RAEW matrix example

Post 1

- Activity 1 is allocated to Post 1 as its primary activity. The post description states that the incumbent must:
  - Have the expertise (E: competence and competency) required by Activity 1
  - Execute Activity 1 with a normally full workload (W), ie dedicating 100% of working time
  - Be delegated appropriate authority (A) to make decisions for at least 80% of the execution instances of Activity 1 (with the discretion to refer the most complicated or ambiguous ones to a superior, or even a peer post)
  - Be expected to be the responsible (R) person for the productive execution of Activity 1 and for the quality of its outcome
- The incumbent of Post 1 is expected to contribute some of their time (w) to the execution of Activity 2, for which they must have/acquire a minimum level of expertise (e), with limited authority (a), bearing responsibility (r) only for their own part of the execution and outcome of Activity 2.
- Post 1 is well balanced with respect to RAEW.

Post 2

- Activity 3 is allocated to Post 2 as its primary activity. The post description states that the incumbent must:
  - Have the expertise (E: competence and competency) required by Activity 3

- Execute Activity 3 with a normally full workload (W), ie dedicating 100% of working time
- Be delegated appropriate authority (A) to take decisions for at least 80% of the execution instances of Activity 3
- Be expected to be responsible (R) for the productive execution of Activity 3 and for the quality of its outcome

- The incumbent of Post 2 is expected to contribute some of their time (w) to the execution of Activity 1, for which they must have/acquire a minimum level of expertise (e), with no authority (-), bearing responsibility (r) only for their own part of the execution and outcome of Activity 2.
- Post 2 is well balanced with respect to RAEW.

Post 3

- Activity 2 is allocated to Post 3 as its primary activity. The post description states that the incumbent must:
  - Have the expertise (E: competence and competency) required by Activity 2
  - Not bear any workload (-) for the execution of Activity 2, which indicates that this post solely involves the management of other posts, such as Post 4, in the execution of this activity
  - Be delegated appropriate authority to make decisions for at least 80% of the execution instances of Activity 2
  - Be expected to be responsible (R) for the productive execution of Activity 2 and for the quality of its outcome
- Post 3 is not well balanced with respect to RAEW. In modern organisations, all executive posts should bear a certain productive workload. For a supervisory post in a contact centre, for example, this could be the preparation of the roster of the contact agents and the substitution of someone who has fallen suddenly ill until a replacement agent appears for duty.

Post 4

- Activity 2 is allocated to Post 4 as its primary activity. The post description states that the incumbent must:
  - Have a low level of the expertise (e: competence and competency) required by Activity 3
  - Bear a full workload (W) for the execution of Activity 2

> Be delegated no authority to make decisions for any execution instances of Activity 2

> Be somewhat responsible (r) for the productive execution of Activity 2 and for the quality of its outcome

- Post 4 is not well balanced with respect to RAEW. It obviously demands an operative with inadequate expertise and no authority who is being managed by Post 3. In modern organisations, operatives should have adequate expertise relating to their main activity and be allocated authority for making decisions regarding the routine instances of their activity. Posts without any authority should be rare.

Adopting the RAEW model, successful executives delegate authority and push responsibility down to the level of execution of processes, subprocesses, atomic activities and projects dictated by activities, taking into consideration the risks, controls and internal audit systems involved in decision making and, any applicable, regulatory obligations.

They avoid having posts demanding expertise without imposing productive duties or posts with workload without demanding the necessary expertise or, even, posts requiring expertise and workload throughput without delegating to them adequate authority for optimal execution.

RAEW analysis and mapping result in enriched post descriptions. These should be reviewed and revised periodically to be adapted to evidence-based reality, as well as whenever significant changes impact any post, such as:

- Changes to regulatory obligations
- Reengineering and/or automating of the activities allocated to the post
- Revision to risk assessment and compliance requirements
- Reviewing and resolving problem incidents
- Appointing new persons with significantly differing capabilities and cultural fit

Infrastructure mapping

The value streams and process maps are the base for designing physical infrastructures, such as:

- Buildings
- Equipment layout

- Work position layout
- Cabling and wiring design
- Person and moving equipment traffic analysis and design in working areas

Automation architecture

> **Successful executives enhance the productivity of their organisation by optimally automating its processes.**

They strive to dramatically increase:

- Their organisation's **effectiveness** by exploiting the capability of software to always adhere to rules and restrictions
- Their organisation's **efficiency** by exploiting machine (such as computer and robot) capability to work continuously without fatigue
- Their organisation's **quality** by exploiting the capability of machines to achieve constant quality and monitor it

Business process automation (BPA), also known as digital transformation, is advanced technology-enabled automation of processes – usually the complex ones. It can streamline an organisation for simplicity and to achieve high performance, meaning increased service quality, improved service delivery, and contained costs.

Robotic process automation (RPA) is an emerging field within BPA that uses software with artificial intelligence (AI) and machine learning capabilities to handle high-volume, repetitive tasks that were previously performed by humans. These tasks can include queries, calculations, and maintenance of records and transactions.

> **Successful executives base their organisation's automation on a holistic process and data architecture, and on a sound development methodology, acknowledging that this is absolutely necessary to avoid poor automation system quality and mismatch and lack of compatibility between the various automation systems.**

The automation architecture covers core production processes for both physical product and asset production activities, and all relevant abstract activities; and support, staff, managerial and leadership processes.

Unfortunately, a significant percentage of automation efforts prove futile, the main reason being that they are based neither on a holistic process and data architecture nor on a sound development methodology (analysis, design, construction, testing, transition and commissioning).

Information systems architecture

Successful executives base their organisation's abstract process automation on a holistic information systems architecture that covers all kinds of activities.

Production information systems are the systems that help the organisation's people increase their productivity in executing all types of processes. The production IS architecture is derived by normalising the process–data interaction matrix using the degree of affinity between the data creation and updating actions.

Personal and collaboration information systems are the systems that help people in their personal tasks, such as word processing, archiving, and presenting, and in cooperating between themselves, with their external stakeholders, and with other people and entities, such as collaboration tools, email and computer telephony integration (CIT).

Business intelligence (BI) systems use the production and the collaboration data to prepare and present information for increasing the productivity of managerial and leadership processes. BI systems statistically process the raw data and combine it to present actual results of important aggregate and compound KPIs in various numerical and pictorial ways; compare them to planned targets; extrapolate into the future; build planning scenarios; and enable drilling down to various aggregation levels using any combination of useful parameters.

Successful executives use BI systems to brief themselves and their people; to interrogate the various arguments; to reach deductions and conclusions; to achieve alignment; to formulate and revise plans; to monitor and review actual performance; and to analyse deviations and revise plans. They exploit modern tools, such as artificial intelligence and machine learning, to enhance forward-planning, such as product and services promotion and sales planning, customer retention campaigning, risk assessment, and so on.

Information systems management

> **Successful executives recognise that information is a corporate asset and information systems are a vital enabler for increasing process and people productivity, and that they must be managed with due attention, like all other assets and enablers.**

They ensure that information is managed via a holistic approach covering both internal and external information as well as ethically acquired competitive intelligence (CI). They ensure that it is based on evidence; that it covers both raw and derived data; that it is safe and made available on a need-to-know basis, when sensitive. They further ensure it is made available to all internal stakeholders, so that they can be productive and feel comfortable, and to all external stakeholders on a need-to-know basis. They also ensure that it conforms with all applicable legislation, such as the European Union's General Data Protection Regulation (GDPR).

Lastly, they ensure that information systems are:

- Managed in conjunction with process management
- Based on a holistic information systems architecture that covers all kinds of information systems, such as production systems, support systems, data warehousing and mining systems, BI systems, and personal and collaboration systems, which are based on the organisation's process and information architectures
- Developed or acquired and maintained through the use of a consistent methodology by coherent development teams, comprising:
  - **Business developers**, ie executives and operatives who know well how the organisation operates
  - **Process and data architects**, ie staff post holders who maintain the process and data architectures of the organisation
  - **Systems developers**, ie people who specialise in analysing business needs, designing or adapting information systems (software, information technology hardware, and electronic communications systems), and constructors/programmers who specialise in writing, adapting and tuning the code
- Functionally managed by the process owners who must, as a rule, be executives (line managers) and who should own the functional specifications of the information systems, as developed by the development teams

Successful executives also ensure that the organisation's ICT infrastructure is managed by an (internal, external or combined) expert organisation.

Generic subprocesses

Contemporary management and leadership theory and practice, as well as extensive research, show that successful organisations manage methodically and consistently various generic processes that help them comply with the obligations imposed by external legislation and regulations, as well as voluntary internal regulations. They also help to enhance the effectiveness, the efficiency and the quality of their processes, the quality of the value they create and deliver to their various stakeholders, and the quality of management and leadership practice.

These processes include:

1. Culture management
2. Governance management
3. Risk management
4. Business continuity management
5. Environmental management
6. Health and safety management
7. Quality management
8. Innovation management
9. Project management
10. Programme management
11. Performance management
12. Business planning, budgeting, monitoring and review
13. Internal audit
14. Process management

Many organisations try to manage the generic business subprocesses as independent, standalone processes. This proves to be wrong. They all need to be managed on two levels:

- **On a methodological, consultative/training/coaching, coordinating, monitoring, auditing and reporting level, as well as for certain of the above subprocesses, such as for business planning, review and revision, which require aggregation and/or ad hoc execution, it is done by delegating them to specific staff posts.**
- **On a day-to-day operational and strategic level, by the executives and operatives carrying out the organisation's core, support, staff and executive (management and leadership) processes, realising its mission through value streams, and vision through strategic projects.**

> Successful executives ensure that each process is designed so that it includes, as embedded subprocesses, all applicable generic subprocesses, and that these are covered in the respective post descriptions.

The above generic business subprocesses are analysed in detail in the next chapter. However, we introduce below those that we believe need to be initiated and driven with emphasis by the top and senior executives, as management activities, due to their nature.

Optimising processes

> Successful executives acknowledge that by maintaining optimal process design and automation, they ensure high productivity and quality and that this is done regularly.

Our experience reinforces the truth of the following adage:

'With excellently designed and automated processes, the (few) outstanding employees excel, the (many) average ones achieve very good performance, while the (few) not satisfactory ones are expelled by the system.

With poorly designed or automated processes, the (few) outstanding employees achieve very good performance, the (many) average ones show poor results, while the (few) not satisfactory ones pass below the radar, spoiling the organisation.'

> Successful executives ensure that each and every process embeds, in a suitable manner, as many of the above generic processes as required and conforms to appropriate design standards based on an appropriate methodology; includes appropriate KPIs measuring its productivity, ie its effectiveness, its efficiency and the quality of both its operation and its outputs; includes an embedded subprocess for periodic review and revision of its design and performance, with respective KPIs; and has a formally appointed owner, who, as a rule, should be the responsible executive (line manager) whose post description mandates the execution of the process, including its generic subprocesses.

Reengineering the business

Changes in technology, customer or market requirements, standards, competition, or even executive management or ownership, dictate the need to radically change the way the organisation operates, and hence the need for business reengineering – commonly called, rather narrowly, Business Process Reengineering (BPR).[32]

Business process reengineering is necessary when one or more processes need to be redesigned from scratch. This is usually necessary in the context of digital transformation or, more simply, process automation. It may also be dictated by disruptive technological inventions or by regulatory changes.

Business reengineering is necessary not only when processes are redesigned and/or automated, but also when other related organisational elements must be redesigned in parallel, such as post descriptions and reward schemes.

It should be carried out rarely since it causes significant disruption. Whenever required, it should be managed as a major strategic programme.

Successful executives formulate and execute business reengineering programmes in the context of realising the organisation's vision or effecting significant organisational change.

Improving processes – Kaizen

Kaizen is based on the philosophy: 'Today is better than yesterday and tomorrow better than today.'

Systematic process management demands regular review and revision of processes, usually at a low level, ie at the level of activities, tasks or procedures and related data and performance definition and specification, including the introduction or modification of KPIs. In this way, process productivity is continually optimised and the need for process reengineering is kept to an absolute minimum – usually, though not always, dictated by external or internal disruptive changes.

32 Hammer M. (1996) *Beyond Reengineering.*

Successful executives ensure that the activity of systematic process improvement is embedded in the specification of every process, reflected in the related post descriptions, and executed using methods such as Kaizen and techniques like quality circles.

Deploying policy – hoshin kanri

Another method used for continual process improvement is hoshin kanri, or policy deployment. This method dictates that processes be managed by using appropriate indicators, setting target values for their performance, regularly measuring actual performance, analysing deviations, and taking corrective measures for process improvement and execution as well as for improvement of input materials and services.

In a formal sense, hoshin kanri (the compass) only refers to the alignment of breakthrough goals and objectives that take the organisation to a new level (sometimes called kaikaku), while stretching objectives on KPIs aligned with these goals are part of daily management of kaizen. There is not much concern, in practice, with distinguishing hoshin kanri from daily management and kaizen: they are both part of the company's commitment to continuous improvement. In some ways, hoshin kanri is not particularly different from many tools used by other companies in their attempts to align corporate, business unit, and individual goals. Familiarity with those tools may lead many people to be somewhat sceptical about hoshin kanri; while compelling at the theoretical level, such tools have a decidedly mixed record in practice. However, there are some subtle but absolutely critical differences that distinguish between checking off on achieving metrics (MBO) and thinking deeply about innovative ways to achieve results (hoshin kanri).

EXAMPLE[33]

Hoshin kanri is the process by which Toyota manages the direction of the company, aligns goals, and controls deviation from those goals. The system of alignment starts with a business vision from the top of the company. That vision is cascaded down through every level of the organization, so that everyone has his personal goals and responsibilities and knows how those actions support the topmost vision.

33 Liker J. K. and Convis G. L. (2012), *The TOYOTA Way to Lean Leadership: Achieving and Sustaining Excellence Through Leadership Development.*

There are three main differences in the way Toyota executes *hoshin kanri* that account for its success as compared to the Management by Objectives/cascading goals that are too frequently practiced at many organisations. The first difference is the way in which the *hoshin* goals are identified and vetted. Specifically, the corporate *hoshin* is developed through an intensive process of data gathering and consensus building engaged in by the 20 to 30 top leaders within Toyota, people who have intimate knowledge of the present state of the company at all levels—knowledge built by spending time at the *gemba – the production site.* This is a substantive difference from the five- or eight-member executive teams that so often set goals in large companies without having much insight into how work actually gets done and what opportunities for improvement there may be.

The second difference is the level of collaboration and give-and-take that occurs as the goals are cascaded down through the organization and get turned into innovative approaches to process improvement. Hoshin kanri uses the term "catch-ball" to describe this process. In essence, the process of setting goals and targets in support of the corporate hoshin is a two-way conversation, not a one-way mandate. Senior leaders (at whatever level of the company) engage the next level of leaders in considering what goals are achievable and what would be the best options for approaches to achieving them.

The third difference in Toyota's approach is the point at which the company engages all levels of the organization in hoshin kanri. At Toyota, the company invests in developing leadership first; leaders then develop more junior people, so that everyone, from team members up to senior leaders, has the requisite skills needed to engage in the process of cascading hoshin goals and identifying the means that will be used to achieve them. This is why Toyota can use the catch-ball process and engage more junior leaders in real discussion and innovation: it trusts the leadership skills of these junior leaders. The requisite skills for self-development and kaizen include standardized work and problem solving done in the right way so that it engages and develops others; and it takes years to bring a company to the point where these skills are strongly enough in place that engaging all levels of the organization, especially the team members doing the value-added work, in hoshin kanri can be done. If the leadership of a particular group, plant, or even country is not yet sufficiently developed, Toyota doesn't use the hoshin kanri process in its complete form of top-to-bottom participation. It uses a top-down structure that is more similar to Management by Objectives.

Depending on the nature of the process, tolerance levels (bands with upper and lower thresholds) are used as performance indicators, targets are set, actual performance is measured, and threshold target values are periodically revised.

> **Successful executives employ Hoshin Kanri to deploy policy for the improvement of performance management.**

Modelling for business excellence

> **Successful executives follow a holistic approach to the continuous, systematic improvement of the operation of the organisation they head, by adopting a proven excellence model such as the European Foundation for Quality Management (EFQM) Business Excellence Model.**

This model is widely acknowledged as an effective tool for enforcing a high-quality, high-productivity, all-embracing management and leadership system. Its implementation pays back quickly and ensures, *inter alia*, continuous high-quality process management and people leadership.

The model specifies five enabler criteria and dictates the identification and use of performance indicators for each, based on suitable guidelines:

- Leadership
- Strategy
- People
- Resources and partnerships
- Processes, products and services

It also specifies four results criteria and dictates the identification and use of respective performance indicators for each, based on respective guidelines:

- Business results
- Customer results
- People results, ie employed executive and operative results
- Society results, ie actual results of the impact on related communities and the wider society

The performance indicators can be either objective or subjective depending on their nature and must be accompanied by appropriate measurement methods.

The model demands periodic self-assessment with the use of these performance indicators and scoring that allocates varying weights to the different criteria groups. The maximum theoretical score is 1000 and is distributed in the form of relative weights to the nine criteria groups. An organisation rarely scores above 500 at first self-assessment – usually much less. The few organisations that win the European Excellence Award score in the region of 800.

Balancing KPIs and targets – Balanced Scorecard (BSC)

Another effective method for managing the organisation is the introduction of balanced objectives and goals, especially at the strategic level, to achieve alignment.[34] This approach is not all-embracing like the EFQM model. It does not usually go down to the lowest-level process decomposition, ie to the level of atomic or team activities, which are as crucial as the high-level ones and the strategic projects.

Developing business intelligence

Successful executives use real, objective, evidence-based information in carrying out their managerial and leadership activities, as we stress in the respective chapters.

They use scorecards or dashboards presenting, in a way that guides decision-making, the most critical corporate KPI actual values in regard to targets, allowing drilling down to successive levels of increasing detail, via intermediate (ie grouped, statistical or production) information to raw (non-statistical) production data.

Identifying process competence and competency needs

To recruit or appoint the most suitable persons for carrying out productively each organisational process and further developing their competences and competencies, it is essential to identify and define the requisite competences and competencies for each process (or subprocess), role and post.

34 *Kaplan R. and Norton D. (2006) Alignment: Using the Balanced Scorecard to Create Corporate Synergies.*

These definitions help to design and implement personal development plans, both at placement and at annual personal assessment for development, aiming at bridging any gaps between actual and evolving requisite competences and competencies.

The process of process management

Managing processes and all related organisational matters, as we have exposed previously, falls within the realm of the duties, and hence the post description, of all executive posts. It is, in effect, a subprocess of their management process. The process of process management is in essence a meta-process specifying what process management is, why, when and how it should be carried out, the relevant state-of-the-art standards (eg currently BPMN2.0), methodologies, techniques and tools, as well as the required competence (knowhow) and competency (eg high interpersonal, analytical and synthetical qualities) to optimally carry it out. It also specifies the dependencies between process management and business process on one side and between process management and information/automation systems management on the other side.

The need for expertise in process management

It should not, however, be expected that all executives of an organisation have the competence and competency to manage effectively their processes beyond their obligation and capability to manage their execution.

As for most of the other generic subprocesses, organisations must allocate the process management process to a specific executive or, depending on their size, to a particular department. In small organisations, it may be one of the roles of the human resource manager or the HRM department.

Such a process management role must be seen, like the many other staff roles, as an internal consultancy role with the objective of introducing methodologies, teaching and coaching executives (line managers) and their people, advising them, auditing their relevant work, and reporting to the top executives and the board of directors, precisely as the internal auditor, the chief risk officer and the chief quality officer should do.

The process management officer must be, by objective necessity, the advisor and the liaison between the business process owners and the information analysts, ie between the business units and the information systems management unit.

We dare say that extensive research and our long experience prove that the majority of the failures of automation or computerisation and digital transformation projects (which cost organisations, directly and indirectly, billions of dollars, pounds or euros, loss of business, and frustration every year) are mainly attributed, in the great majority of organisations, to a lack of formal process management process and respective posts and competent incumbents.

Formal process management methodologies and practitioners

It is a proven fact that the languages of the business people, those who own and execute the business processes, and of the information technology (IT) and the information systems (IS) people, those who develop and maintain the process-automating software, are entirely different. Furthermore, in the majority of cases, both sides lack a formal methodology.

The majority of university graduates with degrees in computer science and related subjects are not taught any systems development methodologies, and their teachers do not have adequate experience in real-life systems development with the application of any formal methodology.

Process management is rarely, if at all, taught in universities, and process management practitioners are seldom employed, either permanently or as consultants, during process reengineering or automation, computerisation, or digital transformation.

Process management practitioners are the people who speak both languages (business and informatics: application software or information systems) and understand both process management and information systems development methodologies to an adequate extent. They are obliged to speak the business language and present and specify the business processes in a way that is univocally understood – on one hand, by the process owners and the business operatives and, on the other, by the information systems developers so that whatever system they develop or customise (using an off-the-shelf software application) will accurately reflect the business process and the related data, as well as its rules.

Successful executives acknowledge that:

- Process management is a prerequisite for business success.
- Well-designed processes contribute significantly mainly to the effectiveness, but also to the efficiency and quality, of executing the organisation's mission and, hence, its processes for creating and delivering value, and for innovation.
- Effectively automated processes contribute significantly mainly to the efficiency, but also to the effectiveness and quality, of the organisation's capability to create and deliver value.
- The many real-life automation failures are due to inadequate specifications of business requirements – to the inability of the business executives and operatives to specify how they operate, in other words, to describe thoroughly their processes and their data, and the inability of the software (IS and IT) developers to identify and understand the business requirements.
- The introduction in their organisation of the process management process, both as a generic subprocess and, hence, as a role in all executive post descriptions, and as a formal staff process and, thus, a role allocated to a suitable staff post and its incumbent, is a prerequisite for success.

They therefore ensure that this process is managed formally and systematically, as with all other processes and generic subprocesses, using an effective methodology and software tool – ideally integrated with a computer-aided software engineering tool.

In summary

Successful executives acknowledge that an enterprise business architecture is a powerful tool which enhances their capability to manage and lead successfully the organisation they head, and they use it effectively.

They map their organisation in a holarchical way, ie they map the various enablers of the organisation as (semi-)autonomous interdependent architectures, each of which must be managed autonomously as a *holon* (a whole); and they use architectures as components of a harmonious whole, usually called an enterprise business architecture or EBA.

They use the organisation's EBA and its subordinate architectures to describe, in a clear and comprehensible way:

- How value is created and delivered to the organisation's stakeholders to their satisfaction and delight
- How its mission is decomposed into value streams, and what the interdependencies between the values streams are
- How its value streams are composed of interdependent processes, and what the interdependencies between the processes are
- What the outputs and inputs of each value stream are
- How each process is decomposed into subprocesses and activities
- Which data (information) is related to each process, and what the interdependencies are between the processes and the data and between the various data entities
- What the characteristics and attributes of each process and each data entity are
- Which rules govern the processes and the data entities
- Which competences and competencies are required for the optimum execution of each process
- Which KPIs enable the effective management of the productivity (ie the effectiveness, the efficiency and the quality) of each process and the quality of its outcome
- How the various processes, subprocesses and atomic activities are delegated to work roles, and how the work roles compose work posts that can ensure empowered and productive process execution (including the management and leadership processes) with balanced expertise, workload, authority and responsibility (RAEW)
- How the work posts are organised into a process-centric organisational structure (chart)
- How the work posts are thoroughly described and the performance of incumbents is assessed through applicable process KPIs, personal expertise application, and development performance, and how these are rewarded
- How the various non-human assets and resources are organised so that the value streams and processes are productively and competitively executed

- How the organisation strives for sustainability and mission evolution via knowledge, product, process and business model innovation, and the realisation of its vision through the execution of strategic projects
- How the management and leadership processes are decomposed into executive activities, as exposed in this and the following chapters

Figure 3.3 (read bottom–up) presents the various components of an enterprise business architecture.

Vital questions

1. Does your organisation recognise the importance of building and maintaining an enterprise business architecture comprising a comprehensive set of architectures for the various enablers and resources making up its value streams and their components?
2. If yes, has it done this, and does it put it to good use?
3. If no, does it maintain any partial architectures, for example a process architecture, a data architecture (ERD), process–data interaction matrices, an information systems architecture, and a post-process/activity RAEW architecture?
4. Does your organisation maintain any other kind of organisational architectures?
5. Does your organisation define, in detail, its processes, and does it map them together with their dependencies? If yes, does it use a dedicated software tool for this?
6. Does your organisation define its data and its interaction with its processes in a data model?
7. Does your organisation base its digital transformation projects on its process–data interactions?
8. Does your organisation define its KPIs based on its processes?
9. Does your organisation use its process mapping to define its work roles, work posts and organisation chart?
10. Does your organisation use its process definitions for performance management?
11. Does your organisation use a business excellence model?

Infrastructure Architectures	Automation Architectures	People Architectures
R&D Equipment	**Competitive Intelligence (CI) Architecture and Systems**	**Rewards Model and Schemes**
Personal Productivity Devices and Tools	**Business Intelligence (BI) Architecture and Systems**	**Realistic Organisation Chart** (adapted to People Capabilities)
Office Equipment and Furniture	**Personal and Collaboration Productivity Systems and Tools**	**Ideal Organisation Chart** (Process-centric)
Communications and Information Technology (CIT)	**Administrative Information Systems** (Applications and Equipment)	**Post Descriptions** (Activities, Expertise, Authority, Responsibility, KPIs, Rewards)
Movable and Transport Equipment	**Production Automation**	**Posts *v* Activities RAEW Matrix**
Production Equipment	**Automation Architecture**	**Process Execution Roles**
Real Estate (Buildings, Warehouses, etc)	**Process – Data – Rules Architecture**	**Process Competences and Competencies**
Operation's Geography	**Data Architecture**	**Process Description** (incl KPIs)

Process Architecture
(Workflow and Dependency Diagrams)

Value Streams
(Value Creation and Delivery Chains)

Value Cycle
(Financial Sustainability Cycle)

Purpose and Values – Culture and Mission

Figure 3.3: The organisation's business model and architectures

CHAPTER FOUR

GENERIC BUSINESS SUBPROCESSES

Successful executives comprehend and manage the business requirements of this challenging environment by embedding in their organisation's processes all necessary generic subprocesses.

What is a generic subprocess? Why should an organisation manage its generic subprocesses? Who is responsible for implementing the generic subprocesses in an organisation?

As we have already outlined in previous chapters, processes are distinguished by their nature into core, support, staff, management and leadership processes. Core, support, and certain staff processes are specific to the organisation's purpose and mission, and even its vision, and the study of these lies outside the scope of this book. We cover those staff processes closely related to the management and leadership processes in the respective parts of this book.

Whatever the nature of a process, it must be designed to ensure that important generic business requirements are met. Some of these are imposed by legislation and regulations, others by regulatory authorities, certain others by internal rules and codes, while others still by management and leadership practice. Meeting these requirements can be achieved by embedding in each process all applicable generic subprocesses.

Successful executives ensure that in designing, reviewing and revising the organisation's processes, all applicable generic subprocesses are seamlessly embedded in the relevant process.

We therefore briefly present the most important of these in the next sections.

Business process optimisation

> **Successful executives know that by maintaining optimal process design and automation, they ensure high productivity and quality.**

They ensure that each process has:

- Suitable design standards based on an appropriate methodology.
- All applicable generic subprocesses.
- Suitable KPIs measuring its productivity, ie its effectiveness, its efficiency and the quality of both its operation and its outputs.
- Competence and competency specification based on the latest theory and practice, which are reflected in the descriptions of the posts mandated with the execution of the process.
- All available technology tools that can maximise its productivity.
- An embedded subprocess for the periodic review and revision of its design and performance, with respective KPIs.
- The requisite execution environment that enables the operatives holding the posts mandated with its execution – who should have the requisite expertise: competence, competency, fit, implementation capability and willingness – to execute it most productively.
- An owner. As a rule, this should be the executive with the hierarchical duty of executing, managing and optimising the process.

EXAMPLE

International standard ISO 9001 dictates that processes must be continually upgraded based on the results of audits. For a process, this upgrade can take various forms :

- Upgrade of its procedures
- Introduction or modification of its KPIs
- Upgrade of its competence and competency specifications
- Modification or replacement of its automation hardware and software
- Drastic reengineering from scratch

Culture management

Culture management is, as we repeat in many places in this book, one of the vital components of the leadership process of every successful executive – as shown by extensive international research and our own long experience.

A legitimate question springs to mind:

Why include culture management among the generic business subprocesses?

Well, because only within a uniform and stable culture can executives manage and lead an organisation to achieve and maintain long-term success in creating and delivering value.

> Building and maintaining a productive and innovative culture has certain *sine qua nons*:
>
> - The organisation must build and maintain its culture around one common set of values, a code of ethics that is adopted, preached, implemented in the organisation's language and reflected in its KPIs, and lived by the great majority of its people.
> - This set of values and the way it is implemented in the organisation's language, be that its slogans, its oral, written and electronic communication, its marketing and advertising material and campaigns, its statements of mission, vision, and even its guidelines for executives' formal and informal, internal and external speeches, must be managed systematically.
> - The induction and training of newcomers and existing people needs to reflect the same set of values.
> - The various subcultures, which are unavoidable, reflecting the personalities of each executive and their team, must also revolve around the common set of values.

In view of the above, an organisation needs to set up and maintain a culture framework and ensure that the organisation's culture is focused. Thus arises the need to introduce the generic subprocess of culture management.

> **Successful chief executives recognise this need and undertake themselves, ideally in cooperation with the chairperson of the board of directors, the culture management subprocess. They are assisted by the chief executive team, the general management team, and staff posts, depending on the organisation's size, complexity, and geography.**

This is not dissimilar to the generic quality management or risk management subprocesses, the only difference being that culture management is a leadership activity and, therefore, a *sine qua non* component, a subprocess, of the leadership process of all executives, which again needs to be managed systematically.

Governance management

Governance, usually referred to as corporate governance, can be described as a set of policies, principles and guidelines to support the responsible management and control of the organisation.

> **Successful executives aim not only at complying with governance rules, regulations and codes, but also at applying best practices in the field of governance.**

The aims of governance are to give to the board of directors, which represents directly the shareholders and indirectly all other stakeholders, control over the executive management and ensure that legislation, regulations and policies are implemented, to steer management towards efficient and transparent methods of conducting operations, to ensure integrity, and to facilitate financing of future investments.

The governance of an organisation is becoming ever more complicated due to pressures and obligations raised by governments, public independent, national and international authorities, stock exchanges, financing institutions, non-governmental organisations, the media, the public, and the organisation itself.

Introducing the respective codes and regulations, interpreting them, implementing them throughout the organisation and ensuring that they are observed demands systematic management. The ultimate responsibility for implementing governance within the organisation – often referred to as corporate responsibility – is borne by the board of directors, which needs to both implement it in its own operations and ensure that it is implemented throughout the organisation.

Successful chairpersons ensure that the board's governance sub-committee functions effectively, ensuring that governance is systematically managed and reported. They also cooperate with the chief executive officer and their chief executive team to provide executive support to the board in following governance developments and in ensuring that management comprehends what is expected from it regarding governance.

EXAMPLE

John Lewis Partnership Plc[35]

Extract from the Terms of Reference for the Corporate Responsibility Committee of the Partnership Board (Approved by the Partnership Board on 9 September 2015)

'Responsibilities

1. *The Committee is responsible to the Board for the oversight of the Partnership's Corporate Responsibility Policy and corporate responsibility objectives, ensuring these are consistent with the Partnership's obligations under the Constitution towards partners, customers, suppliers, competitors, the environment, and the communities in which it operates, and are effective in safeguarding the Partnership's corporate reputation.*
2. *In discharging its responsibilities and duties, the Committee will have due regard to the Partnership's Constitution and in particular Principle 4 (Members), Principle 5 (Customers), Principle 6 (Business Relationships), Principle 7 (The Community) and Section 3 (Responsibilities to others) of the Constitution and promoting the success of the Partnership for the benefit of Partners as a whole.*

Duties

Monitoring performance and risk

1. *The Committee will receive reports and review activities from the Head of Corporate Social Responsibility, the John Lewis Partnership Environment Steering Group, the Divisional Corporate Responsibility Committees, and others (including external stakeholders) as necessary in order to monitor the performance of the Partnership's corporate responsibility obligations as set out in the Corporate Responsibility Policy.*

35 www.johnlewispartnership.co.uk/content/dam/cws/pdfs/about-us/governance/corporate-responsibility-committee-tor.pdf

2. *The Committee will review management's assessment of the effectiveness of the Corporate Responsibility Policy and how well specific corporate responsibility obligations and risks are being managed against key performance indicators and satisfy itself that there are adequate resources and management reporting to support such activity.*
3. *The Committee will review the Partnership's response to those external developments and emerging risks which are likely to have significant influence on the Partnership's ability to conduct its business responsibly and enable it to maintain and safeguard its reputation.*
4. *The Committee will review the effectiveness of the Partnership's procedures for maintaining and safeguarding the Partnership's corporate reputation.*
5. *The Committee will report to the Board as appropriate.*

Narrative Reporting

1. *The Committee will approve the corporate responsibility elements of the Partnership's Annual Report and Accounts.'*

Successful chief executives ensure that governance management is introduced in the organisation as a generic subprocess and mandated to the chief executive's posts, according to specialisation, and to all executives, as part of their management activities. They further undertake, themselves, the overall responsibility and coordination of the various aspects of governance management. They even ensure that, where applicable, governance is reflected in KPIs.

Stakeholder relationship management

An organisation exists to create and deliver value to its stakeholders. The founding stakeholders may constitute one group with few members – in many cases, only one. As the organisation acquires flesh and bones and becomes fully operational, it acquires various other stakeholder groups, such as:

- Employed executives
- Employed operatives

- Non-executive directors (ie non-executive members of the board of directors)
- Suppliers
- Partners and associates
- Lenders and creditors
- Small shareholders
- Regulators
- Customers
- Communities affected directly or indirectly by the organisation's operations
- Evaluators (eg journalists and mass media, consumer associations and specialised publications)

Each stakeholder group, sometimes even a group within a group, has its own needs, demands, expectations and aspirations, and therefore a different value must be created and delivered to its members. In many cases, these demands and expectations are in conflict and hence the respective values need to be balanced in a widely acceptable way. Furthermore, each stakeholder group speaks its own language and requires different handling.

Successful executives design and manage systematically the organisation's relationships with each stakeholder group, covering the whole lifecycle of these relationships.

They ensure that an appropriate stakeholder relationship management subprocess is embedded in most, if not all, processes as applicable for related stakeholder groups, with its own KPIs, targets and monitoring methods.

They maintain, where appropriate, service level agreements (SLAs) governing the respective relationship management subprocess, taking into consideration that, depending on the nature of each stakeholder group, this subprocess may influence the design of any number of the organisation's core, support, staff, management and leadership processes and their other generic subprocesses.

They define specific staff posts that act as custodians of the relationship with one or more stakeholder groups, depending on the importance of each stakeholder group. These officials act as internal consultants and auditors for the various process owners, who retain the responsibility for their process, in regard to their stakeholder relationship subprocess.

EXAMPLE

Forward-looking organisations:

- Introduce KPIs measuring the expectations and satisfaction of each stakeholder group: customers (consumers, patients, students, etc), owners/shareholders/investors/creditors, employees, suppliers, partners, sellers, communities (in which the organisation operates and, depending on its nature, in which its suppliers, partners, and sellers operate, and where customers consume the value delivered to them by the organisation)
- Set targets for these KPIs
- Regularly measure the actual situation
- Analyse all identified deviations and take corrective actions
- Continually upgrade the related processes, products, and services, and the expertise and plans of executives and operatives

Stakeholder relationship management has its own information requirements, which must be reflected in the process–data mappings and the relevant information systems.

Nowadays, most organisations maintain a Customer Relationship Management (CRM) system. Many, however, ignore the systematic relationship management of other important stakeholder groups, such as the employees, the shareholders, the community, the regulators, the suppliers, and the media.

Successful executives ensure that stakeholder relationship management is governed in accordance with the ethical values of the organisation. These values should be duly communicated to the external stakeholders and reflected clearly in all information exchange and contacts, and in related KPIs.

They employ the organisation's code of ethics in balancing the value to be created and delivered to each stakeholder group to achieve a broadly, though ideally unanimously, accepted golden mean, since the interests of the various stakeholder groups and, consequently, the respective expected value, are often in conflict.

Risk management

The world is becoming ever more complex and open to ethical and unethical competitive activities and actions. Internal and external risks are soaring by the day: poor or even bad-quality raw materials, faulty software, low-quality equipment, human errors, human subversion, illegal actions, embezzlement, cybercrime, environmental dangers, workplace hazards, terrorism and other risks present themselves, usually in a concealed manner. Their adverse results shout loudly and clearly, to the detriment of the organisation and its reputation. Ignoring them exposes the organisation and its stakeholders to further small and large risks.

Successful executives in the modern world ensure that each and every process of the organisation and, in many cases, specific processes of its suppliers, partners, sellers and customers, is designed to manage inherent, probable, and even improbable internal and external risks.

In managing these threats, they identify all possible risks; assess the adverse impact of each; take appropriate measures to eliminate as many as is technically and financially feasible; hand over to external parties as many as possible of those that cannot be mitigated; of those left unresolved, take out suitable insurance against as many as are insurable at a reasonable cost; and self-insure against the rest by costing them and putting aside adequate funds.

Successful executives ensure that a suitable risk assessment and, where possible, a risk management subprocess is embedded in each and every process and is thus reflected in the respective role and post descriptions. They further ensure that it is taught to responsible incumbents and its implementation is monitored with suitable KPIs.

Depending on their type and size, organisations may create a Risk Manager post, or even a Risk Management department. We would stress here that the manager and management titles are misleading and are frequently misunderstood. These are staff posts and the incumbents act as internal consultants, advising and ensuring that risk assessment and risk management subprocesses and measures are embedded in each and every process; that these subprocesses are well documented; and that the incumbents of the relevant posts understand them fully and know how to implement them. This group of staff posts may also act as internal auditors monitoring the implementation of these subprocesses. However, the responsibility for their implementation should always lie with the executives, ie the line management that own and execute the (parent) process, up to the CEO and the board of directors, which should have a risk management committee.

It must be stressed that risk management is not a generic process relevant only in big organisations. It concerns all organisations from the biggest and most complex to the smallest and simplest, as the example below shows. It also shows that there exist methodologies and tools that can help executives manage risk effectively.

EXAMPLE

Erik's Hair Salon[36]

Hairdressing has always been an important part of Erik's life. Back in the mid-seventies, his parents opened a small hairdressing business. Today, the salon remains a family concern. He says:

'Running a busy unisex salon with ten employees involves much more than cutting, styling or colouring hair. There are key safety issues to consider, too. Hairdressing products can carry risks of eye or skin irritation for both staff and customers. Even something as commonplace as shampooing carries risks for everyone in the salon.

Water, through the wash basins, is a major area of risk – people might slip on wet floors.

And with wet work – when staff are constantly shampooing 20-30 times a day – there's a risk of occupational dermatitis, a major issue in our industry.

Until recently, completing a Health & Safety Risk Assessment for the salon was a headache. It was quite complicated – and it wasn't very clearly set out.

But now, thanks to the example risk assessments available on the UK Health & Safety Executive website, I feel much more confident that I'm submitting the right paperwork. There's an online example for a hairdressing salon that we use, which takes away any possible inconsistencies. The examples give you clear, basic headings – and the process is much easier to understand.

For us, the example risk assessments have simplified everything. It's made it all a lot clearer.'

---

36 www.hse.gov.uk/risk/casestudies/hairsalon.htm

Experience shows that the most difficult and challenging aspect of managing risk is identifying it. Some risks are known from experience, some are easy to see, but some are not so obvious.

Successful executives create and maintain an organisation-wide culture in which people are always alert and looking for risks while performing their other duties.

Business continuity management

In assessing and managing the risks faced in the various processes of the organisation, the executives should ask whether its operation, ie the realisation of its mission for producing and delivering value, may be jeopardised in any way. They should ask also whether the operations of its external stakeholders, be those suppliers, partners or customers, may be endangered if their organisation's operation is inadvertently discontinued.

Successful executives ensure that business continuity is maintained by their organisation, at a reasonable cost; as well as its suppliers, partners and sellers to the extent that it affects its operations; and its customers to the extent that their operations depend on the products and services delivered to them by the organisation.

To this end, they should ensure that a suitable subprocess dealing with business continuity is embedded in every process, alongside the risk management subprocess.

The business continuity management subprocess has a broader spectrum than the risk management one. It views the value chain, or one or more value streams, in a holistic way and assesses the impact of every process on the operation of the whole internal value chain or stream and, where applicable, on the extended value chain. It includes the activities of formulating and maintaining disaster recovery plans and testing them. It has its own characteristics and KPIs.Depending on their type and size, organisations may establish a Business Continuity Manager post. We stress here that the manager title is misleading and is frequently misunderstood. This is a staff post and the incumbent acts as an internal consultant, advising and ensuring that the business continuity subprocess and its measures are embedded in each and every process; that these subprocesses are well documented; and that the incumbents understand them fully and know how to implement them.

Business continuity managers may act as internal auditors monitoring the implementation of the subprocess, but the responsibility for its implementation should always lie with the executives, ie the line management, that own and execute the (parent) process, up to the CEO and the board of directors who approve the business continuity policy of the organisation and monitor its implementation.

EXAMPLE

An electronic communications provider:

- Takes extensive measures to ensure a high probability of business continuity. It maintains both equipment and network physical and geographic diversification and duplication, and it avoids single points of failure for its non-human assets and for its experts
- Safeguards its financial viability and, hence, its business continuity, by insuring its assets and its employees
- Takes extensive measures to ensure the business continuity of its business customers regarding their electronic communications by offering them separate feeds to each of their sites from different electronic communications centres

Successful executives ensure that their organisation develops and maintains sound disaster recovery plans that include provisions for business continuity if any risk materialises. They develop consensus among their fellow executives and within the departments responsible for implementing and maintaining disaster recovery plans. They furthermore ensure that the disaster recovery plans are regularly tested so that they do not become futile exercises on paper.

Environmental management

In today's world, the impact of the operation of every organisation on the environment is a significant factor influencing its success, its reputation and, consequently, its brand.

Its significance cannot and should not be underestimated, not only because of applicable legislative obligations but also because stakeholders and society at large are becoming increasingly sensitive to environmental hazards and adverse effects of corporate activity.

Successful executives ensure that a suitable environmental impact assessment and, where possible, an environmental management subprocess is embedded in each and every process and is thus reflected in the respective role and post descriptions. They further ensure that this is taught to responsible incumbents and its implementation is monitored with suitable KPIs.

Once again, depending on their type and size, organisations may establish an Environmental Manager post. Again, the manager title is misleading and is frequently misunderstood. This is a staff post and the incumbent acts as an internal consultant, advising and ensuring that the environmental management subprocess and its measures are embedded in each and every process having a direct or indirect environmental impact; that these subprocesses are well documented; and that the incumbents understand them fully and know how to implement them.

Environmental managers may act as internal auditors monitoring the implementation of the subprocess, but the responsibility for its implementation should always lie with the executives, ie the line management, that own and execute the main process, up to the CEO and the board of directors who should approve the environmental policy of the organisation and monitor its implementation.

EXAMPLE

In a hotel, the technical or fixed assets manager is responsible for the water supply to all areas. If the environmental impact assessment shows that a significant environmental impact is the huge consumption of water by the facility, guest rooms, kitchen, gardening, pools, etc, then the technical or fixed assets manager must take measures to reduce consumption without compromising the service the hotel is offering. This may be done in a number of ways: fitting taps with timers or flow regulators, water-saving policies for guests and staff, and close monitoring of water meters to swiftly identify any leakages. The idea here is that the line managers are responsible for water consumption and avoidance of loss or overspending and not a third party (eg the environmental manager) who has no authority over the process.

Health and safety management

Nowadays, the health, safety and wellness of the organisation's people are acknowledged of being of paramount importance in every organisation. Many of the health and safety aspects of running an organisation are governed by legislation, with strict rules and severe penalties for any violations.

The importance assigned to the health and safety of all stakeholders is a significant factor influencing, in many ways, the success of an organisation. Talented staff may show a preference for organisations with high health and safety consciousness, and companies may not be able to retain high flyers if the latter consider the workplace to be potentially hazardous or the management indifferent.

Successful executives ensure that health and safety, and even wellness, are systematically managed by embedding, as applicable, an appropriate subprocess within every process, which is reflected in the respective role and post descriptions, and that this is taught to responsible incumbents and its implementation is monitored with suitable KPIs.

Depending on their type and size, organisations are required by law to establish a Health and Safety Officer or Manager post. We stress that, in this case, the manager title is not misleading. Health and safety officers/managers bear considerable responsibility, though they hold a staff post, and the incumbents act as internal consultants, advising and ensuring that:

- The health and safety management subprocess and, depending on the organisation's policy, the wellness management and measures are embedded, as applicable, in each and every process.
- These subprocesses and all applicable rules and regulations are well documented.
- The executives and the operatives of the organisation understand them fully and know how to implement them.

Health and safety managers/officers are obliged by law to act as internal auditors monitoring and reporting on the implementation of the legislation and whichever related standards the organisation has adopted. Hence, the responsibility for their implementation, in this case, lies with both the health and safety officer and the executives, ie the line management, that own and execute the (parent) process, up to the CEO and the board of directors who should review the health and safety policy of the organisation and monitor its implementation in parallel with the implementation of all relevant law.

EXAMPLE

As we have seen with environmental management, the health and safety risk associated with a process must be managed by the process owner, ie the line manager. In a factory, the line manager is responsible for ensuring that machinery is equipped with the necessary protection guards and that these are not bypassed, that people use their personal protective equipment as required, that the area is clean and that people are not overexposed to adverse conditions.

Quality management

The impact of the quality of an organisation's products, services and servicing on its operation, as perceived by the related stakeholders, is crucial for its success and its longevity. This is true not only for the value produced and delivered to external stakeholders, eg customers, but also to the value delivered to internal stakeholders, eg executives and operatives.

Besides being an objective characteristic of a product or service measured with specific systematic methods and tools, quality is frequently a subjective characteristic, as perceived by direct or indirect stakeholders. In many cases, it may even be both a subjective and an objective characteristic, and its performance indicators may have entirely different values at a particular point in time, since the subjective impressions of product and service recipients may be different to objective measurements. The term 'quality' also incorporates the notion of meeting implied characteristics.

EXAMPLE

You may require a ruler that measures in inches or centimetres and is 30 centimetres in length, but needless to say, its edge must be straight. This is an implied need that may never be specified by the client but is still a requirement.

Quality must be an inherent element of a product or service and, therefore, of the processes that design, produce and deliver them and service their recipients (that is, of all processes constituting the value chain, from the beginning of the supply chain to servicing the recipient stakeholder, ie the customer), and of all associated external processes and products and services, at both ends of the value chain. These can be processes producing raw or semi-finished goods, equipment, input services, support services, staff services, production services, and after-sales services.

Quality nowadays is thought to be a *sine qua non* component of the productivity of a process, the other two being effectiveness and efficiency, and has two dimensions: the quality of the execution of the process, and the quality of its output – a tangible product, a service or a piece of information.

Its significance cannot and should not be underestimated, not only because of applicable legislative obligations but also because stakeholders and society at large are becoming increasingly sensitive to and demanding of the quality of products, services and servicing.

Successful executives ensure that the quality management subprocess is embedded in each and every process and is thus reflected in the respective executive or operative role and post descriptions; that this is taught to the responsible incumbents; and its implementation is monitored with suitable KPIs.

Depending on their type and size, organisations may establish a Quality Manager post. We stress that the manager title here is misleading and is frequently misunderstood. This is a staff post and the incumbent acts as an internal consultant, advising and ensuring that the quality management subprocess and its measures are embedded in each and every process; that these subprocesses are well documented; and that the incumbents understand them fully and know how to implement them.

Quality managers may also act as internal auditors monitoring the implementation of this subprocess, but the responsibility for its implementation should always lie with the executives, ie the line management, that own and execute every process, up to the CEO.

EXAMPLE

In a call centre, it is the responsibility of the call centre manager to ensure that 80% of the calls are answered after the second ring and that all calls are answered within five rings. How many times the phone rings before being answered is one element of the quality of the service that the call centre offers.

Innovation management

An organisation without creativity and innovation has no future. It's at a dead end. To be successful and sustainable, an organisation must innovate continuously by:

- Designing new products and services
- Redesigning its products and services
- Improving and redesigning its processes
- Inventing new business models
- Reviewing and revising its mission and its vision

> **Innovation can no longer be a circumstantial, ad hoc event.**
>
> **It must be a continuous process resulting in a series of innovations. Productive innovators use process management to execute innovation, to hone their own and the organisation's innovation competency, and to increase the innovation productivity, ie its effectiveness, its agility, its speed and its efficiency, as well as the quality of its outcome.**
>
> **The ability to execute innovation is at least as important as the innovation itself, and the link between innovation and execution, in today's highly disruptive, technological world, can only be accomplished with systematic process management.**
>
> **Successful executives ensure that innovation is managed as part of process management through continuous process improvement or reengineering; through relevant KPIs, embedded in the performance indicators of every process, usually as improvements to other performance indicators; and through zero-based process redesign exercises.**

They encourage and provoke people to ask questions and make radical suggestions, and they hold group meetings with the purpose of drastically changing products, processes and business models. They never insult or discourage any person for expressing radical ideas. On the contrary, they reward them for any ideas that are adopted.

They ensure that for core and staff processes aiming at the design of new services, products and business models, innovation is being managed as part of each process by:

- Formulating specific innovation KPIs
- Setting respective target values
- Systematically monitoring actual results
- Reviewing plans and revising them whenever necessary
- Including innovation management within the regular duties of executives

EXAMPLE

The new CEO of a small electronic equipment designer encourages its people to devote half an hour a day to thinking outside of the box, conceiving improvements to its processes, its products and its services, or new ones. They hold weekly meetings at which they present their ideas, which are openly discussed and, where feasible, these are adopted and their ideators rewarded. No contribution is discouraged or criticised.

Innovation managers, if necessary, hold staff positions and act as internal consultants.

Successful executives appoint an innovation manager with the mandate of introducing modern creativity and innovation methodologies, training the people of the organisation, and catalysing the implementation of innovation.

Innovation management has not traditionally been considered a standalone element of scientific management. We, however, consider it a crucial component of the management and leadership processes.

Project management

Successful executives recognise that projects are different from processes and ensure that they are managed differently, by considering project management as a separate process, or as a generic subprocess of the core, support, staff, management or leadership processes of the organisation.

Process versus project

A process is a permanent (typically mission-dictated and, hence, routine) sequence of interdependent activities, each consuming/using one or more resources (employee time, energy, machine time, money, etc) to convert inputs (data, material, parts, etc) into outputs (services, products, assets, information or knowledge), in a standardised manner. It is part of the business-as-usual working mode of an organisation. It is mature, to a good extent. To make its resource consumption worthwhile, it must add value to the organisation.

A process is staffed by people who have been trained and are knowledgeable of the work methods used and the people with whom they must cooperate. They are expected to function efficiently and effectively and to produce results according to precise specifications. They must be competent at what they do, will usually perform their activities for lengthy periods of time, and work under a stable culture and with well-established interdependencies. The performance of a process is measured through KPIs using pre-agreed targets, and its operatives are assessed (at least partly) in terms of how well they perform within the process, ie how well their competences and competencies match those demanded for the optimal execution of the process, and whether they are being put to productive use.

Process management refers to the activities of planning, coordinating and monitoring the execution of the process. Constant incremental improvement is a part of process management – eg the Kaizen way. If the process is found to be severely inefficient and/or ineffective, it is likely it should be redesigned or reengineered. The process owner is the manager of the process and the person to be credited with or held responsible for the performance of the process.

By contrast, a project is a temporary assignment and usually has a temporary structure, aiming at creating a new, unique product, service or result. It has a defined beginning and end, and a predetermined amount of resources to be used. It has a specific recipient – a customer – for its final product, either internal or external to the organisation. When its purpose has been achieved, the project has no reason for existing and it is terminated.

Depending on its nature, it is executed by performing either stable, well-structured processes, or ad hoc processes.

Internal projects

An internal project is outside the usual operation of the organisation and has an internal customer, the board of directors, a high-level executive, or an internal organisational entity. It is used to realise (part of) the vision of the organisation or to react to an unexpected need, threat or opportunity, such as a disruptive technological innovation or a disaster, or to realise a significant improvement, or respond to a regulatory or a major financial change. It belongs to the strategic level of operations.

The people populating the project team usually come from various functions and disciplines and may not have worked together in the past. They are borrowed from their regular posts and are returned to these once the project ends. Due to the nature of projects, sensitive issues often arise, such as conflicts due to group dynamics, which must be addressed. The project team members are chosen based on their competences and competencies; they must complement each other and be able to work as a single body, as a team, and deliver results. A good team fit and a positive team spirit must be achieved for the project to deliver.

The success of a project is measured by its end result: its deliverable. Specifically, a project's degree of success is judged by answering, at the end of the project, the question of whether the purpose of the project has been fulfilled according to the description, requirements and specifications set at the beginning; whether this has been done on time and within budget; and whether it is acceptable to the internal client(s).

One-off internal projects may entail ad hoc processes that, due to their nature, are not systematically designed and managed. Such projects include, for example, research projects carried out by an organisation or a university for the first time.

EXAMPLE

A car manufacturer has a systematic process for managing the design of new models but employs an ad hoc process for designing a concept vehicle, based on entirely different principles.

Projects for external customers

Depending on the nature of the mission of the organisation, it may routinely execute projects for external stakeholders; for example, when it constructs custom buildings based on customer designs, which obey standard principles. These projects are tactical and not strategic. They have stable processes and are systematically managed.

Managing external projects is similar to managing internal projects, with the significant exception that these projects are managed as part of core processes and are staffed (semi-)permanently with the same people.

EXAMPLE

A contracting company building houses to customer drawings has several core processes, such as: quantity surveying; estimation, quoting and bidding based on the customer's architectural specifications; formulating contracts for successful bids; project managing the building of each house; purchasing materials and services; warehousing on site; quantity surveying actual works; invoicing against architect work certificates; receiving payments; and commissioning each house. Each process is carried out by the same people, except for the real building project, which is carried out by an ad hoc team, set up from a pool of people depending on the type, size, complexity and schedule of the contract.

The company has a quality assurance team comprising specialised civil, mechanical, and electrical engineers ensuring that the project teams implement the project management methodology adopted by the company as well as high standards of building engineering works.

An organisation may execute ad hoc projects based on new principles employed for the first time. In this case, they are managed as strategic projects.

Organisations, such as consultancy firms, execute strategic projects for clients. These are managed similarly to the internal strategic projects.

Project management methodologies

Project management is a process demanding the application of knowledge, skills, tools and techniques to project activities to meet project requirements. It has five phases:

- Initiating
- Planning
- Executing
- Monitoring and controlling
- Closing

Project managers are the executives responsible for the smooth operation of and the end result delivered by the project. They carry out the day-to-day planning, coordinating, leading and supervising of the execution and monitoring of the project activities and progress, escalating problems or changes as required to the project steering committee.

In most organisations, while processes are its backbone, through which its mission is achieved, projects are equally important as the tools through which change or innovation is accomplished and the vision is realised. They require a different approach to their structure and management, to people leadership, to closely monitoring progress and results, and to prompt problem-solving.

Successful executives introduce or develop a structured approach to project management, applying a project management methodology and tools so that both tactical and ad hoc strategic projects are managed productively.

They ensure that:

- The methodology is governed by the organisation's codes of ethics and governance, in the same way that they govern process management.
- This methodology is taught to people, regardless of whether it is their main regular role, or a circumstantial role in parallel with the regular roles defined in their post description.
- Project managers report to the executive who bears the responsibility for the systematic project performance monitoring, review and reporting.

Programme management

On occasion, organisations will need to realise a major change, the effects of which will transcend the whole or a large part of the organisation. Such a change can be a major acquisition or buy-out, a merger, a significant business process reengineering or digital transformation programme, or a significant culture change programme initiated by a new CEO or owner.

Managing such a change, which affects many of the organisation's people, is referred to as programme management. This is a one-off major strategic project and is different from managing a confined tactical, or even a minor strategic project, in which a relatively small number of the organisation's people are involved.

As a rule, traditional project management methodologies prove to be inadequate for programme management.

In their efforts to manage such a major change, programme managers fall into two different types. First, there are those who focus on project management methodologies, spending most of their time and effort on tasks, charts and metrics. While this scientific management approach has some positive aspects, and structure is necessary for success, this type of programme manager often falls short when it comes to delivering the specified programme results.

The other type of programme manager takes a different approach, emphasising activities around relationship-building and driving stakeholder engagement. This type of programme manager practises people leadership.

While it is necessary to apply a project management methodology and follow defined processes, successful programme managers elevate their performance by aligning, engaging and leveraging their stakeholders to drive results. The programme managers who take this approach change the game by finding a way to leverage their own and their people's competences and competencies to adapt to the changing environment and needs of the organisation's stakeholders.

> **Successful executives select their programme managers carefully so that they are not only productive managers but also effective leaders, and empower them, ensuring that they believe in and apply the same values.**

We would stress here that successful project managers do employ elements of leadership. However, programme management, involving many more of the organisation's people and/or aiming at effecting a major change, demands a significantly higher level of leadership competency and implementation.

EXAMPLE

The board of trustees of a medium-sized traditional university was forced to admit that the productivity of the organisation was inadequate, its quality of learning and research was slipping, and its slim financial reserves were fast depleted. They appointed a new executive president with the explicit mandate to carry out a major reengineering programme.

The new president appointed an experienced external consultant as programme manager and, on their advice, appointed a fully fledged programme management structure including a steering committee, headed by themselves, and a multidisciplinary programme team led by the consultant, to execute the programme. The members of the team were selected based on their expertise and knowledge of the university processes and their Belbin role capabilities to ensure that the group could function as a team.

The team successfully carried out the programme: they redesigned, to a small or significant degree, most core, support and staff processes. Those most drastically reengineered were:

- The teaching–learning process
- The research processes
- The bidding for research funding process
- The general fund-raising process

Performance management

For years, executives have been striving to invent better theories and practices in regard to how to best execute the mission of the organisation they head and realise its vision. In other words, to find better ways to create and deliver value, immediately and in the future, to its stakeholders: the owner(s)/shareholders, creditors/investors, customers, employees, partners/suppliers, and their community.

One of the many techniques they have invented is performance management. Its overall purpose is to contribute to the achievement of high performance by both the organisation and its people. High performance means reaching, exceeding, and stretching goals and targets for achieving value for money, measured as the degree to which the specified characteristics of the produced and delivered products and services are met, and whether the expectations of the various stakeholder groups are satisfied.

Nowadays, great significance is attributed to the various elements of performance management that organisations incorporate into their processes. Unfortunately, many executives consider these to be bureaucratic and time-consuming and do not give them adequate consideration.

Successful executives see performance management as a two-faced coin:

- **On one side, they embed performance measures, such as KPIs, in every process of the organisation and, therefore, in every post description, and use them in managing the processes, leading the people, planning, and monitoring performance.**
- **On the other side, they use compound performance measures, derived via aggregation and statistical analysis of process performance measures, as business intelligence.**

In this way, they ensure that every individual, every team, every department, every division, and the organisation at large, *know how they are* performing and whether and to what level their stakeholders are satisfied.

Furthermore, performance management serves as a tool for people management, especially for continuous improvement, as well as for introducing performance-based reward schemes, which must be employed carefully due to possible weaknesses. Where employees are driven solely by 'soft' motives, such as learning and development of their skills, they often fail miserably. We elaborate on this issue in the performance management section of Chapter Five.

> **Performance management is significant because it establishes a framework for the organisation's people – in particular, the executives – to plan, act, execute, monitor and review their work while, at the same time, they are able to assess and agree on aims and concerns that arise while accomplishing the mission, creating and delivering value, and realising the vision of the organisation, ultimately achieving longevity and sustainability.**
>
> **This enables both sides, those managing/leading and those being managed/led, to have clear objectives that help them both execute their processes creating and delivering value and develop and grow themselves.**

> **Successful executives ensure that performance management is inherently exercised by all levels of the hierarchy, ie by the executives overseeing the outcome and behaviour of other people (work/team leaders, supervisors, managers, department heads, division heads, general managers, up to the CEO) and by the operatives executing each and every process and project.**

Sometimes, the term 'performance management' is used in lieu of the traditional appraisal system. This is wrong. Performance management encompasses a much broader management and leadership concept.

A performance management system is combined with a formal business model and, therefore, with a systematic 'plan, act, monitor and review' cycle approach, as is, for example, the EFQM Business Excellence Model in combination with the Management-by-Objectives and/or the Balanced Scorecard performance management systems.

While introducing performance management, we feel the need to remind our readers that it must be an all-encompassing management and leadership umbrella duty, linking the fundamental duties of the executives, namely:

- Managing culture
- Managing processes and subprocesses
- Leading and managing people
- Managing mission and vision

All executed continuously and consciously and, to a large extent, concurrently.

EXAMPLE

The newly appointed CEO of a medium-sized European city water board decided to introduce the Business Excellence Model of the European Foundation for Quality Management (EFQM) and invited their people to carry out its first self-evaluation, under the guidance of a small multi-disciplinary team headed by an external expert consultant who trained the team and presented to everybody the relevant methodology.

The result of the self-evaluation was disappointing – just 270 points out of a theoretical maximum of 1000.

The lowest marks were given to the soft enabler and result criteria: leadership, people, culture and policy, suppliers and partners, and community. The process and customer criteria scores were not as bad, though still not satisfactory.

The CEO invited their people to propose KPIs for all areas. The proposals were discussed openly in various fora from the floor level to the executive committee. A significant number of new KPIs were adopted and their measurement methods introduced, targets set, actual results measured, deviations analysed, and corrective actions implemented.

A second self-evaluation was carried out two years later. The results were unexpected: the score went up to 630 out of 1000, a 133% increase on the first self-evaluation. A year later they were recognised for excellence by EFQM and were awarded five stars.

The CEO asked people whether they would like to introduce a reward scheme based on performance, and to participate in the European Quality Award competition two years later. The great majority accepted both proposals. They proposed and introduced additional KPIs measuring personal, team and departmental performance, and personal development performance, as well as benchmarking against competitors for various soft criteria.

Two years later, the company was a finalist for the EFQM Excellence Award and became the EFQM Prize Winner in Developing Organisational Capability.

Internal audit

Internal auditing is a *must* in every modern organisation. It presents itself in two forms:

- As an independent support process: an objective assurance and consulting activity designed to add value and improve an organisation's operations. It helps an organisation accomplish its objectives by bringing a systematic, disciplined approach to evaluating and improving the effectiveness of risk management, control, and governance processes.
- As a subprocess embedded in every other process of the organisation: realised as internal control activities, at best safeguarding the productive parts of the process from errors, mistakes, misuse, deception and illegal actions, while at least monitoring check-points to promptly highlight these dangers.

Depending on their size and nature, organisations may have an internal auditor or even an internal audit department carrying out the internal audit process and advising and monitoring all other departments on the existence, need for, or adequacy of internal audit systems embedded in their processes.

Internal auditors act either autonomously, following their own activity plan, or reactively carry out investigative work on the instructions of the board of directors or the CEO. They may also be triggered by whistleblowing. In certain cases, they may be proactively asked to give their opinion before any major or high-risk decisions are taken.

Successful executives ensure that:

- **The internal audit process, as executed by the internal auditor and/or the internal audit function is seen as an independent standalone process; is managed to achieve high productivity (effectiveness, efficiency and quality); and has its own rules, KPIs and business plans and reports.**
- **Internal audit systems are embedded in all core, support and staff processes of the organisation.**

EXAMPLE

Until recently, the internal auditor in a public organisation was considered by executives and operatives to be a kind of policeman, with the result that they avoided any productive cooperation with the internal audit department.

A young executive was appointed as internal auditor, following the retirement of the previous incumbent. After consulting the chairperson of the board and the CEO, the new IA explained to the organisation that their role would be to:

- Act as an internal consultant to executives/process owners for improving the various organisational processes with an emphasis on the internal audit procedures
- Audit mainly processes and projects – their design, planning and execution – leaving the financial and accounting audit to the external auditors
- Assist the board and the executives in investigating abnormalities and suspicions of fraud or violations of legislation or regulations

Within two years, the attitude of the executives and the operatives had changed utterly. They were competing for the services of the internal auditor and their staff. The internal procedures of the organisation improved significantly, minimising errors and weaknesses.

Business planning and budgeting

Successful executives plan effectively the production and delivery of value as dictated by the organisation's mission, to realise its purpose, by ensuring that it transcends the whole organisation. They acknowledge that business planning is not adequately effective when executed in a vacuum by the top executives and their office staff without iterative exchange of planning proposals and scenarios, both vertically, from the bottom to the top of the organisation, and horizontally, between interrelated/interdependent processes and functions, until alignment and harmonisation are achieved.

In effect, they treat it as:

- A staff process exercised by the organisation's (ie the corporate) planning and budgeting department staff.

- A subprocess for all executive posts, from the CEO and the board of directors down to the bottom-level line managers. They consider it a fundamental element of the management and leadership processes, as we shall see in the respective chapters.

The reason we consider business planning and budgeting as a generic subprocess is that it needs to be specified in detail and be accompanied by specific methodologies and tools, and included in the description of all executive posts as a specific role with its own KPIs. As such, it needs to be managed like all other processes and generic subprocesses, by specifying the competences, competencies and KPIs required for its optimal execution.

To this end, the business planning (sub)process covers elements including:

- Collection of real data with accuracy and thoroughness, both from within the organisation and from the market, as ethical competitive intelligence (CI)
- Analysis of the data through the use of scientific tools, such as SWOT (strengths, weaknesses, opportunities, threats) and PESTLE (political, economic, social, technological, legal and environmental) evaluation
- Formulation of planning scenarios
- Risk analysis
- Formulation of short-term operational plans and rolling budgets
- Formulation of mid to long-term strategic plans and zero-based budgets, including the formulation of the organisation's vision and the review and revision of the organisation's mission
- Monitoring of actual results and analysis of any deviations from the planned targets
- Identification of effective compound organisational KPIs
- Specification and operation of business intelligence (BI) systems, assisting executives effectively at all levels in carrying out their management and leadership processes

Successful executives ensure that this generic business planning subprocess, or at least a subset of its elements, is included in the description of the various executive posts.

Evidently, this subprocess, like many of the other generic subprocesses, needs to be applied periodically to itself, so that organisations can upgrade systematically their planning and budgeting process.

Strategic versus operational planning

Business planning covers, as we have already mentioned and will explore in detail in the next chapters, operational planning, ie the execution of the (current) mission, and strategic planning, ie the formulation and realisation of the organisation's vision.

We remind you here that a *strategy* means merely a *method* for achieving a purpose, a mission or a vision. The strategy for realising an organisation's mission is the method of, or approach to, executing its processes and its projects. A successful and sustainable organisation has stable processes, and in carrying out its business planning process it merely plans the volume and the quality at which its processes will be executed. It does not need to refer to strategic planning unless it desires to effect change – to innovate.

An organisation engages in strategic planning when formulating its vision and strategic projects for realising it, ie for improving its processes, its products and services, and its business models, and for inventing new ones – in short, for effecting change. Strategic planning is entirely different from operational planning, which by nature is based on tradition, on the status quo, and aims at realising the short-term targets of the organisation by executing its processes as they are already defined. By contrast, strategic planning looks towards the future, towards the unknown. It demands thinking outside of the box, breaking away from tradition.

To be able to do this, executives need to stand on solid ground. They need clarity on the current situation of their organisation and its environment. This can only be accomplished by achieving and maintaining a clear view of the organisation in terms of its processes, its data, its business and competitive intelligence, its structure, the competences and competencies of its people, its performance and, most significantly, its culture.

Successful executives achieve clarity through systematic process and information management. In this way, they not only execute successfully the organisation's mission but also lead their people in effectively visioning the future of the organisation and themselves within it, and in formulating and realising an ambitious vision with its strategic projects, conceiving and executing continuous improvement and innovation.

Enterprise business architecture (EBA) management

Successful executives acknowledge that managing the organisational architectures is a complex but necessary and fruitful activity. They ensure that process and function owners manage their partial EBA with the assistance of the person(s) in charge of maintaining the aggregate EBA, hence the need for EBA architect staff positions.

EBA architecting is, on the one hand, a generic subprocess embedded in the management process and, therefore, allocated to each and every executive post; and, on the other hand, a staff process closely intertwined with a number of other staff processes, such as business process management, information systems development, business planning and performance management.

Successful executives build and maintain the EBA of the organisation they head, not only as the foundation of its management and leadership models but also as the primary tool for achieving clarity within the organisation, covering its value streams, its infrastructures, its processes, its KPIs, its mission, its vision, its plans and strategic projects, and the management of change.

In doing so, they apply a number of principles, such as:

- Looking at the organisation through the eyes of the various stakeholders to whom value is delivered, starting with the customers, asking questions about what value they expect, of what quality, at what time, and at what price. In this way, the main value streams are built with their processes and respective KPIs.
- Ensuring that the organisation's mission and its realisation plans are consistent with its value streams, its processes, its KPIs and its targets, and that its vision is consistent with its purpose and its mission evolution, in the form of process, product, service and value model innovation.
- Streamlining the organisational structure so that it is process-centric, enabling optimised execution of its end-to-end processes.
- Ensuring that the culture of the organisation is based on its values and transcends, harmoniously, its various architectures.

- Striving for alignment in value creation and delivery to the organisation's stakeholders and, subsequently, to achieving engagement in realising its mission and its strategic projects, and commitment to action and ownership of processes, projects and targets.

In doing this, they must meet certain challenges, such as:

- Overcoming inertia and resistance due to tradition, by engaging all people in open dialogue, innovation and change implementation.
- Surpassing resistance to transform a functional organisational structure into a process-centric one.
- Avoiding the adoption of too many concurrent change projects, which the organisation does not have the capacity to execute, and thus avoiding the frustration caused by their likely failure.
- Avoiding a mismatch between a performance-based reward scheme, the process KPIs, and the business plan targets.

Process management

Managing processes and all related business matters, as we have explained previously, falls within the realm of the duties, and hence the post description, of all executive posts. It is, in effect, a subprocess of their management and their leadership processes.

It should not, however, be expected that all executives of any organisation have the competence and competency to manage their processes effectively. As with most of the other generic subprocesses, organisations need to assign the process management process[37] to a specific executive or, depending on size, to a particular department. In small organisations, it may be one of the roles of the human resource manager or other HRM department posts.

A central staff process management post must be seen, as with other similar ones, as embracing an internal consultant's and an auditor's role with the objective of introducing methodologies, teaching and coaching executives and their people, advising them and auditing their relevant work, and reporting to the top executives and the board of directors, exactly as the internal auditor, the chief risk officer and the chief information officer should do. In addition, this staff post must build and maintain the aggregate corporate process architecture.

37 The Business Process Management Group (2005) *In Search of Business Excellence*.

> **Furthermore, the process management officer must be, by objective necessity, the advisor and the liaison between the process owners and the information system analysts/designers, ie between the business units and the information systems management unit. Both research and our own experience prove that most of the failures of automation, computerisation and digital transformation projects (which cost organisations, directly and indirectly, billions of dollars, pounds or euros, loss of business, and frustration every year) are attributed, in the great majority of organisations, to the lack of formal process management and respective responsible posts and incumbents.**

It is a proven fact that the language of the business people, those who own and execute the business processes, and the information technology or information systems people, those who develop and maintain the process-automating software, are quite different. Besides, in most cases, both sides lack a formal methodology.

Many university graduates with degrees in computer science and related subjects are not taught any systems development methodologies, and their teachers do not have any experience in real-life systems development with the application of any formal methodology. Process management is rarely, if at all, taught in universities and process management practitioners are seldom employed, either permanently or as consultants, during process reengineering or computerisation.

Process management practitioners are the people who speak both the business language and the information systems language, and understand both methodologies to an adequate extent and depth. They are obliged to speak the business language and present and specify the business processes in a way that is understood univocally by, on the one hand, the process owners and the business executives and operatives and, on the other, the information systems developers, so that whatever system they develop or customise (using an off-the-shelf software application) will accurately reflect the business process and the related data, as well as its rules.

The many real-life automation failures and the findings of our own research support our firm belief that all organisations need to introduce process management as a subprocess, and hence as a role, in all executive post descriptions, and as many operative posts as is reasonable; and process management process as a formal staff process, and hence role, allocated to a suitable post and its incumbent.

The execution of this process must be managed systematically, as with all other processes and generic subprocesses.

Successful executives ensure that:

- Their organisation builds and maintains its process architecture as a vital component of its organisational architectures.
- Each process is described thoroughly including its interdependencies with other processes and data, and allocated formally to a process owner, ideally the executive in charge of the execution of the process.
- For every process, suitable KPIs are identified together with appropriate mechanisms for measuring actual values; target values are set as components of operational and strategic business planning; actual values of KPIs are measured; deviations between targets and actual values are identified and analysed, deviation reasons are identified, and corrective action is taken; and design reviews and updates are regularly carried out for both improvement and automation purposes.
- The process architecture is managed systematically by a dedicated process manager role which they allocate, depending on the size and complexity of the organisation, to either a dedicated post (the process manager) or to a multi-role post, such as the personnel manager or the information manager, who acts as internal consultant to process owners and liaison between them and the information systems management function.

In summary

Whatever the type or purpose of an organisation, it must ensure that important generic business requirements are met. Some of these are imposed by legislation, others by regulatory authorities, certain others by internal regulations and codes of practice, while others still by management and leadership practice. Meeting these requirements can be achieved by embedding in the organisation's processes all applicable generic activities.

The world is increasingly complex and stakeholders ever more demanding. Legislation and regulations are becoming more numerous and complicated, competition is becoming shrewder and more aggressive, and technology and innovation faster and more disruptive.

Therefore, executives must concentrate on realising their organisation's mission, creating and delivering value to its stakeholders – ideally to their delight – and this will prove increasingly demanding and challenging. They cannot afford to devote unlimited time to meeting, in an ad hoc manner, any applicable generic business requirements, such as risk, business continuity, environmental, personnel health and safety, and quality management, as well as internal audit.

Successful executives ensure that these generic business requirements are dealt with systematically by seamlessly embedding them as subprocesses in the organisation's processes so that they are effectively and efficiently executed and managed while executing the core, support, staff, management and leadership activities making up the organisation's value streams and processes. They define suitable KPIs in addition to those measuring the performance of the organisation's enablers and the level of stakeholder satisfaction. They set ambitious targets, monitor actual results and take all necessary corrective or improvement action.

Table 4.1 presents the most important generic business subprocesses.

Table 4.1: Generic subprocesses

1.	Culture Management
2.	Governance Management
3.	Stakeholder Relationship Management
4.	Risk Management
5.	Business Continuity Management
6.	Health & Safety Management
7.	Environmental Management
8.	Quality Management
9.	Innovation Management
10.	Project Management
11.	Programme Management
12.	Performance Management
13.	Internal Audit
14.	Business Planning, Budgeting, Monitoring & Review
15.	Enterprise Business Architecture Management
16.	Process Management

Vital questions

1. Does your organisation recognise the importance of systematically managing generic business subprocesses?
2. Does your organisation maintain a map and detailed descriptions of generic business subprocesses? If yes, which ones?
3. Does your organisation maintain a process architecture and, if yes, does it include generic business subprocesses within it and in each process description?
4. Does your organisation define and map its processes in detail, including their generic subprocesses? Does it map their dependencies? Does it map the interdependent data? If yes, does it use a dedicated software tool?
5. Does your organisation define KPIs measuring the performance of generic business subprocesses?
6. Are generic business subprocesses covered by the information systems automating the organisation's processes?
7. Does your organisation's business intelligence (BI) system cover generic business subprocess KPIs?

PART II
MANAGEMENT AND LEADERSHIP

CHAPTER FIVE

MANAGING THE ORGANISATION IN EXECUTING ITS MISSION AND VISION

Successful executives manage their organisation as both a static and a dynamic coherent holarchical system comprising semi-autonomous subsystems. They manage:

- **Its design, its construction and its operation**
- **Its values, its philosophy, its culture and its governance**
- **Its mission, its value streams and its enablers**
- **Its data, its information, its knowledge and its wisdom**
- **Its vision, its creativity, its innovation and its sustainability**
- **Its posts, its staffing and its people's capabilities, growth and affairs**
- **The value and the lifecycle of its customers, its products and its services**
- **Its customer and its other stakeholder relations**

They plan, budget, staff, organise, direct, coordinate, execute and report.

To manage is to accomplish. Used as a verb, 'accomplish' usually implies that something is being done. Used in the past tense, it often indicates that something has been achieved successfully, even though we may need to express that something has been poorly managed.

We use the term executive(s) to refer to the persons who are appointed to head an organisation or an organisational entity within an organisation with the mandate to create and deliver value to its stakeholders, fulfilling the organisation's purpose.

To help our readers clarify what successful executives do and how they do it, how they ensure that their organisation is successful, and remains so, long term, we distinguish their roles as managers and as leaders. We do this despite the fact that to be successful they must seamlessly combine the two roles and, occasionally, even merge management and leadership into one integrated role.

In this chapter, we focus on the management role of the executive, using a fictitious, virtual model of an organisation to elaborate on this role. We ask you to imagine that our virtual organisation is similar to an actual organisation, with only one difference. Instead of being staffed by human resources, it is populated only by 'robots' with the exception of you, the executive. This may seem an extreme simile. We employ it to stress that in architecting and blueprinting the organisation and its operation, one can approach an ideal system.

In the subsequent chapter on leadership, we revert to our actual organisation, populated by human beings with all of their strengths, weaknesses and dynamism.

In their role as managers, successful executives perform two sets of management processes.

They comprehend, design and automate, to the maximum feasible degree, the operations of the organisation, and ensure that their robots are programmed to execute productively (ie effectively, efficiently and to the specified quality) their processes, projects and plans.

They also plan, in detail, the operation of the organisation over a specific time period (usually the short term); direct, coordinate and monitor the execution of the plans and projects; continually adjust the plans, responding to external and internal parameters, to create and deliver the value specified by the organisation's mission; and execute the strategic plans, dictated by the organisation's vision, to achieve the specified deliverables, which will lead to the evolving mission that is envisaged (Figure 5.1).

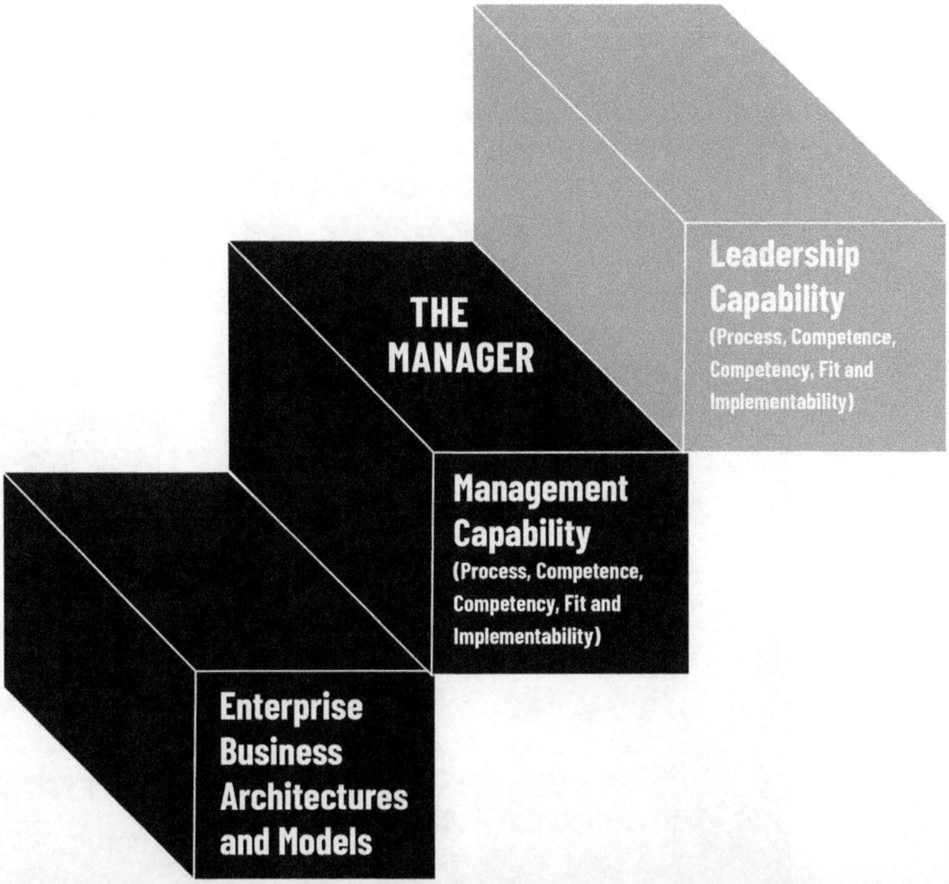

Figure 5.1: The effective and efficient manager

Architecting and blueprinting the organisation's functioning

To programme the operations of the organisation, successful executives must comprehend all of its aspects thoroughly.

They draw blueprints depicting the static organisation from all possible angles and then create dynamic flowcharts of all its operations:

- The acquisition and reception of resources
- Their transformation by the organisation's enablers into outputs, ie into created value
- The delivery of the created value to interested stakeholders

Successful executives formulate the enterprise business architectures that we have outlined in the previous part of this book; they document, in useful notation, the architectures and all their relationships correctly and thoroughly; they design and document all value streams, processes and workflows, their inputs, outputs and rules, accurately and thoroughly, in useful notation so that they can be turned into software and machine programs; they automate the workflows, to the most technologically and financially feasible degree. They program the robots, as ideal virtual people, that will execute, precisely as designed, the organisational processes, so that:

- **They comprehend the organisation as outlined above, ie they acquire the competences (knowhow) required for the optimal execution of the processes.**
- **They comprehend, ie they acquire, the competencies (imitating, as closely as possible, the human qualities) required for the optimal execution of the processes. In other words, they imitate the best people executing the respective roles.**
- **They comprehend, ie they are programmed with, the plans for the creation and delivery of value over a set time period, as dictated by stakeholder needs and expectations, market conditions, and organisational capacity.**
- **They could even be furnished with artificial intelligence (AI) enabling them to self-heal program glitches, overcome unforeseen problems, minor changes in inputs and plans, and improve their processes, adapting to evolving needs and conditions.**

They acknowledge that their organisation must deliver in terms of satisfying the needs and the expectations of its stakeholders in comparison to its competitors and in light of market developments.

They therefore embed in the organisation's architectural descriptions and programmes suitable metrics, including key performance indicators (KPIs), which enable the inclusion and setting of targets in the plans, which they then use to direct process execution and monitor the organisational performance by comparing the actual values attained for each indicator against the planned targets. In this way they are able to detect variances, or lack of variances where they should exist, identify their causes and effect adjustments, changes and corrections.

To analyse the causes of the variances, negative or positive, they decompose the indicators down to comprehensible parameters of the organisation's assets, resources, enablers, activities and outputs, be those goods, assets, services, information or knowledge.

Thus, ultimately, they create and use a detailed hierarchy of indicators corresponding to the hierarchy of the organisational architectures from the top value streams down to atomic activities and their inputs, enablers and outputs.

In essence, this analysis comprises the management activity we call performance management.

Successful executives, in architecting the organisation, take into consideration the diverse roles or models that the various enablers and stakeholders can play or implement.

These can be:

- Individuals
  - As rational actors
  - As emotional actors
  - As social actors

In our virtual robot-staffed organisation only the rational role is applicable. The rational role executes the management process as it is described in this chapter. The emotional and social roles execute the leadership process as it is described in the next chapter.

Successful executives move continuously and seamlessly between the rational, emotional and social roles maintaining the optimum balance demanded by the prevailing conditions.

- Organisations
  - As machines
  - As brains

- As individual entrepreneurs
- As networks
- As partnerships of experts

- Processes
  - Systematic
  - Directed
  - Organic
- Society
  - Economic
  - Sociological
  - Ethical
  - Political
  - Legal
  - Historical

The management process

> **Management, in its broader sense, is what orchestrates a set of available interrelated enablers within an organisation to accomplish a specific purpose, such as a final product or service, creating and delivering value to interested stakeholders. It can be compared to the central intelligence and the central and peripheral neural subsystems of a living organism, the dissemination of actuating signals to the various interrelated enablers in structured sequences, and the receipt and processing of monitoring feedback signals in continuous or continual loops.**

In the evolution of humankind, management, which only became structured in the twentieth century, has passed through the various stages that mark the evolution of all other human activities.

The systematic development of management has progressed and is now described in a broad body of both dedicated and general literature comprising thousands of books, papers and articles. It is taught in hundreds of universities, specialised colleges and institutions, and expert classrooms, seminars and workshops, and discussed in conferences and symposia. It is the subject of continuous research by many scientists and practitioners around the planet.

It has grown to be one of the crucial elements of the concerns that humanity is most occupied with. Its socio-economic importance has been increasing ever since humans realised that raw materials and energy resources are limited and can only be best exploited through productive management, and that individuals' development, goals, welfare and happiness are highly influenced by the *hierarchy* of their working environment.

It concerns all the activities of an organisation, from policymaking at the board of director level, to the way operatives perform their duties.

Management, as a process, can be decomposed into a number of subprocesses answering the primary fundamental question of *what* executives do, in their management role. It further provides various methods, procedures and techniques answering the second fundamental question of *how* they do it.

The high-level management subprocesses are:

1. Designing the organisation as a productive system capable of creating and delivering the intended value
2. Directing, coordinating and controlling the construction of the organisation
3. Planning the operation to create and deliver the targeted value
4. Directing, coordinating and controlling the operation of the organisation and the execution of the business plan(s)
5. Monitoring the execution of the designs and the plans and revising them, as needed, to improve productivity, ie effectiveness, efficiency and quality of operation and output
6. Planning the evolution of the organisation towards an envisaged, evolved or new mission – ie formulating its vision and its strategic plans – to continue creating and delivering the currently specified or envisaged (evolving or new) value into the foreseeable future, ensuring the organisation's sustainability
7. Directing, coordinating and controlling the strategic projects, dictated by the organisation's vision, and their execution
8. Monitoring the execution of the strategic projects to improve their performance and ensure the creation of their deliverables, and revising the strategic plans, as needed, to ensure that the vision remains current and feasible

Designing the organisation

In previous chapters, we have discussed the structure of an organisation and its representation in various static and dynamic architectures. An organisation usually starts small and simple and evolves over time, either organically or via merging. Later, it may contract, either organically or by spinning out certain parts of the organisation or by splitting into two or more organisations, vertically and/or horizontally.

As we have seen, an organisation comprises a number of value streams decomposed into processes, subprocesses, down to atomic activities, carried out as roles by individual machines or persons, each with its own specifications, ie data and information, knowledge and plans, inputs, operating enablers, and outputs.

> **Successful executives acknowledge that designing, tuning and adjusting the organisation so that it can productively create and deliver value is one of their fundamental subprocesses and, hence, roles.**

The organisational design subprocess itself needs to be defined. The specific competences and competencies that are required need to be identified, acquired and continuously improved, and the subprocess should be carried out in a systematic way, like any other organisational process.

Organisational design is an activity that transcends the whole organisation, being a subprocess assigned to all executives, at all levels, with input from:

- All operatives, for continuous improvement (eg using the Kaizen method, as we shall see later)
- Internal business intelligence that analyses and presents performance and, in particular, deviations between actual results and targets and the causes of those deviations
- Competitive intelligence that presents developments in the market and the competition
- Internal and external innovation in products, services, business models, enabling technology and methods, as well as new knowledge resulting from research, discoveries, and inventions
- Suggestions from specialised staff mandated with organisational design and the continuous updating and upgrading of the same

The competences and competencies required for specific aspects of this activity may necessitate the use of external expert services.

> **Successful executives acknowledge that, due to its nature and impact, the organisational design falls, to a varying extent, within the portfolio of all executives from the top to the lowest hierarchical level. They further ensure that it is included in all executive post descriptions and exercised effectively.**

Directing the construction of the organisation

The organisational design needs to be implemented by executing specific projects, as dictated by the nature of the design and as set out within the business plans of the organisation, depending on available resources and tolerable disruptions of productive operation, if unavoidable.

The design and the corresponding implementation projects can affect any mix of:

- Value streams
- Business models
- Fixed assets, such as buildings and workspaces, technological infrastructure (such as electrical, electromechanical, energy and data networks), fixed machinery, and movable property (such as furniture and vehicles)
- Process and data specifications
- Process automation (such as information technology, software and robotics)
- Work post specifications and organisational structures
- Executive and operative competences and competencies
- Staffing
- Geographical dispersion

Again, the competences and competencies required by projects implementing specific design aspects may necessitate the use of external services.

Unfortunately, many executives ignore the organisational design and its implementation, believing that the two roles do not fall under their post specification; or, they delegate them to subordinates who are not capable of executing them effectively, efficiently, and at the required quality. Such negligence has grave consequences in the long term since it results in a sub-optimal organisational system which cannot attain maximum operational performance no matter how good the resources and enablers may be.

Planning the operation of the organisation

Successful executives, when translating the organisation's purpose into value to be created and delivered to its stakeholders, formulate its mission and set the top-level goals for the medium term, in general terms, and for the short term, in detail.

The short-term goals are then decomposed top–down into specific targets for the outputs of the core production and delivery processes of the organisation and, based on those, targets for the support, staff, management, and leadership processes.

These targets take the form of planned values for outputs, inputs, enabler capacities and other performance indicators. They are included in the organisation's business excellence model.

Based on these targets, further target values are set for all variable parameters of the dynamic operation of the organisation, and of the static resources and other enablers, not only within the organisation but also for any enterprise extension on either or both ends, ie for the materials, equipment and services on the supply side, and the products and services on the delivery side.

In executing the organisation's mission, the top executives formulate its vision, prescribing how its mission will evolve in the medium to long term. In addition, it determines which strategic projects need to be executed to effect short-term improvements or replacements/additions to its current products and services portfolio, processes, assets, resources, and enablers. Therefore, besides operational plans, the organisation also formulates plans for executing these short-term strategic projects.

The plans are developed by the various organisational entities through iterations of vertical interaction between the top executives and the executives of the various organisational entities (see arrows two, three, four and eight in Figure 5.2), and through iterations of horizontal interaction between the internal entities and the closely related supply and sales partners (see arrows five, six and seven in Figure 5.2). This is repeated until a consistent integrated business plan with its subordinate budget is finalised and approved by the top executive team and, where required, by the board of directors.

As we have seen, from various angles, successful executives acknowledge that their ultimate mandate is the creation and in particular the delivery of value, executing the mission of the organisation. Thus, they formulate plans for the foreseeable future, usually at a high level for the medium term and in detail for the short term, ie for twelve to thirty-six months. To plan ahead, successful executives first of all map and assess the current state of affairs of the organisation, and then set its goals, objectives and targets for the planning horizon.

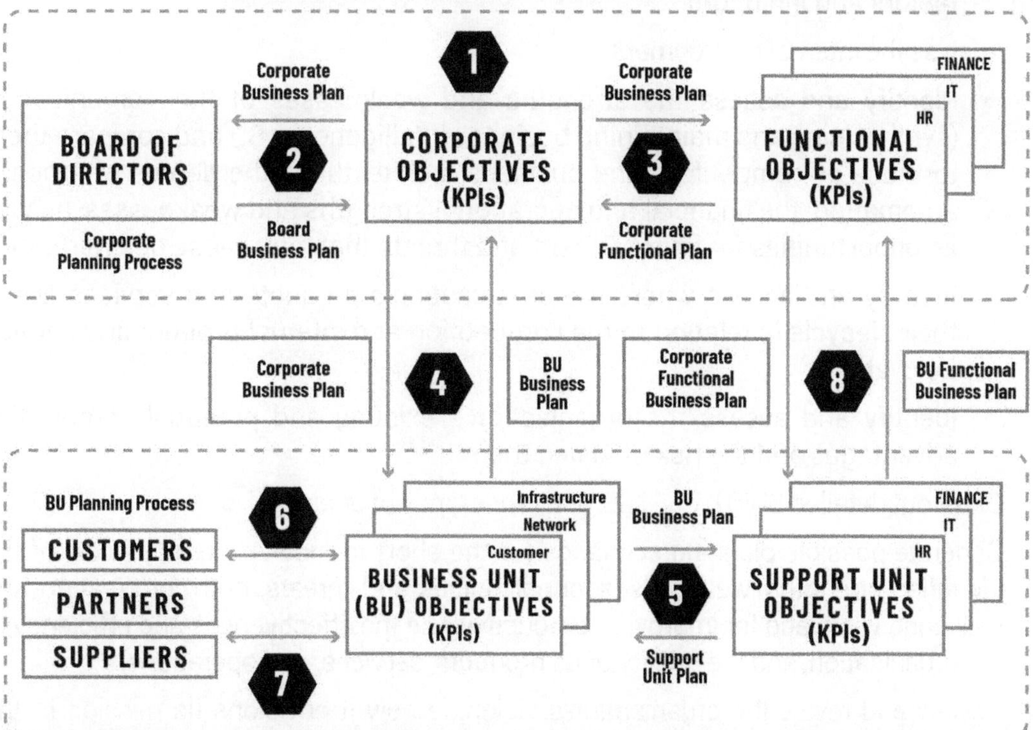

Figure 5.2: The business planning cycle

1. Analyse the needs and prospects of the organisation's various stakeholders for both the short and long term.
2. Analyse the external environment:
   - Identify and assess the strengths and weaknesses of competitors by maintaining ethical competitive intelligence (CI).
   - Identify and assess technological developments, especially disruptive ones.
   - Identify and assess the market and the organisation's customers with respect to their value to the organisation, the churn and acquisition trends, the customers of the organisation's competitors, as well as potential new markets and customers and their demographics.
   - Identify and assess the sellers and suppliers of the organisation and its competitors, as well as potential new suppliers, wholesalers and retailers, their products and services, and their logistics, delivery and quality control processes.
   - Identify and assess the geopolitical and economic environments.
   - Identify and assess opportunities and threats, as well as probable key success factors and inhibitors.
3. Analyse the internal environment:
   - Identify and assess the strengths and weaknesses of their organisation (synthesising and maintaining business intelligence – BI) and compare them to those of competitors: the business architectures, the degree of process automation, the financial and operational strengths and weaknesses, as well as opportunities for improvement and threats that may cause deterioration.
   - Identify and assess where the organisation's products and services are in their lifecycle in relation to the competition and internal product and service innovation.
   - Identify and assess the organisation's existing and potential competitive advantages and the risk of losing them.
4. Carry out detailed SWOT, PESTLE, and other types of analysis.
5. Generate possible planning scenarios for the short to medium term, in view of the identified strengths, weaknesses, opportunities and threats, both for creating and delivering value and for improving productivity (ie the effectiveness and efficiency of the organisation, and the quality of its products, services, and operations).
6. Review and revise the organisation's vision, ie how it envisions its mission in the medium to long term.
7. Generate possible planning scenarios for strategic projects to be executed in the short term that will contribute towards the realisation of the organisation's vision.

8. Carry out risk analysis and assessment for the various scenarios.
9. Finalise the short-term business plan by selecting the optimum scenario, the one which carries a level of risk that is acceptable to the main stakeholders and a profitable/viable budget.

The organisational business plan is decomposed into partial business plans for the various organisational entities, so that each entity has a clear mandate to execute in the short term.

In raising the plans, executives and operatives employ various techniques and tools that are closely tied to the management and leadership model of the organisation. A sample of such techniques and tools is given later in this chapter. The purpose is to achieve better operational accuracy and, hence, a higher probability of achieving the short-term goals, and to enable better performance management.

Successful executives adopt rolling business plans and budgets that cover eighteen to thirty-six months and are updated every three months. Similarly, they update yearly their medium-term plan and review and revise their mission and vision.

Directing the operation of the organisation

Once the business plans are approved, successful executives manage their execution effectively.

In our theoretical robotised organisation, this would be achieved by robots implementing the automated processes and projects. In such an organisational environment, executives would simply monitor the execution of the short-term plans and review and revise them as required in response to unforeseen internal and external changes (that cannot – yet – be assimilated and processed by the robots).

In the real world, however, executives lead human beings with their competences, competencies, their strengths and weaknesses, their cultural and team fit, and their implementability circumstances in executing their processes in a real-world environment with its continuous unforeseen evolution and its many disruptive developments.

In the next chapter, on leadership, we discuss extensively how successful executives lead their people in productively executing the organisation's processes and implementing its plans.

Monitoring the operation of the organisation

Monitoring operations and the execution of plans is part and parcel of the management subprocess of performance management, which will be extensively explored later in this chapter.

Control, though considered by the supporters of Scientific Management as a function of management, is partly an activity of Performance Management based on business intelligence (BI) and partly an activity of leadership, as we shall see.

> **Successful executives acknowledge and ensure that the activity of managing the execution of the mission is performed continuously by updating both the external competitive intelligence and the internal business intelligence so that the organisation can respond quickly to significant and disruptive changes.**

Managing the various value streams

> **Successful executives ensure that everybody in the organisation comprehends its mission and, in particular, how value can be created and delivered to the various external and internal stakeholders.**

They achieve this by ensuring that not only the *formally* responsible executives in the organisation, but as many operatives as possible comprehend the various value streams and that the responsible executives manage them at an optimum level by collecting and analysing real, accurate and thorough data and building possible scenarios for their development.

These value streams, as we have already mentioned[38] in Chapter Two, are, for example:

1. Product/service inception-to-development (R&D – product/service innovation)
2. Lead-to-order (order acquisition)
3. Order-to-cash (order fulfilment)

---

38 Martin J. (1995) *The Great Transition: Using the Seven Disciplines of Enterprise Engineering.*

4. Request/complaint-to-service (customer service)
5. Manufacturing-to-distribution (operations and logistics)

By managing all meaningful value streams, the organisation identifies and adopts useful KPIs, which are complemented by the business process KPIs to help maintain an effective and efficient performance management system.

Managing the processes, data, information and knowledge

Successful executives acknowledge that process management is an indispensable management subprocess the value of which has increased exponentially with the advent of process automation (such as administrative computer applications, computer-aided design, automated manufacturing and robotics), and that it is necessary for managing the day-to-day operations as well as for continuous improvement.

They ensure that it transcends the whole organisation from the floor level to the very top. In this sense, it covers not only the core, support and staff processes but also the management and leadership ones, as well as the workings of the board of directors and the process management process itself.

Effective process management requires top executives to ensure that an owner is appointed for each and every process. In a process-centric organisation, the owners should be the executives of the organisational entities. In non-process-centric organisations, senior executives should be appointed as process managers and be given sufficient authority to manage their processes.

Executives, up to the chief executive (CxO) level, need to monitor, using appropriate KPIs, their management and leadership processes, while the chairperson of the board needs to manage and monitor the operation of the board using formal methods for planning, monitoring, assessing and improving.

Managing projects

> **Successful executives recognise that projects differ from processes and manage them according to each one's specific characteristics.**

Projects versus processes

As we have already seen in previous chapters, processes are, as a rule, stable. They have specific characteristics, such as periodicity and seasonality. They are carried out by stable organisational structures and people who execute them in a repetitive manner. They are either continuous or continual. They are not time-bound in the sense of having a beginning and end date, though they do have deadlines.

Projects, by contrast, have a specific beginning and a specific end. They are executed by a specific team, established specifically for each project. Each project is designed and planned in an ad hoc manner to produce a specific result for a particular internal or external customer. Each project is executed through a number of processes, certain of which may be well known to the organisation and hence mature, while others may be employed only for the specific project and thus be unknown to the organisation and, in a sense, experimental.

> **Successful project executives manage all necessary project management activities and lead the project team members in implementing them effectively, efficiently and promptly, at the prescribed quality, creating and delivering the specified outcome.**

In contrast to process managers, project managers more frequently face unforeseen inhibitors and depend more on critical success factors. To be successful, therefore, they need specific additional management and leadership competences and competencies. It's for this reason that we expand on project management in this chapter and on team leadership in the next.

Projects fall into two categories:

Tactical projects formulated under a stable mission process

Typical examples are building construction projects executed by a civil engineering organisation, or heating, ventilation and air-conditioning projects implemented by an electromechanical engineering company. Other examples are consulting firms undertaking client projects, and law offices working on projects or cases.

Tactical projects are designed, planned and executed as subprocesses of organisational processes and are managed productively, following a formal process management methodology. Though they have different blueprints, tactical projects use repetitive processes and project managers can manage them, at a significantly lower risk, by implementing formal project management methodologies and leading their people, who usually have a high level of competence and competency in the process they execute.

Strategic projects to realise the organisation's vision

These are, as a rule, projects with a temporary ad hoc structure aiming at creating a new, unique, or significantly improved product, service, process, knowledge, or business model.

Unlike processes and programmes that may have been active in an organisation for many years and have reached a certain level of maturity, each strategic project is a fresh start and might involve the implementation of specific processes for the first and only time. From the project or programme manager's point of view, the management of the project is also a new requirement that needs to be addressed. Every project or programme is something new, but this does not mean that one cannot build on prior experience or use a formal project management methodology, suitable tools, and best practices that have been successful in the past.

Strategic project managers are required to manage projects, at a significantly higher risk, by not only implementing formal project management methodologies but also by leading their people to acquire an adequate level of competence and competency in the new processes they must execute.

In managing strategic projects, successful executives exploit all of their previous work and life experiences and balance, as needed, and in a flexible way, their scientific, artistic and craftsmanship management roles (as outlined below), drawing on best practices and guidance from available sources.

Often-missed aspects of project management

Various project management approaches, methodologies and best practices are available worldwide. The reproduction of these methodologies lies outside the scope of this book, though we will discuss some often-missed aspects of project management.

A project exists for a reason. Therefore, among its stakeholders exists a client. When a project aims at pushing the organisation significantly towards its vision, its client is usually top-level management. If it is an implementation-level project, effecting, for example, a process improvement, its client may be a department or a group of users, or even the entire workforce of the organisation, becoming a change programme.

Maintaining client agreements

> **Successful project executives acknowledge that it is imperative that the team and the client have exactly the same perception of the value that the project is mandated to create and deliver over its duration or at its completion.**

It is sometimes the case that, while initially there is consensus regarding what the project outcomes will be, and the perception of the value to be created and delivered is relatively stable, over the course of executing the project or programme, and in light of unforeseen events, obstacles and new challenges, the project or programme is transformed into something other than what was initially designed and planned. In this case, it must be confirmed that the client continues to recognise and accept the value to be created and delivered.

> **Successful project or programme executives ensure that the project team does not unilaterally decide to make changes that will affect the end result.**

They ensure that proposed changes and the reasoning behind these are communicated to all affected stakeholders and agreement is reached. They acknowledge that if this is not the case any work done by the project or programme team may be pointless and even detrimental to the organisation and/or client.

Project staffing

Successful executives staff projects so that the chosen persons can function as coherent teams, by ensuring that they can play all necessary roles and have an excellent cultural and character fit.

We will discuss project staffing in more detail later.

Handling clashes within project teams

A serious problem that often presents itself within project teams is cultural and other kinds of clashes between team members, arising from, for example, different priorities, personal agendas, or even latent grievances. This is not uncommon, especially when team members are not selected on the basis of correctly identified background, competences, competencies, track record and team fit, and when the team lacks specific essential roles, such as an effective leader, a planner, or a finisher. This can also occur when the team has too many members competing for the role of leader or when no one is assigned the role of the leader.

No formal project management methodology can prepare the project or programme manager for this. If intense cultural conflicts arise in the team, the project or programme may fall apart as cooperation collapses. The best remedy, in this case, is prevention through effective leadership and prompt action.

Similar to running the organisation's operations, leadership is crucial when it comes to the human factor in project management.

Suffice it to say here that the team members must be selected based on both their expertise (ie their competences) and their personal qualities (ie their competencies), but also on their team and cultural fit, ie their ability to work together and comply with the organisation's code of ethics.

In case there appear strong rivalries, hidden agendas or even divergent strong beliefs and values, then it is better to sacrifice expertise for the benefit of the team fit. If these cannot be prevented, then the only option may be to change one or more team members and/or add new members as soon as the problem is identified, to save everyone involved unnecessary pressure and frustration.

We discuss, in detail, various leadership aspects of project management in Chapter Six.

Managing project schedules

No matter how well-prepared, the Achilles' heel of most projects and programmes is time management. Even though the project deadlines might be reasonable, feasible and agreed, and the project or programme managers determined to stick to them, it is not always up to them. The ability to meet deadlines depends on the team's collective effort, the input of other departments or people, products or services from contractors and suppliers, and often internal or external customer input and interventions.

It is imperative that the project or programme managers communicate the importance of meeting deadlines to all affected parties, as well as the effects of delays. It is even more important that they talk the talk and walk the walk by completing their reviews on time and answering queries promptly so that the team is not delayed on their account.

Further, the project or programme manager must account for the review time necessary for all deliverables when the time schedule is formed, and for the possibility that each deliverable may need a couple of iterations before it reaches an acceptable status.

These are but a few project and programme management issues that, no matter what methodology is being employed, tend to pop up and can place the project or programme in peril. The best teacher in project management is experience.

Successful project or programme managers are usually those who have had their fingers burnt in the past and have formulated or adopted an effective and efficient methodology.

Managing the execution of the vision

Successful executives review the organisation's vision annually in response to and/or in anticipation of disruptive changes, and formulate or revise strategic projects for its realisation.

Managing strategic projects

Successful executives manage strategic projects either within the organisation or by establishing ad hoc structures. They staff them with their best people, exercising the best project management practice. They often use external consultants to assist them with these projects. In extraordinary cases, they even contract out strategic projects.

Managing the contemporisation of the mission

Successful executives embed the wins of the strategic projects in the organisation by continually contemporising the organisation's mission. They do this by introducing new and upgraded products and services, and ditching those that are reaching their end-of-life; by improving or reengineering processes; by extending or contracting markets; by targeting new customer segments and dropping existing ones where their value is falling below their break-even point; and by inventing new business models.

Management competencies and roles

Although for reasons of clarity we present in this part of the book the management aspect of the job of executives as purely scientific, we must stress that life is too complex to be described algorithmically. Even if, at a point in time, the organisation is architected precisely and its processes are designed and constructed with accuracy and thoroughness, and are perhaps even automated, the actions of formulating business plans, implementing them, running the organisation's processes and executing its projects by leading its people (ie managing and leading the organisation) prove to be part science, part art, and part craft.

In their scientific role, successful executives:

- Base their tasks on logic
- Rely on real facts
- Systematise and repeat their tasks
- Make decisions deductively
- Formulate plans, which are by necessity short term, based on actual facts
- Systematically analyse and evaluate
- Avoid getting stuck as a result of being too rational, over-analytical and consumed in endless assessment

In their artistic role, successful executives:

- Base their tasks on imagination
- Rely on creative insights
- Pursue novelty
- Make decisions inductively
- Formulate strategic plans through visioning
- Systematically model and design through conceptualisation
- Avoid getting lost in their imagination and visioning

In their role as craftsmen, successful executives:

- Base their tasks on experience
- Rely on creative, practical experiences
- Are utilitarian
- Make decisions iteratively
- Formulate strategic plans through venturing
- Learn dynamically by acting and experimenting
- Avoid getting stuck in past practices and experiences

Executives demonstrate different styles depending on the particular mix of the three roles each assumes and plays.

> **Successful executives exhibit flexibility in their management and leadership style by changing the mix of the three roles they play, depending on circumstance. They demonstrate specific personal, interpersonal, informational and action-oriented management and leadership competencies.**

They are reflective and think both tactically and strategically; in addition to their subordinates they manage, in a balanced way, their duties, their stress, their time, their information, their career and their boss. They are well informed, they interrogate and comprehend the issues and the intelligence at hand, and they disseminate and present it in a comprehensible, structured way so that their audience tune in at the same wavelength and understand it in the same way.

They analyse, evaluate, conceptualise, model and present information and knowledge in a comprehensible and actionable manner. They communicate effectively, both in writing and orally – they listen, speak, dialogue, brief and present until a reasonable consensus is reached. They design, plan and set the agenda, goals and targets. They break down issues into actionable parts, which they prioritise and schedule efficiently.

They delegate, allocate resources and authorise, in a balanced way. They network, organise, build productive teams, cooperate, collaborate, represent, negotiate and promote. They monitor and review actual results, analyse deviations, identify their causes, take corrective action, and revise in a realistic way the business plans.

The natural work flow of successful executives proves that management and leadership activities are intertwined into a holistic executive process. Management activities become ever more effective as executives improve their competence, their knowledge and experience, about the management activities, their methods, techniques and tools, and the context of the specific organisational environment and sector. They certainly prove even more efficient when executives possess specific competencies, such as high IQ and very good analytical and synthetical capability. They, however, become exceptionally more efficient and hence productive, as executives improve their leadership competence and competency – as it will be made obvious in Chapters Six and Eight. Conversely, executives who exhibit strong leadership competence and competency, but poor management competence, prove unproductive and often disastrous, destroying stakeholder value.

Performance management

Successful executives manage the operational and strategic performance of their organisation by monitoring the actual results of executing both its tactical plans, ie the creation and delivery of value through process execution, and its strategic plans, ie the improvement and innovation aimed at realising the organisation's vision through strategic project execution.

They manage performance by employing proven approaches, such as the Balanced Scorecard or the European Foundation for Quality Management (EFQM) Excellence Model, which enable them to manage in a balanced way the various aspects of the organisation.

Proven performance management models dictate that it is not sufficient to manage the performance of one or a few restricted aspects of the organisation, such as its finances and/or its customer satisfaction. Instead, they demand that performance management looks at the organisation in a holistic way, at all of its static and dynamic aspects.

This means that KPIs must be identified and adopted, and then respective targets set, actual results monitored, variances analysed and conclusions fed back into planning, for:

- All of the organisation's enablers:
  - Its non-human assets
  - Its processes, data, information and knowledge
  - Its people (their competences, competencies, cultural fit and performance)
  - Its partners and suppliers
  - Its culture, policies and rules
  - Its leadership and management
- All its stakeholders and its outcomes:
  - The created and delivered value, in financial or social terms
  - Its customer satisfaction
  - Its people satisfaction
  - Social satisfaction, eg its community perceptions
- All its evolutionary activities:
  - Its governance
  - Its incremental improvement and reengineering
  - Its learning
  - Its creativity and innovation
  - Its sustainability

Successful executives manage their organisation systematically, ie they manage holarchically each and every one of the organisational enablers (including the relations with all stakeholder groups and, where possible, individuals) and the whole organisation as a holistic system.

Compare this to the human body as a whole organism and as a system comprising various organs, which are *holons*, ie whole, as organs and, at the same time, parts of the organism – a higher-level *holon*. Thus, one can consider the *holons* as semi-autonomous, though so tightly interrelated with other *holons* that they cannot stand on their own outside the system.

Specific aspects of management

Under the generic term 'management process', we include below what we call 'executive corporate processes'. These are generic subprocesses aimed at ensuring the organisation is effectively and efficiently governed and managed at all levels. They are usually executed collectively.

They are herein distinguished from the executive activities, which aim at ensuring that executives (line managers) at all levels carry out, in a balanced way, all of their management and leadership duties, and from the organisation's core, support and staff processes, which aim directly at realising the organisation's mission and executing strategic projects that contribute to realising the organisation's vision.

Stakeholder relationships management

Successful executives acknowledge that an open dialogue with the organisation's key stakeholders is crucial if they are to respond to the international market and technology trends, and to customer expectations.

Successful executives consider anyone having an interest in their organisation to be a stakeholder. Key stakeholder groups include consumers, customers, employees, governments, shareholders, investors, creditors, local communities, the media, NGOs, partners, suppliers and trade unions.

Successful executives manage the relations between these groups and the organisation, both at the level of the board of directors and at their own level, in both structured and ad hoc ways.

Executives, and the board of directors, need to identify and use specific KPIs for setting targets; for collecting and analysing information about their expectations, impressions, and assessment of the organisation and the value it creates and delivers to the various stakeholder groups; for identifying the reasons for any deviations; and for revising business plans to not only improve results and relations but also to achieve consensus and alignment.

Though, as a rule, the external representation of an organisation belongs to the duties of the chairperson of the board, the CEO and their top executive team need to assist and complement the chairperson in managing these relations successfully.

Managing regulation and compliance

As life and technology progress, they become ever more complicated and states and supranational organisations regulate at an increasing degree and over a broader spectrum the various entrepreneurial sectors.

Regulation imposes restrictions and rules on assets, processes, input materials, products, and services, and must be complied with.

In their efforts to minimise the impact of regulatory changes on their organisation's operations and costs, successful executives manage systematically the relations with all relevant regulatory bodies, either directly or via sector representative bodies. They also manage compliance in a systematic way using applicable KPIs.

Managing partners and suppliers

A great many organisations nowadays operate as extended enterprises, depending critically on their suppliers, partners and sellers. Extending, where applicable, the organisation in the supply chain on the input side, and in the delivery chain on the value delivery side, as well as outsourcing non-core processes, is the result of continuous efforts to increase productivity without unilaterally sacrificing the interests of any of their stakeholder groups.

Successful executives consider their suppliers, partners and sellers to be members of their organisation and pay due attention to managing the organisation's relations with them, using suitable KPIs and service level agreements (SLAs).

They treat partners, suppliers and sellers as stakeholders and, therefore, ensure that both they and the organisation enjoy the value that is specified and agreed, for their mutual long-term benefit. They support them to the extent of helping them improve their processes, when relevant and applicable, and especially their interfaces with the organisation.

Managing the board of directors and its relations with top executives

The board of directors directs, supervises and represents the organisation. The chairperson, the vice chair, executive directors, dependent or independent non-executive directors, and the leading independent director must be equal, both in expressing their opinion and in voting.

Being the head of the organisation, the board reflects the organisation and so needs to operate effectively and efficiently. It must have well-defined processes with KPIs, objectives, goals, targets and performance measurements. For the processes to be productive, requisite competences and competencies need to be identified and any gaps must be bridged via development or replacement.

The chairperson* must not only manage and lead effectively and efficiently the board but also its relations with the CEO and their top executive team, without undermining them, and with the organisation's environment: shareholders, investors and bankers, regulators, customers and customer associations, and community representatives.

*Kakabadse A. and Kakabadse N. (2008) *Leading the Board*.

The board must be well structured with committees responsible for core processes, such as recruitment and emoluments, risk management, and internal audit.

Finally, the board must identify and live the organisation's values and ensure their spread throughout the organisation by defining its code of ethics and empowering and supporting the top executives in cultivating a culture based on this code.

The role of the chairperson in modern organisations cannot be understated. Extensive international research shows that it is indeed critical. Many organisations have failed because of their chairpersons' inability to execute effectively their board-chairing process. Successful chairpersons exercise specific duties and disciplines, acknowledge that their role is absolutely different and distinct from the role of CEO, and act in accordance with their role description.

They manage the board's operations, as a small organisation, executing, in essence, all management processes as described in this chapter. They lead their board, executing the leadership process as described in the next chapter. They manage the board's and, especially, their own relations with the CEO, and manage the organisation's relations with external stakeholder communities.

Successful chairpersons are effective in:

- Delineating authority and responsibility boundaries
- Ensuring that all board members make sense of all corporate issues, interrogating exhaustively the surrounding arguments
- Influencing responsibly the outcome
- Preaching, demonstrating and living the organisation's values (its code of ethics)
- Developing themselves and their board both individually and collectively as a coherent team
- Ensuring that the organisation has and effectively enforces forward-looking codes of governance and compliance, as well as any other codes dictated by legislation and good practice

We stress that, in the existence of a CEO, the (non-executive) chairperson may not and should not act as an executive, but must act solely as the manager and leader of the board of directors.

Successful board chairpersons exhibit the competences and competencies of successful executives and execute the same management and leadership processes in heading the board, and only the board.

Successful CEOs have a thorough understanding of the role of the (non-executive) board's chairperson and cooperate with and support the chairperson so that they complement and assist one another in heading the organisation. They do this striving for a productive delineation of work, authority and responsibility boundaries while recognising that such relations are dynamic and depend on both the chairperson's and their own personalities. Experience shows that organisations in which there is a dysfunctional relationship between the chairperson and the CEO are doomed.

Executive/management committee management

The executive committee comprises all or most of the organisation's chief (executive) officers (CxOs), such as the chief financial officer (CFO) and the chief technology officer (CTO).

Wherever Anglo-Saxon company law applies, this committee is a corporate instrument aiming at collective consultation, strategic and tactical decision-making alignment, and specific action/duty/project allocation. It is not a legal instrument and does not imply collective responsibility.

In central and northern European countries where two-tier company law pervades, the executive or management committee has collective decision-making powers and hence collective responsibility, while the board of directors acts as a supervisory council.

Successful CEOs manage the agenda of this important committee and lead it as a cohesive team in, inter alia, shaping and disseminating the corporate culture, as we shall see later.

Managing the organisation as a system

Successful executives manage their organisations as coherent systems, at least to the extent of applying the same values and codes of ethics and governance and in cultivating and maintaining a uniform culture.

To the maximum feasible degree, they construct a process-centric organisation. They place particular emphasis on managing the interfaces between the various organisational entities, especially when value streams/processes, by necessity, transcend more than one entity, despite all efforts to place each end-to-end process under the same roof.

Where applicable, they use KPIs and SLAs to manage these interfaces.

Governance management

Modern governance theory and practice dictate that corporate governance should be broader than what is defined by mandatory corporate governance codes. It should be based on the formal (or informal) corporate code of ethics, which comprises the corporate values and their application and should define corporate responsibility. The latter supersedes corporate social responsibility, which has been rightly demoted to the level of public relations and cannot stand alone outside corporate responsibility.

Culture management

Culture transcends every action, relation and behaviour in an organisation, from the boardroom to the floor level and the field. It is reflected in the words, the body language, the work execution mode, and the relational behaviour of each and every person in the organisation, both individually and collectively.

Ideally, it is the coherent, harmonious sum of the inevitable micro-cultures that form under a set of common corporate values. In reality, it is, unfortunately, often a cacophony of micro-cultures based on divergent values with clear positive or negative consequences for the organisation's short and long-term results and sustainability.

Successful executives spend time and energy effectively managing the culture of the organisation in a coherent way based on the corporate code of ethics, maintaining a balance with their other duties. They live and demonstrate the values of the organisation and they lead their people in accordance with these values, as we shall see in the next chapter.

They know that managing the culture of their organisation is one of their main executive activities, as important as managing the business processes and leading their people in executing the organisation's mission, in visioning its future and in striving for sustainability.

Corporate risk management

A healthy organisation should strive not only for short-term results but also, simultaneously, results in the medium and long term. As such, identification of long and short-term corporate threats and risks, development of policies and plans to mitigate and/or manage these, execution of plans, systematic review of results and revision of plans must be a formal management subprocess.

Risk management should be a formal activity of both the board of directors and the executive committee and, depending on the size of the organisation, be supported (via advice, consulting and auditing) by a formal organisational post or unit. As a support subprocess, it should be embedded in all core, support and staff corporate processes, and be an executive responsibility.

Successful executives ensure that risk management is embedded in all of the organisation's processes.

Brand management and branding

Brand management, in the sense of managing the organisation's image, should be considered an essential part of culture management and, hence, pervade all processes relating to all stakeholders.

Successful executives recognise that brand management does not coincide in any way with the narrow subprocess of advertising, which belongs to the product and service value stream management process.

Branding, which has a broader meaning than brand management, may be considered a component of culture management in its broader sense. It depends absolutely on the organisation's values and the degree of their active adoption and enforcement by its people in all their actions and behaviour.

Customer value management

> Successful executives view the organisation's customers as stakeholders and strive to create and deliver to them the value that satisfies their needs and expectations.

They ensure that their satisfaction is achieved and monitored with the use of suitable KPIs, the setting of ambitious targets, the analysis of any deviations in actual results, the identification of the causes of deviations, the prompt revision of product and service specifications, and the formulation and execution of plans to effect corrections and improvements.

They implement an effective customer relations management (CRM) system aiming at satisfying short and long-term customer needs, service, and contact. They strive for customer loyalty and commitment.

They implement an all-embracing customer value stream from the design, production and sales to after-sales support for products and services.

> Successful executives systematically manage the customer value lifecycle, recognising that customer retention is critical to both the organisation's reputation and its bottom line, and that it always costs far less than winning back churned customers.

Product value management

Similar to the other value streams of the organisation, the lifecycle of products and services must be managed systematically, with the use of suitable KPIs, from inception through development to launch, delivery, servicing and continual improvement or upgrade until their substitution with new innovative products and services.

> Successful executives manage systematically the product value lifecycles and strive to create positive value for as long as possible by continuously upgrading. They ensure that each product is replaced or improved promptly, before it falls below its break-even point.

Marketing, sales, after-sales and churn management

The marketing process must be tightly coupled with sales and after-sales service, as most marketing campaigns do with all kinds of Customer Contact Centres. Up and cross-selling must be combined with churn and retention management.

> **Successful executives manage all these activities as subprocesses of product value management and customer value management, using suitable KPIs.**

Information, knowledge and wisdom management

Processes and projects are productively executed and managed through information. Information becomes useful knowledge only when it is made available to, and used by, the organisation's people in carrying out their tactical and strategic duties. People without information are blind, and information without knowledgeable people is useless data. Being vital resources, information and knowledge must be managed systematically.

> **Successful executives manage and lead using evidence-based information, also called real-world evidence (RWE).**

Nowadays, there are vast volumes of valuable data of widely varying quality. Data-gathering technology that enables RWE has exploded in recent years. The sources of RWE are innumerable. The legitimately available data is collected in many formats: structured data, eg from databases; unstructured text, eg from emails; images, eg from websites; printed literature; photographs and video recordings; and voice, eg from legal recordings, such as those made in contact centres.

> **Successful executives develop a holistic information architecture and implement it with the aim of data reuse, thoroughness and consistency.**

By centralising data management, storage, access and analytics, executives gain significant benefits:

- Data structures are used and reused across many processes and projects with different sources being managed centrally.
- The processes for data collection, processing and quality assurance are standardised and optimised.
- The rules governing the processes and data are standardised and reflect the organisation's decision-making model.
- Tools for advanced analysis are used by multiple organisational entities, teams, and persons.
- Tools for communication and collaboration make the results, analysis, insights and publications of each entity or project available to other entities and teams, to be applied in new ways and areas.
- Business intelligence (BI) and competitive intelligence (CI) are optimised.
- Decision-making is supported by clean and consistent data and analytics.
- The benefits of data and information-sharing multiply over time.
- The return on the investment grows exponentially.

Successful executives ensure that the information architecture is in harmony with the process architecture and the decision-making architecture so that interdependencies are consistent and the lifecycles of both the processes and the data are complete and systematically managed together.

Static information (about assets, enablers, products, services, people, customers, suppliers, partners and the environment)

Successful executives have profound knowledge and understanding of their organisation and ensure that information is effectively and efficiently managed.

Executives acknowledge that information is the lifeblood of the organisation. It supplies its various organs with oxygen and nutrients and takes away whatever is not useful anymore, through data cleaning.

They collect information in a systematic way, they ensure that it is complete and correct, and they use it to not only comprehend their organisation but also to communicate with and align their people. They establish and maintain a business intelligence system that collects, analyses and presents evidence-based information, targets and actual results, at various levels and combinations, enabling both overview and drilling down to any required level. In this way, they keep everybody up to date on their business environment and the organisation as a whole so that they feel responsible and in control.

To this end, executives design all processes to ensure they collect all useful information; they keep this information correct, up to date and safe, and make it available to all who need it.

> **Successful executives use the organisation's business intelligence system to keep all organisational information in a useful structure, so that executives and operatives can retrieve it at the level that is useful for monitoring the organisation, decision-making and forward-planning.**

Operational information

Similarly, executives collect, process and make available all dynamic information relevant to the execution of operational plans and strategic projects.

Production data must be stored in a manner that enables statistical processing and regression and even the building of trends and scenarios for forward-planning.

> **Successful executives ensure that not only the actual values of all KPIs are collected and kept, but also that tolerance levels are monitored and jeopardy reports created, at real or near real-time, so that operatives and executives are informed about deviations in a timely manner and can take prompt corrective action.**

Competitive intelligence (CI)

> **Successful executives ensure that their organisation collects and processes, in an ethical way, information about the economy, demographics, the market, technology, and their competitors. They use this in managing the various value streams and lifecycles, such as of the products, services and customers.**

Business intelligence (BI)

Successful executives ensure that the organisation introduces and maintains a BI system that enables users at any level to retrieve, in a user-friendly way, any combination of data they need for managing their operations and projects and for planning ahead.

Productive BI systems can be used by executives and operatives in any way they deem useful, without the need to resort to information technology (IT) expert assistance. These systems enable the production of compound high-level actual result indicators and the drilling down, with any combination of parameters, to any useful level, all the way to raw data. Where artificial intelligence (AI) is used, they enable the building of forecasting scenarios that can predict the future with unprecedented accuracy.

EXAMPLE

Unilever[39] publication extract:

'Unilever delivers AI-assisted decision-making to users. Unilever's CIO explains how the organisation is using software tools to bring reliability and trust back to its use of data.

Unilever is one of the world's largest consumer goods companies, operating in over 190 countries, with its products used by 2.5 billion consumers every day. With that scale, comes an enormous amount of valuable data. However, getting to grips with that data to deliver value for business functions isn't straightforward, as its CIO explains.

Unilever is now deploying a wide array of tools, including artificial intelligence (AI), machine learning and business intelligence (BI) capabilities, in an attempt to bring trust back to the data and to put data in the hands of users, aiming at allowing for AI-assisted decision-making to become commonplace across the organisation in the context of digital transformation. However, the CIO stresses that Unilever doesn't want to deploy technology for technology's sake. Instead, it focuses on the business value. She stresses:

39 https://diginomica.com/2018/05/25/unilever-teams-microsoft-deliver-ai-assisted-decision-making-users

"One of the things I like to say to my team is, why are we doing this? For anyone that's a CIO or CTO, you know you get requests for hundreds if not thousands of projects. You really need to look at that and ask yourself, what business value are you giving back?

So, let's talk about the business value. What is the size of the opportunity? At Unilever, our BI systems have primarily over the years focused very well on looking back in history. And now we have the enormous opportunity to predict the future.

And with some of the new technology that we are employing, we are improving the accuracy of our forecasting, which is a big deal. We have seen improvements with lean inventory metrics; we can even spot slow moving goods before they become slow moving."'

Knowledge (methodologies, patents, production systems, machines, software, etc)

Successful executives manage the organisation by maintaining architectures, models, blueprints, methodologies and plans using standards and notations that enable common understanding, alignment, and continuous improvement. In the same way, they maintain and guard the organisation's intellectual property.

Executives use conceptualisation, effective modelling and sound methodologies to ensure that all their people, processes and automation systems speak the same language and communicate on the same wavelength.

Wisdom

Successful executives maintain and cultivate the organisation's wisdom through ethics and values, culture, governance codes, dilemma solution cases and mentoring, in a managed way.

Executives employ the services of the organisation's elders and even its pensioners so that their knowhow and experience, but also their competencies, are passed down to their successors.

The values they adopt and the culture they cultivate enhance cooperation and collaboration, as well as teaching, coaching, mentoring and learning. They foster a culture of open, sincere discussion and they help their teams reach widely accepted deductions and conclusions and, ultimately, decisions. They employ their codes of ethics and governance as well as their past experience to solve dilemmas.

Innovation management

Process, product, service and business model innovation are prerequisites for sustainability. Only through continuous innovation can an organisation sustain competitiveness and, ideally, a series of parallel and/or successive temporary monopolies, which will ensure its future health and reinvention for the sake of its stakeholders and the community.

Successful executives manage innovation with the same rigour as all other leadership, management and business processes, based on the organisation's values and focused on continuously creating and delivering value to its customers and other stakeholders.

Managing non-human resources

Successful executives systematically manage the assets of the organisation as enablers of the creation and delivery of value.

Managing non-human asset lifecycles

Successful executives ensure that the lifecycle of non-human assets is managed productively using suitable KPIs. They further make sure that all assets used as enablers of process(es) are owned and managed by the process owners to achieve optimum productivity considering their acquisition, operation, repair and replacement costs, depreciation, obsolescence (due to technological evolution), as well as product/service development, and production needs and disposal.

Non-human assets must be managed for effectiveness, integrability, safety, reliability, serviceability, maintainability, environmental impact elimination or minimisation, operation simplicity, energy efficiency and expandability, as applicable. Conformance with international and local standards, legislation, regulation, codes and guidelines must also be taken into account.

Managing non-human asset integration

Successful executives ensure that the organisation's assets are in harmonious integration so that all assets are productively used.

They also manage the risks associated with single points of failure, thus ensuring business continuity and keeping disruptions to a minimum, if not eliminating them.

Managing logistics

Successful executives today consider logistics an integral part of the organisation's value streams. They manage logistics systematically using suitable KPIs and external and internal SLAs to optimise external and internal handovers and interfaces.

Managing the supply chain

Successful executives consider the organisation's supply chain an integral part of its value streams and manage it systematically.

This can include assisting or, at least, advising suppliers and partners on innovation, how to improve their products and services, and how to optimise their own processes to produce and deliver value for money to the organisation. They also minimise procurement, warehousing and logistics costs by enforcing just-in-time (JIT) delivery.

Managing the extended enterprise value streams

In the same way, successful executives manage the delivery side of their organisation, for both sales and after-sales service, using KPIs and SLAs.

EXAMPLE

Automobile manufacturers specify the look and feel of their resellers' outlets and the level and quality of their service, both of which they subsidise.

Managing human resources (HRM)

They say that the people of an organisation are its main asset. We say that the organisation is its people. However many of its processes an organisation may outsource; however many of its premises and equipment it may rent; however much money it may borrow, it continues to be its people, as few or many as they may be.

Successful executives manage the organisation's people systematically ensuring that they are fit for the job they are delegated, and that the organisation creates and delivers to them the value they are due and which satisfies their expectations, at a competitive level. They do this while recognising the organisation's values, which should coincide, to a high degree, with each person's own values.

In doing so, they strive to optimally employ their management competences and competencies.

Successful executives, in parallel, lead the organisation's people in devoting their best selves to the creation and delivery of the value specified by the organisation's mission. In doing so, they exert themselves in optimally executing their leadership competences and competencies, as we will elaborate on in the next chapter.

Managing roles, posts, RAEW and organisational structure

> **Successful executives architect the organisation they head by basing its post specifications on the operative and executive roles its people must play to optimally execute the organisation's value streams and processes.**

They architect the organisational structure so that its posts are allocated various roles in such a way that each post maintains an optimum balance of the required expertise (ie competences, competencies, culture and team fit), the demanded workload, the allocated authority, and the expected responsibility (RAEW). They group the posts in a process-centric way, striving to keep the execution of end-to-end processes within value streams under the same organisational entity.

They review and revise the roles, posts, and organisational structure whenever they review and revise the organisation's processes, which they do regularly as part of process management.

Managing the staffing of the organisation

Organisational post staffing

> **Successful executives staff the organisation they manage and lead by selecting for each post the candidate who (a) satisfies as closely as possible the post specifications, and exhibits the capability of developing themselves to bridge any identified gaps; (b) fits the culture of the organisation and, where applicable, the team they will join; and (c) is willing to devote, and capable of devoting, their best self, by using their competences and competencies, to create and deliver value by executing the processes, projects and plans allocated to their post.**

They execute the staffing activity for recruitment, transfers, and promotions by selecting the best candidate for each post, using scientific tools such as assessment centres, psychometric, personality and simulation tests, and structured interviews. They ensure that the selection process and criteria are known and understood by everyone. When absolutely necessary they can deviate but should explain why.

Successful executives acknowledge that the execution of many processes is rarely uniform. On the contrary, many processes present a fluctuating workload.

As a result, executives allocate to many posts:

- One or more main (sub)processes to which incumbent post holders are mandated to devote the bulk of their efforts and time, and for which they must possess, at a high level, the necessary competences and competencies, be delegated the required executing authority, and be expected to undertake the *primary* responsibility for the results and the execution productivity (effectiveness, efficiency and quality).

Plus:

- One or more other (sub)processes or atomic activities to which the post incumbents are called to devote, circumstantially, efforts and time *in addition to* the workload of their principal (sub)process, with or without any executing authority and with minor responsibility. The post incumbent is required to possess to an adequate degree the competences and competencies required, respectively, for these *secondary* (sub)processes.

The allocations are depicted in a RAEW matrix by presenting the allocation of both the main and the secondary (sub)processes/atomic activities, as well as the related competencies, competences, authority and responsibility, as explained in Chapter Three. They use small letters for the secondary (sub)processes in contrast to capital letters for the main (sub)process allocation (Figure 3.2).

They include, in the post descriptions, the allocation of all secondary (sub)processes and the related competences, competencies, authorities and responsibilities, if any. They also ensure that, where the execution of the supplementary (sub)process(es) demands collaboration between all primary and secondary process allocation incumbents, those incumbents are managed and led as a coherent team by the primary process owner. This duty is specified in the respective post descriptions.

Project and ad hoc team staffing

> **Successful executives staff projects and teams so that they can be productive. They ensure that the project or team members can play successfully all necessary roles, such as those identified by the Belbin test, in a balanced way.**

In staffing projects and ad hoc teams, they take into consideration the workload of each individual and the potential negative impact their absence may have on their department and regular work.

Managing competences, competencies, cultural and team fit, and implementability

> **In managing performance, successful executives ensure that the performance of each of their people is assessed for personal development, ie gaps between the exhibited and requisite competencies and competences are identified, reasons for deviation analysed and, where gaps are judged bridgeable, personal development plans (PDPs) are formulated.**

They furthermore ensure that PDPs are executed in the most appropriate way: via in-class or out-of-class group or personal training, coaching or mentoring. Where competency/competence gaps are considered severe and unbridgeable, every effort is made to retrain and transfer people to other, more fitting posts before deciding to compensate and release them.

Managing PDPs extends to cover group and team training, coaching and mentoring not only for bridging competence and competency gaps but also for career development, preparing people for future personal, team and corporate needs.

Managing KPIs, targets and variances

> **Successful executives manage their people using applicable KPIs, setting SMART (specific, measurable, achievable, relevant and time-bound) targets, monitoring real results, identifying and analysing deviations, and revising targets as necessary.**

They ensure that besides covering output and behaviour (as in cooperation, collaboration, and servicing external and internal customers and other stakeholders), targets cover personal development achievements and the implementation of competences and competencies.

People performance management

In managing people's performance, successful executives ensure that their assessment is clearly distinguished into:

- Assessment for development and building of personal development plans
- Assessment for posting and promotion
- Assessment for reward

They ensure that these assessments are carried out separately, with special care taken to not mix the assessment for development and the assessment for reward, though some output from the former is used as input for the latter.

Successful executives ensure that personal and group assessment for development is considered a management subprocess and is informally carried out by their superiors on a continual basis, even though it is formally executed periodically, eg yearly, semi-yearly or even quarterly, when the execution and success of the current PDP is assessed and, if necessary, revised or a new one formulated.

To this end, executives at all levels must keep a critical incidents diary for each person and team under their jurisdiction and ensure their entries are formally, though confidentially, communicated to the affected person(s) as soon as possible after each positive or negative critical incident.

Furthermore, successful executives ensure that it is clear to everybody in the organisation that the assessments for development and for reward are distinct and kept separate from each other and from any assessment for posting, ie for promotion or transfer. For the latter, the description and demands of the post to be filled will apply, irrespective of whether some of the output of other assessments may be applicable as input to the assessment for posting.

Reward management

Reward management is a delicate process and can easily produce negative results. It requires a certain maturity of operational performance management and widespread credibility.

Successful executives ensure that the organisation's reward schemes are based on the assessment of both objective performance measures, based on personal, team, departmental and/or organisational results, and personal development and capability implementation results, which are weighted according to the level of the post and its relative power in influencing organisational outcomes.

Objective performance-based rewards – operational performance management

Successful executives introduce a performance management system based on a mix of performance evaluations using:

1. **Operational KPIs**

   These are the KPIs for the various value streams or processes of the organisation. They relate to both the competences and the competencies of the people of the organisation, and their degree of implementation.

2. **Behavioural KPIs**

   These are the KPIs for the behaviour of the organisation's people. They assess the competences and the competencies of each person in the organisation and the degree to which the person puts them to productive use. It also assesses the degree to which each person is working to improve their competences and competencies.

3. **Value delivery KPIs, targets and actual results**

   These are the KPIs for the value delivered by the organisation to its stakeholders.

When using the European Foundation for Quality Management (EFQM) Excellence Model, which is essentially a holistic implementation of the Management by Objectives (MBO) approach, successful executives relate KPIs to:

- **Value delivered to the stakeholders for whom the organisation was established**

  In for-profit organisations, the KPIs pertain mostly to financial results. In not-for-profit organisations, they relate to social value indicators. In progressive organisations, KPIs relating to learning, creativity, innovation and sustainability are also measured and taken into consideration. Most of the actual results considered relate to targets set against KPIs. The social indicators relate to both objective and subjective results.

- **Value delivered to the organisation's people**

  These KPIs measure the degree of happiness of the people of the organisation – happiness being a measure of various components, such as salary satisfaction, wellbeing, and wellness. They are mostly subjective, measuring the impressions of the people concerned. Forward-looking organisations also measure actual results in relation to targets set against objective KPIs, such as the mean salaries of the various groups of people, their fringe benefits and their working environment in comparison to other organisations in the same and other sectors.

- **Value delivered to the organisation's customers**

  These KPIs measure the customers' degree of satisfaction. They are mostly subjective, measuring the impression of the customers and whether they pay willingly for the value delivered to them or other beneficiaries (as is the case for philanthropic organisations). Successful organisations also measure the actual results in relation to targets set against objective KPIs, such as value for money, functionality, duration of useful life, and safety.

- **Value delivered to the society affected by the organisation**

  These KPIs measure the degree of satisfaction of the communities and the society affected directly or indirectly by the organisation. They are mostly subjective, measuring the impression of the population, of interested groups, and of the communities affected by any part of the extended organisation, ie not only by its operation but also by its supply and delivery chains. Successful organisations also measure actual results in relation to targets set against objective KPIs, such as employability, environmental impact, ethical impact, legality, and financial impact.

- **Process and project KPIs**

  These measure the organisation's internal productivity and innovation.

The various KPIs and the respective targets and actual values are grouped in Balanced Scorecards (BSC) with appropriate weightings. These are broken down into:

- An organisational BSC
- Departmental BSCs
- Individual performance appraisals

Reward scheme management

The operational performance management system directly affects the people performance management system.

> **Successful executives formulate emolument schemes that reward the organisation's individuals as if they were shareholders of the organisation (besides being salaried or contract employees). In this way, their emoluments are calculated based on a compound index in which weights are attributed depending on the breadth of each individual's contribution and responsibility, ie the degree to which each affects the organisational results, as well as their team and individual performance.**

These schemes have thresholds below which no bonus above basic salary is awarded. In this way, people participate explicitly in the profit-making of the organisation and also, implicitly, in its losses.

EXAMPLE

No bonus will be given if the actual value of the organisational compound BSC index is lower than 80% of the target value (irrespective of being profitable); partial bonus will be awarded if it lies between 80% and 100%; and proportional bonus will be paid if greater than 100% with a cap at, for example, 130%.

The reward index of each individual is usually affected by two groups of factors:

1. The weights of their organisational impact, departmental impact and individual performance, where the higher up an individual is in the hierarchy, the higher the weighting of the first two factors, and the lower the weighting of the third. For the CEO, for example, only the organisation's results may count, while for operatives, their personal performance could have a weight of 60% or more, with the rest divided between the departmental and organisational results.
2. The other factors are usually the organisational achievement as a percentage of the overall target applying to all people; the departmental achievement applying to all members of the respective departments, as a percentage of the respective target; and the personal achievement, within performance brackets.

High flyers, for example those with high potential and/or extraordinary performance, may be awarded an additional percentage, from between 5% to 10%.

Ultimately, emoluments are calculated by multiplying the universal bonus index by each individual's fixed salary and adding the bonuses calculated, as described above, on the basis of organisational, departmental and personal achievement.

Personnel administration

> **Successful executives ensure that their people's affairs are productively administered.**

They ensure that:

- Their personnel records are kept in an orderly and safe manner, in compliance with the relevant legislation and regulations.
- Their people's health and safety are looked after to the highest degree and in compliance with the relevant legislation and regulations.
- Personnel insurance is efficiently managed.
- Personal assessments are carried out promptly and productively in accordance with internal policies and regulations, with strict confidentiality and with the use of modern techniques, tools, and distinct methods for:
  - Personal development with the formulation of personal development plans (PDPs)
  - Promotion and placement
  - Rewards

- Personal and group development plans are implemented.
- Employee relations are managed within the organisation's culture of strong ethical values.
- Compensation and benefits are administered properly, in compliance with the relevant legislation, internal policies and regulations, and any applicable contracts or trade union agreements.
- Personal support is provided promptly and successfully as needed within the organisation's culture of strong ethical values.
- The post descriptions and the organisational chart are continually updated.
- Trade union relations are managed productively.
- Methodologies and techniques for people management, leadership and administration are continually modernised and used across the organisation.

Managing sustainability

Successful executives strive for sustainability via concrete actions that help their organisation fulfil its purpose and mission in the long run, by creating and delivering value that delights all of its stakeholders.

They build the organisation's sustainability agenda on the organisation's values, setting high ethical and governance standards on which they base their culture, policies and guidelines, wherever the organisation operates.

They understand sustainability in two ways:

- The sustainability of their organisation
- The sustainability of the environment and the organisation's enablers

They strive to achieve sustainability for their organisation by carefully and respectfully managing its non-human enablers, successfully executing its mission and pursuing continuous improvement. They formulate an ambitious vision, translating it into strategic projects and executing these productively, promptly contemporising the organisation's mission by continually incorporating strategic wins.

They strive to contribute to the sustainability of the environment and the organisation's enablers by ensuring that the organisation complies with local legislation and regulations as well as their own high ethical standards, and demand the same from their suppliers, partners and sellers, wherever they operate. They ensure the organisation delivers value, in a balanced way, to all its human enablers, acknowledging that they are vital stakeholders.

In the above context, executives aim at maximising the value delivered to the organisation's stakeholders and the benefits to the society, and at eliminating, or at least minimising, any negative impacts on people, the economy, and the environment. In case the latter is inevitable, they offer satisfactory compensation.

Executives also introduce KPIs and targets aiming at realising sustainability.

Successful executives achieve sustainability by continually contemporising the organisation's vision, by continuously effecting improvements, achieving innovation, executing strategic projects, and embedding all wins into the organisation's processes, products, services and value models. They further contemporise the organisation's mission for creating and delivering increasing value to its stakeholders within a virtuous evolutionary circle.

Ultimately, they acknowledge that sustainability can only be achieved through a holistic approach to wellbeing that calls on organisations (and societies at large) to pursue economic, social, and environmental objectives in an integrated manner.

EXAMPLE

An excellent example is Stora Enso[40] of Finland and Sweden – perhaps the oldest enterprise on the planet, with roots in the fourteenth century. Its outstanding sustainability agenda focuses on four pillars and nine areas:

Human Rights – integrated in all areas

Social:

- Employees and broader workforce – caring about all the organisation's people
- Community – helping communities be resilient
- Business ethics – playing fair

40 www.storaenso.com/en/sustainability

Environmental:

- Materials, water and energy – using natural resources with care
- Carbon dioxide – combating global warming
- Forests, plantations and land use – respecting the local environment

Economic:

- Customers – helping customers be sustainable
- Suppliers – choosing like-minded partners
- Investors – rewarding investors sustainably

The changing views of executive philosophy and practice

Today's organisations are facing a social crisis. The confidence of the public in private, public and state-owned organisations has gradually diminished. The phenomenon appeared first on the western side of the Atlantic Ocean in the 1970s and has since spread, albeit slowly, all over the world.

Many now believe that an organisation is not merely an economic entity but a social and political one too. This is a concept that imposes a different consideration and a new environment, in which many management systems are made inapplicable.

The globalised technological era in which we are living is continually altering people's perceptions of what is truly valuable. These alterations occur in, among other areas, the economics, management, leadership and social role of modern organisations.

The inertia of our socio-political system is, however, so great that our culture is now reformed through crisis. Since its formation after the Industrial Revolution, our culture has been dominated by:

- The intense development and use of the scientific method
- The amalgamation of scientific and technological advance
- The intense division of workforce associated with specialisation
- A dominance of economic judgement in social policy, acquisitive materialism in private life, and religious ethics at work

Unfortunately, abundance and piling-up of goods leads, in many countries, to environmental decay, pollution, materials and energy shortage, and increased concentration of wealth. The efficiency of industrial engineering may lead to dehumanisation.

Universal means of destruction become more effective and may be easily manipulated by small groups.

The new culture, looming on the horizon, sees reality quite differently. The basic economic concepts are redefined:

- **Productivity is redefined to include gains in education and innovation, new management methods, inspiring leadership, and the pursuit of happiness.**
- **Cost is redefined to include both economic and environmental cost, while wealth is redefined to include environmental enhancement and happiness.**
- **Income is also redefined, and is now subordinate to happiness.**

Meanwhile, the informed and aware citizen challenges the rationality of the organisational decision-making environment. The concept of corporate social responsibility, after having occupied a significant position within the organisation's brand management during the last decades of the twentieth century, is collapsing following the stock exchange scandals and the financial crisis of the first two decades of the twenty-first century. It is rightly being replaced by an evolving holistic corporate responsibility.

The notion of corporate responsibility is thus extended to include:

- Creating and delivering value to all the organisation's stakeholders (not only to shareholders and investors)
- Contributing definitely and positively towards helping society at large achieve its goals

Forward-thinking organisations are called upon to participate in the creation of the new culture in a threefold way:

- **By conforming to the evolving business ethics**
- **By fostering changes in social standards**
- **By fostering internal management and leadership adaptation**

Successful executives acknowledge that the organisation's mission is to create and deliver value to all its stakeholders with value understood to be aimed at improving their happiness and not only their financial conditions.

Happiness in this respect covers the criteria used in the annual World Happiness Report*:

- Income, in the sense of purchasing power
- Working environment, in the sense of avoiding dystopia
- Health, in regard to health insurance and services
- Personal development
- Participation in decision-making
- A pension that can maintain desired standards of living
- Personal financial and psychological support in times of need

*www.worldhappiness.report/faq This report is prepared via a sampling survey in practically all countries. Dystopia is used as the imaginary country that has the world's least-happy people. The purpose in establishing Dystopia is to have a benchmark against which all countries can be favourably compared (no country performs more poorly than Dystopia) in terms of each of the six key variables, thus allowing each sub-bar to be of positive width. The lowest scores observed for the six key variables, therefore, characterize Dystopia. Since life would be very unpleasant in a country with the world's lowest incomes, lowest life expectancy, lowest generosity, most corruption, least freedom and least social support, it is referred to as "Dystopia," in contrast to Utopia.

An overview of the evolving management and leadership philosophy and practice is presented in Table 5.1.

Table 5.1: An overview of the changing management and leadership philosophy and practice

The Past	The Present – The Future
Assumption that a manager's sole responsibility is to optimise stockholder wealth	Profit still dominant, but modified by the notion that an executive must create and deliver value to all stakeholders
Performance measured only against economic indicators	Performance measured, in a balanced way, using indicators relevant to all stakeholders and enablers
Emphasis on quantity	Emphasis on quantity and quality
Authoritarian management	Combined management and leadership
Short-term intuitive planning	Long-range comprehensive, structured planning
Entrepreneur manager	Renaissance manager-cum-leader
Control	Control plus creativity and innovation
People subordinate	People dominant
Workers as rented labour	Employees-cum-shareholders
People as human resource	People as stakeholders
Financial accounting	Financial, human resources and social accounting
Caveat emptor	Ombudsman
Centralised decision-making	Decentralised and group decision-making
Concentration on internal functioning	Concentration on both internal and external ingredients of organisational success
Dominance of solely economic forecasts in decision-making	Major use of social, technological and political forecasts as well as economic ones
Organisation viewed as a single system (holistic view)	Organisation viewed as a system of systems within a larger socio-economic system (holarchical view)
Business ideology calls for aloofness from government	Business–government cooperation and convergence of planning
Business has little concern for social costs of operations	Increasing concern for internalising social costs of operations
Scientific management	Value leadership
Excellence management	Cultural (tribal) values-based leadership

Successful executives adopt the forward-looking philosophical management and leadership approach presented in the right-hand column of Table 5.1.

Management techniques

Successful executives use a great wealth of techniques and tools that modern management theory and practice have developed and made available.

An exhaustive exposition of the modern techniques used in executing the various management subprocesses and activities lies beyond the scope of this book. We list below some typical examples:

Designing the organisation:

- Process, information, dynamics, and organisation multi-view enterprise-modelling methodology. This supports the understanding, analysis, and design of business processes aligned with information systems for inter-enterprise integration between companies as well as within a single organisation.

Planning and monitoring the operation of the organisation:

- EFQM Business Excellence Model
- Management by Objectives (MBO)
- Malcolm Baldrige National Quality Award

Managing the execution of the mission:

- Managing the various value streams
  - Value stream management (VSM). This is replacing the functional silo-based organisation, with cross-functional teams tasked with maximising the value created for the customers and the other stakeholders of each value stream.
- Managing the processes, data, information, and knowledge
  - Information engineering
  - Business process management (BPM), BPMNO 2.0

- Managing the decision-making
  - Decision Model and Notation (DMN):[41] a standard approach for describing and modelling repeatable decisions within organisations to ensure that decision models are interchangeable across organisations. It is complementary to the BPMN and CMMN standards.
  - Case Management Model and Notation (CMMN):[42] a graphical representation for expressing a case, as well as an interchange format for exchanging case models across different tools.
- Managing projects
  - Rapid evidence review (RER)
  - Knowledge banks
  - Communities of practice
  - Peer assist
  - After-action review (AAR), retrospective review
  - Knowledge exchange
  - PRINCE2

Managing the execution of the vision:

- Managing strategic projects
  - PRINCE2
  - PERT
  - Critical Path Project Management
  - Critical Chain Project Management

Management competencies and roles:

- Learning management systems (LMS)

Performance management:

- KPIs
- MBO
- EFQM Business Excellence Model

41 www.omg.org/dmn
42 www.omg.org/spec/CMMN/About-CMMN

Specific aspects of management:

- Shareholder/investor management
  - Investor relations manager
- Managing regulation and compliance
  - Compliance management frameworks
- Managing partners and suppliers
  - Partnership management
  - Supply chain management
- Managing the organisation as a system
- Culture management
  - Organisational culture models[43] (E. Schein)
  - Multi-focus model on organisational culture[44] (Hofstede Insights)
  - Culture meter survey[45] (www.culturesync.net)
- Corporate risk management
  - Continuous risk management process (IMA)[46]
  - ERM (COSO)[47]
- Customer value management
  - Customer value lifetime
  - Customer value lifecycle
- Product value management
  - Product value analysis (PVA)
  - Product value management (PVM)
  - Sustainable product lifecycle management (Green PLM)
- Marketing, sales, after-sales and churn management
  - Marketing productivity
  - CRM
  - Churn management

43 www.toolshero.com/leadership/organizational-culture-model-schein
44 www.hofstede-insights.com/models/organisational-culture
45 www.culturesync.net/toolbox/culturemeter-survey
46 www.acqnotes.com/Attachments/Continuous%20Risk%20Management%20Guidebook.pdf
47 www.coso.org/Pages/erm-integratedframework.aspx

- Information, knowledge and wisdom management
  - Information engineering
  - Information management
- Innovation management
  - Innovation management tools
- Managing non-human resources
  - Asset lifecycle
  - Asset integration
  - Logistics management
  - Supply chain management
  - Just-in-time inventory management
- Managing human resources (HRM)
  - Managing roles, posts, RAEW and organisational structure
RAEW matrix
  - Managing the staffing of the posts of organisation
Competency, competence, cultural fit and implementability assessment
  - Managing project and team staffing
Competency, competence, cultural fit and implementability assessment
Belbin test
- Managing competences, competencies, implementability, cultural and team fit
  - Aptitude tests
  - Personality tests
  - In-tray tests
  - 360-degree evaluation
  - Cultural mapping assessment
  - Personal development plans
  - In-class and out-of-class training, coaching and mentoring
  - Managing KPIs, targets, variances and performance management
  - KPIs
  - Performance appraisals
  - Management dashboards

- Performance management
    - Lean management/Six Sigma
    - Benchmarking
    - Balanced Scorecard
    - Business intelligence and analytics
    - Big data analytics
- Reward management
    - Performance-based reward schemes

In summary

Successful executives exhibit outstanding performance in carrying out their mandate, by:

- Acknowledging that business success is creating and, more importantly, delivering value to the satisfaction – ideally to the delight – of the organisation's stakeholders
- Recognising that their mandate covers, holarchically, the management process and the leadership process plus any core, support or staff process (subprocess or activity) that may be delegated to them, and devoting to each the necessary time, effort and passion in a balanced way
- Ensuring that their management process covers, holistically, all management subprocesses (Figure 5.3 bottom–up) and ensuring that they are all executed in a balanced way and with due diligence
- Managing the organisational entity they head effectively and efficiently as an integrated system comprising various enablers in a harmonious whole
- Realising in a high-productivity, competitive way the organisation's current mission within a culture of continuous improvement and innovation of the organisation's business model, products, services, and processes
- Successfully executing the strategic projects dictated by the organisation's vision

<table>
<tr><td colspan="2">Managing Strategic Projects (vision execution)</td></tr>
<tr><td colspan="2">Managing Operations (mission execution)</td></tr>
<tr><td colspan="2">Managing Non-Human Resources</td></tr>
<tr><td rowspan="4">Managing Stake-holders</td><td>Managing Human Resources</td></tr>
<tr><td>Managing Relations with Partners, Suppliers and Sellers</td></tr>
<tr><td>Managing Relations with the State (Regulators etc)</td></tr>
<tr><td>Managing Relations with the Chairperson and the BoD</td></tr>
<tr><td rowspan="12">Managing the Organisation as a System</td><td>Managing Relations and Value Delivered to Stakeholders</td></tr>
<tr><td>Managing Information, Knowledge and Wisdom</td></tr>
<tr><td>Managing Improvement, Creativity and Innovation</td></tr>
<tr><td>Managing Finances</td></tr>
<tr><td>Managing Customer Lifecycle and Value</td></tr>
<tr><td>Managing Product Lifecycle and Value</td></tr>
<tr><td>Managing the Brand</td></tr>
<tr><td>Managing Embedded Generic Business Subprocesses</td></tr>
<tr><td>Managing the Organisation's Processes and Data</td></tr>
<tr><td>Managing the Value Streams and the Organisational Architectures</td></tr>
<tr><td>Managing the Culture</td></tr>
<tr><td>Managing Ethics, Governance, Policies and Compliance</td></tr>
<tr><td colspan="2">The Executive as a Manager</td></tr>
</table>

Figure 5.3: The executive's management process

Vital questions

1. Do you acknowledge that an executive's process must cover the management process, as described in this chapter, in parallel with the leadership process (Chapter Six), plus any other activities that may be delegated to them and which may belong to any core, support or staff process?
2. Do you agree that the organisation's purpose, and hence its mission, is to create and deliver value to its stakeholders, satisfying their needs, ideally to their delight?
3. Do you recognise the need to systematically manage relationships with various stakeholder groups and measure their satisfaction using appropriate KPIs?

4. Do you agree that to create and deliver satisfactory value, the organisation employs a number of value streams, which are made up of processes (processing resources and interdependent data, enforcing discrete rules, and demanding specific competences and competencies) the performance of which is measured via relevant KPIs?
5. Do you agree that the organisation must be viewed as a holistic system comprising human and non-human enablers and resources in harmonious relationships mapped in interrelated architectures?
6. Do you agree that executives can carry out the management process successfully by using thoroughly and holarchically built and maintained organisational architectures, descriptions, specifications and constructs?
7. Do you understand that the term 'holarchical' means that each component can be viewed and managed as a semi-autonomous system while at the same time it is a component (or subpart) of a bigger whole, which itself must be managed holistically as an integrated system?
8. Do you recognise the various management subprocesses or activities as presented above?
9. What is the formal view, if any, of your organisation on the above questions?
10. Does your organisation include in your and other executives' post descriptions explicit reference to the management and leadership processes? Does it specify any other processes or activities? Does it have any relevant, comprehensive training programmes?
11. How would other executives in your organisation respond to the above questions?
12. What is your view on the modern philosophical approach to how an executive should carry out their duties as presented in this chapter?
13. Does your organisation have and nurture a culture that promotes clear and truthful communication, deep and univocal understanding, wide alignment, sincere engagement, results-oriented commitment, extreme ownership, continuous improvement, creative innovation, and productive action?
14. Are you evaluated for development and reward purposes with the use of targets based on KPIs explicitly related to your management and leadership competencies and competences, and the results of your implementation of the same?

CHAPTER SIX

LEADING THE ORGANISATION IN CREATING AND DELIVERING VALUE

Successful executives lead their people in producing and delivering value to the satisfaction and delight of their organisation's stakeholders. They communicate, dialogue, inspire and reach common conclusions within their team. They align, engage and gain commitment from their people around the organisation's values, mission, vision, plans, targets and actions. They gain their people's trust, respect, loyalty and love. They inspire discipline and extreme ownership. They lead their organisation in achieving outstanding sustainable results. They bestow success on their people and take responsibility for failure.

To manage means to take care of the household affairs of a home or an organisation; in other words, to administer them, to plan and execute all necessary activities so that the best value is created and delivered to the stakeholders – being all those who have a legitimate interest in the house.

In a small organisation, this activity may appear to be simple enough to be carried out by the average human to the satisfaction of its stakeholders. This may prove true when few humans are involved in the organisation's activities, and especially when they have a strong common interest, such as when the organisation is a close family business.

As the organisation grows and its activities become more and more complex, its management or administration proves inadequate.

Why?

Because at this point, to create and deliver the best value to its stakeholders, it needs people to:

- Devote their best selves
- Acknowledge their strengths and weaknesses and accept the allocation of those duties (activities, authorities and responsibilities), and hence posts, for which their competences and competencies render them most suitable, ie most productive
- Admit that others may be more suitable for other activities and posts
- Cooperate and collaborate with each other in executing complex and interdependent (sub)processes

Leading is not like managing non-human assets, the processes, policies and rules, logistics, supply and the delivery chains, and even parts of the planning activities, which can be considered mechanistic.

> **To create and deliver the highest value to all stakeholders, in a balanced way over the long term, executives need to lead. In other words, they need to navigate the people of the organisation through their business lives, their development, their growth, their performance and their motivation towards the success of the organisation, and to ensure that the organisation creates and delivers satisfactory value to them in parallel to the other stakeholders.**

It may appear that the definitions of management and leadership are contradictory, even controversial, and lack unison. Is this indeed so?

Management, as we have seen in the previous chapters, comprises the administration of organisational architectures, material resources (such as infrastructure, fixed assets and consumables) and processes, as well as the planning, coordination, execution, control and monitoring of administrative tasks that concern the human workforce, and the interfaces with partners, suppliers and sellers.

Leadership comprises the activities of getting people to employ, at the highest level, their competences and competencies in executing their (sub)processes, projects and plans, in an optimal way, and in continuous development and innovation.

In this chapter, we explore the process of leadership and its evolution over time, analysing it and relating it to the management process.

Leadership philosophy and foundation

Successful executives have a profound understanding of and ability to practise leadership.

They recognise and understand, in many cases instinctively, the differences between leadership and management, and the leadership and management philosophies and principles as they have evolved over time.

Aspiring, young and seasoned executives can become successful by continuously developing their leadership capability, ie their competency and associated management competence (which will enable them to implement their leadership competency) through study and practice. Where necessary, they can seek coaching and/or mentoring from senior internal or even external persons who have excelled in executive leadership in a successful career.

Leader or manager?

Are leadership and management two faces of the same coin? Do they coincide? Are they completely different in essence and in nature? Do they overlap?

These questions have been plaguing researchers, academics, philosophers and executives for decades. The debate is still ongoing and will likely continue indefinitely.

Based on our experiences and our own meta-research, we conclude that management and leadership are intertwined and, hence, difficult to delineate.

Many leadership and management concepts and activities are different and distinct. Others are similar and complementary and can be executed either separately or in combination. Certain others still are closely interrelated and cannot be performed independently. The two concepts are, indeed, two faces of the unique executive's coin, inseparably intertwined through the crystal lattice of the metal alloy.

In this chapter, we present a holistic picture of what leadership is and how successful executives lead their people to create and deliver outstanding results in a holarchical and sustainable way.

We repeat here our definitions of management and leadership, to establish the framework for our exposition. Leadership and management are distinct though complementary processes. Executives cannot succeed by implementing one and ignoring the other.

Successful executives perform both the management and the leadership processes in an intertwined way.

Management comprises the design, planning, organisation and coordination of an organisation's:

- Value streams and processes
- Non-human resources and enablers (infrastructure, fixed assets, consumables)
- Human roles, posts and organisational structures
- Data, information, knowledge

Together, these constitute an integrated system aiming at the production and delivery of value to the organisation's stakeholders and the direction for the execution of processes and projects producing and delivering the planned value.

Leadership is the navigation of people through:

- Their business lives
- Their personal development and growth
- Their becoming socialised, productive members of teams and organisations
- Their developing common understanding
- Their becoming aligned around shared values, purposes and missions, targets and plans
- Their visioning for continuous improvement and innovation
- Their becoming engaged and committed in executing their plans, processes and projects and in achieving targets
- Their executing the plans, processes and projects creating and delivering the planned value to the organisation's stakeholders to their satisfaction – ideally to their delight

Executives should exercise a mix of management and leadership activities in their work. Most do this in a personal, ad hoc way, instinctively, while a few do it utilising a selective, technique-based approach, as taught in their management studies and seminars.

Unfortunately, these are usually delivered by academic teachers, professional trainers, coaches and mentors, who have either never had the opportunity to act as executives themselves or have succeeded as executives without ever having researched and/or studied and profoundly comprehended executive success and failure. They are usually effective in teaching the management side and ineffective in teaching leadership.

At the two extremes, management without leadership is a recipe for mediocrity, whereas leadership without management is a recipe for disaster.

Business and political history is full of corroborating examples.

In extremis, people with strong leadership competencies, a populist philosophy and the 'wrong' values have caused some tremendous catastrophes.

The few successful executives, however, exercise leadership as a holarchical process, integrating it seamlessly and in a complementary manner with their management process into a holistic executive process. They understand the leadership process as comprising specific subprocesses, methods and techniques for exercising those subprocesses, governed by a values-based, people-centric philosophy.

We will first analyse the processes, *what* successful executives do, and then the methods, *how* they do it. We shall dwell only briefly on what they avoid, since most of this comprises the opposite of the successful executive's *what* and *how*.

In the next chapter, we reverse the discussion and focus on the competences and competencies that an executive should have and continuously develop to execute successfully the management and leadership processes. Our goal is to give executives who want to develop themselves and their people a framework for identifying their strengths and weaknesses, usually with the assistance of specialised experts, designing a roadmap for development and planning appropriate actions. These can be in or out-of-class learning, on-the-job coaching and/or mentoring and, above all, on-the-job practice.

Again, we define executives as 'successful' when they achieve organisational (business) success, ie the creation and delivery of value to the organisation's stakeholders to their balanced satisfaction – ideally to their delight – within the scope of the organisation's specified purpose and ethical values, in a balanced and sustainable way.

Successful executives complement the execution of the management process by exercising the leadership process in leading their people.

When we speak about executives leading their people, we mean leading on:

- A day-to-day basis, personally, their close associates, ie their direct subordinates: the next level of executives holding executive organisational posts; the operatives who report directly to them holding purely productive posts; and the staff post incumbents, as applicable within the organisational structure
- A day-to-day basis, indirectly via their hierarchy, all people falling under their jurisdiction
- A planned and an ad hoc basis, all people falling under their jurisdiction
- A planned and an ad hoc basis, personally and through the organisation's people, all other stakeholders who are not part of the organisation but are related, in any way, to the organisational entity they head

The above is always done in parallel with exercising their management process, in a balanced way.

Successful executives recognise that, to be effective, leadership needs to be based on a clear and sound philosophy and on a solid foundation.

Research has shown that the leadership process of successful executives, depending on context, is a balanced mix of:

1. Excellence-based leadership
2. Values-based leadership
3. Culture-based leadership
4. Governance-based leadership
5. Wisdom-based leadership

> **Successful executives lead through teamwork, at first by leading their own team, at whichever level they serve, and, thereafter, by propagating their leadership values, principles and practice across the whole organisation. They do this by delegating and empowering their people, at successive hierarchical levels, in leading via team-work, as we shall see in the next sections.**

Perspectives on the leadership aspects of the executive process

Over time, the process of the persons heading a social entity, for-profit or not-for-profit, or even governmental organisation, and its sub-divisions, whom we nowadays call executives, has been studied and analysed under the terms 'management' and 'leadership'. As we have already seen, the two concepts are distinguished by their purpose, their object, and their philosophy, and each can be analysed based on the activities executed under their umbrella, with their specific methods and techniques.

In this section, we briefly describe the evolution of the leadership subprocess versus the management subprocess of the executive process, through successive evolutions of perspectives.

Scientific Management versus leadership

The first perspective on what the average executives, as well as many academics and researchers, understood to be management or leadership was Scientific Management, popular around the beginning of the twentieth century. It was so-called because it was systematised and prescribed as a learnable vocation.

Its main elements were considered to be:

- Ensuring efficient use of resources so that group activity is predictable and controlled
- Ensuring verifiably optimal productivity and resource allocation
- Measuring, appraising and rewarding individual performance
- Organising (to include such activities as budgeting and staffing)
- Planning, coordinating, monitoring and reporting
- Incentivising
- Controlling
- Directing

These remain valid. When applied to non-human enablers, they can be considered mechanistic, or even algorithmic. They are still the basic elements of the executive process, being their main management tasks. Today, knowing how to execute them effectively may be considered the bulk of knowhow, ie the management competence, expected from executives. It is taught at management schools and MBA courses, as well as in professional courses and seminars.

There was little leadership content in Scientific Management, since it focused on the mechanistic part of the executive process. The people-centric leadership part was restricted mostly to the 'incentivising' activity and, to a lesser degree, to the directing, appraising and rewarding activities, which were to a great extent bureaucratic.

The philosophy of Scientific Management was focused on creating value for the owners, shareholders, investors and creditors, no further. Management philosophy has since evolved dramatically, as outlined in Chapter Five.

Leading people: the leadership process

Scientific Management significantly increased the effectiveness and efficiency of the organisations in which it was systematically implemented. However, it became evident within a few decades that it was inadequate in two significant aspects, and could evolve no further on its own. To increase the value created by organisations and their executives:

- More emphasis had to be given to the navigation of the organisation's people in carrying out their processes and their projects, executive or operational.
- The value beneficiaries of the organisation needed to be expanded to cover all stakeholders, not only the owners, shareholders, investors and creditors.

The process of leading people has also evolved over the years, as we outline below. Management and leadership can be thought of as comprising a pyramid with successive levels of increasing effectiveness and efficiency, based on ever higher standards.

Excellence-based leadership

The Scientific Management movement has significantly increased organisational productivity, wherever it was introduced. It made its appearance first as Quality Management, focusing on continuous process improvement (kaizen). Later, it evolved into Excellence-based Leadership with the addition, as we have already seen, of elements that belong to the process of leading people, such as listening actively, being accessible, managing by walking around, and motivating staff and rewarding improvement and innovation.

For the first time, successful executives introduced excellence models based on business-related values, such as quality improvement, innovation reward, managing by walking around, and people-involvement.

They enhanced teamwork by introducing quality circles to their organisations: teams of people linked by common processes and/or interfaces and handovers, regularly convening with the sole task of solving problems, correcting weaknesses, and initiating improvements to increase performance. This activity broke away from the traditional strict hierarchical lines of command and control and introduced revolutionary – for that time – concepts such as open dialogue, dispute of the status quo, and the possibility of raising bold ideas around a table with bosses and subordinates.

Successful executives basing their leadership on excellence introduced for the first time into their organisation a simple ethical code with values such as participation and open dialogue, collaboration, facilitation and coaching, caring and development, continual improvement, and praising and rewarding feasible innovative ideas.

Values-based leadership

The Excellence-based Leadership movement showed to progressive executives and management teachers, trainers and consultants that leading people around a set of specific values had good results and improved performance.

Thus, the values-based leadership was born, with elements such as:

- Visioning
- Prioritising values
- Formulating and enforcing a value set
- Focusing communication around a vision
- Encouraging high organisational performance
- Encouraging the organisation's people to become self-led creators of value and innovation on the basis of shared values
- Empowering individual employees to own the agreed goals and strive to accomplish them
- Teaching and coaching

Life and organisational experience has shown that, in this era, executives united people in a social structure based on a strong glue. In the worst cases, this glue was force and fear, ie forcefully applied direction. Living under force makes people unhappy, reactionary and unwilling to exert their best efforts. These organisations proved to be ephemeral – they could not achieve sustainability.

> **In the best cases, successful executives glued together the organisation's people using a set of shared values, and inspired their people to devote their best selves and exert their best efforts towards a common purpose.**

Such values are those postulated millennia ago by Aristotle, such as ethos, integrity, objectivity, independence, conflict of interest avoidance, responsibility, sincerity, and respect for people and the environment. Plus, widely accepted human and business values added since, such as: stewardship, caring, compassion, justice, meritocracy, autonomy, liberty, unity, team spirit, teaching and counselling, service, quality, productivity, innovation, excellence, and happiness.

EXAMPLES

- Apple's values include accessibility, education, environment, inclusion and diversity, privacy, supplier responsibility.
- The UK National Health Service's values include working together for patients, respect and dignity, commitment to quality of care, compassion, improving lives, everyone counts.
- Whirlpool's[48] values are shown in Figure 6.1.

> **In essence, successful executives lead their people as a tribe, the members of which are united around a set of shared values, shared beliefs, common customs and common interests.**

48 www.whirlpoolcorp.com/our-company

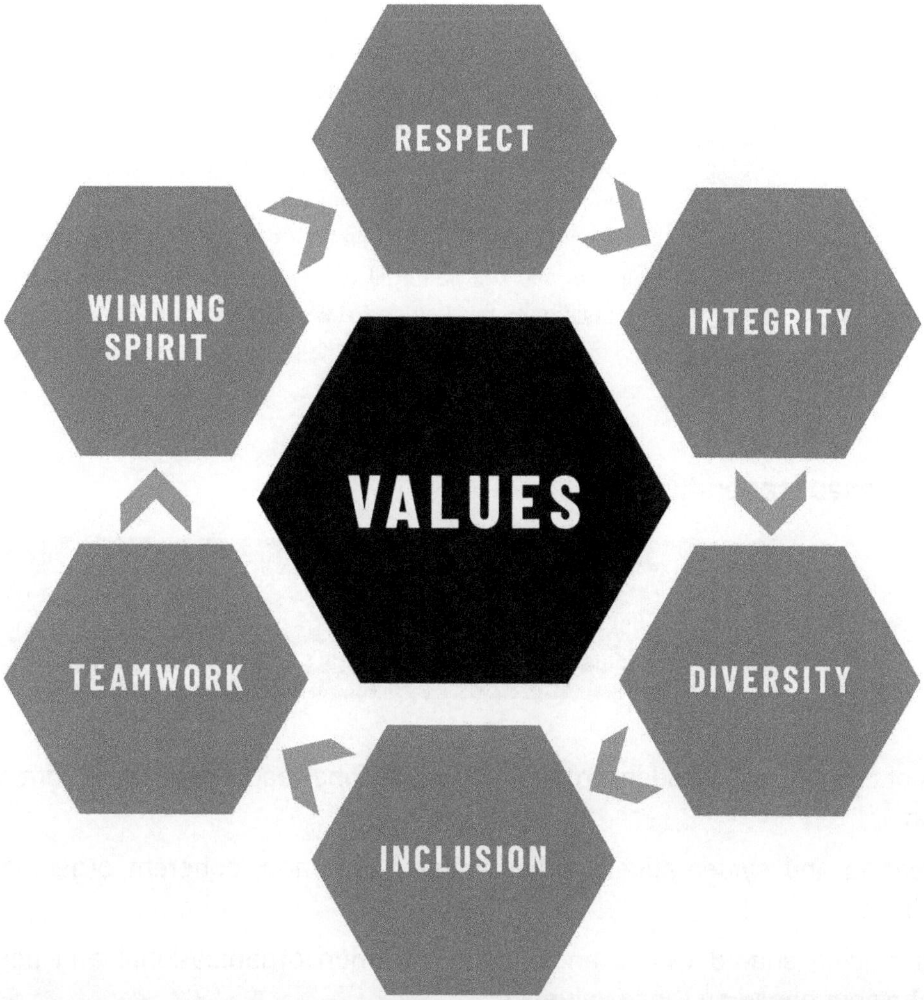

Figure 6.1: An example of a successful value set

They lead the organisational entity they head in formulating and adopting its code of ethics (a set of values, typically four to seven). They preach the values, orally and in writing, in all kinds of formal and informal communication, consultation and negotiation. They live them, they demand that their people live them, and they use them, wherever applicable, as KPIs and in solving operational and strategic dilemmas. They lead their people by example.

The philosophy of values-based leadership ultimately distinguishes this process from the management process. Success in implementing values-based leadership is in helping others become their best selves.

Executives exercising values-based leadership act as stewards of the organisation, its people and its resources, caring for and developing the people they work with and the team they represent. They create and maintain a culture aiming at achieving personal, team and organisational goals. They communicate, emphasise and enforce the adopted values. They lead their people in visioning their future potential and the potential of the organisation. They inspire the organisation's stakeholders to take self-led action. The shared values bind the executive leaders and their people in their common purpose.

Culture-based leadership

Successful executives show that values-based leadership significantly improves performance. They take a step further, beginning to manage culture systematically, based on trust and not on authority and hierarchy.

The era of culture-based leadership, also known as 'tribal leadership',[49] was born, with a focus on:

- Creating and systematically maintaining a common, coherent organisational culture
- Prioritising shared values and, hence, common organisational and personal behaviour based on those values
- Cultivating a shared culture based on trust by sharing governance and team-building
- Ensuring that the organisation's culture is conducive to mutual trust and unified collective action
- Nurturing a growth mindset
- Achieving outstanding results by wholeheartedly implementing personal and collective competences and competencies and devoting one's best self
- Measuring, appraising and rewarding performance

49 Logan D., King J. and Fischer-Wright H. (2008) *Tribal Leadership – Leveraging Natural Groups to Build a Thriving Organisation.*

Our experience and research prove that culture-based leadership can work wonders and that the level of its success depends on the set of shared values and the quality of the relationship between individuals. The best results are seen when **spiritual rapport** is achieved between persons, and when people are liberated through continuous improvement. This is accomplished by:

- Formulating and fostering a code of ethics based on shared moral values
- Cultivating wholeness in a team context
- Inspiring subordinates through stewardship and a service delivery paradigm, and encouraging them to do and promote the same
- Building a knowledge-based organisation
- Encouraging continuous improvement of organisational culture, value streams and processes, enabling technology, growth mindset, competences and competencies, service delivery, performance, and innovation

Culture transcends every individual and collective action, relation and behaviour in an organisation, from the boardroom to the operational level and the field. Ideally, it is the coherent, harmonious sum of the inevitable micro-cultures under a set of common corporate values.

Successful executives, at all hierarchical levels, spend time and energy nurturing a coherent culture based on the corporate code of ethics, the set of shared values, leading the people of their organisational unit, and maintaining balance with their other duties, executive and/or operational.

EXAMPLE

Figure 6.2 shows how Whirlpool[50] nurtures its culture on the basis of its value set.

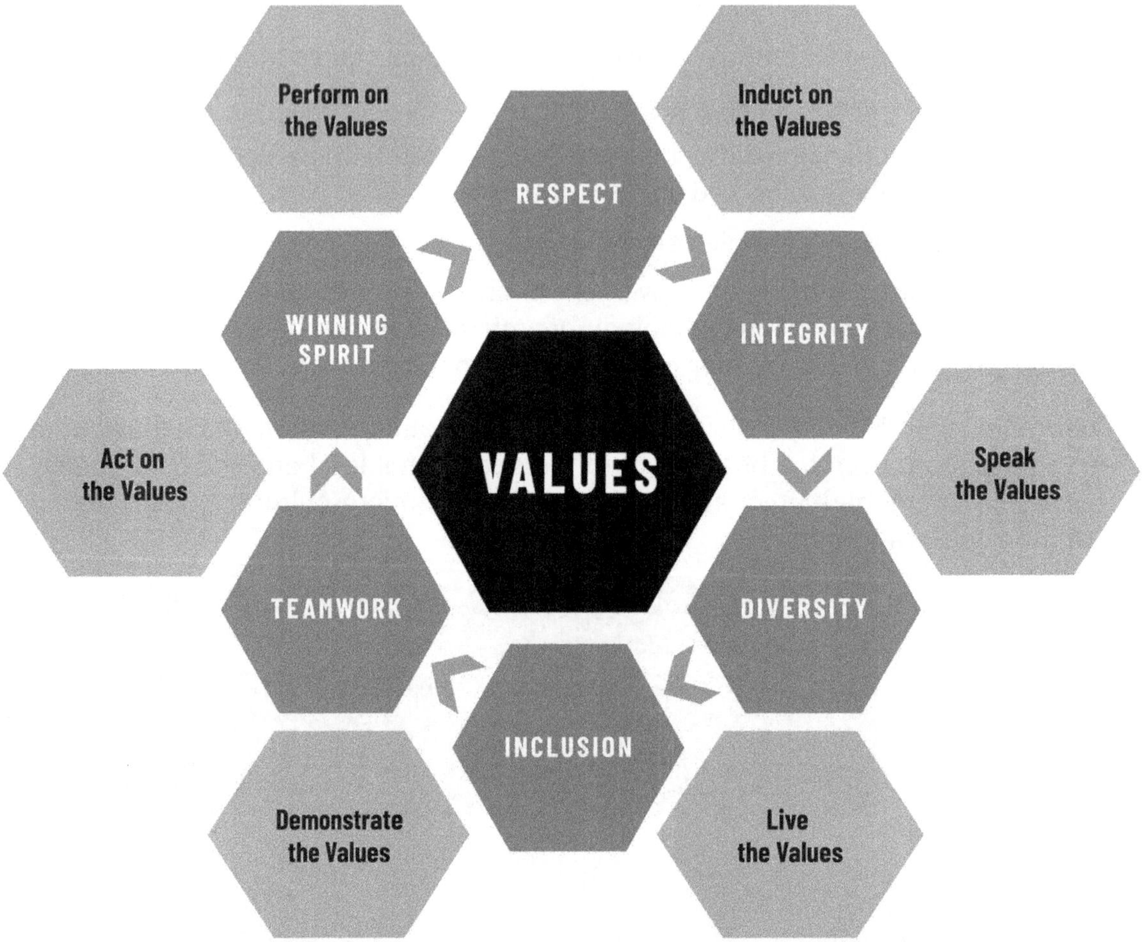

Figure 6.2: Creating a value-based culture

50 www.whirlpoolcorp.com/our-company

Governance-based leadership

> **Successful executives recognise that success does not emanate solely from the people-centric, value-based culture they cultivate but needs, at the same time, sound management of the organisation's architectures and structures. They recognise also that this demands not only seamless value streams, end-to-end processes and integrated data models, but also sound rules. They synthesise these rules into a coherent governance model or architecture and ensure that the rules are enforced and the model is continually updated.**

The governance model covers, among other things:

- All relevant legislation
- All applicable publicly imposed regulations and codes
- All internal regulations and codes
- Related guidelines
- Methodologies governing internal processes

The governance model must be based on the organisation's values, which should not, in any case, violate legislation, regulation and obligatory codes imposed by public authorities.

> **Successful executives strive to implement the governance model into the specification of the organisation's processes and their automation, as mandatory rules, and into the organisation's post descriptions so that their implementation is not ambiguous and vague, but, on the contrary, it is taken as granted by the people.**

Research shows that many organisations enforce strict governance rules but do not introduce a coherent culture model based on a set of values adopted and implemented by the majority, if not all, of their people. In these cases, employees often regard their organisation as a strictly policed state with hierarchically imposed rules, and tend to bend them whenever the opportunity or the need arises. In some cases, they are even pushed to break the rules by the reward system of the organisation itself.

We expand on governance-based leadership later in this chapter.

Wisdom-based leadership

Extensive research[51] shows that successful organisations are led by a team of people who exhibit strong leadership competencies and a broad spectrum of competences. A team that assumes its leadership role by owning the corporate culture: identifying and adopting corporate values; formulating and implementing the codes of ethics and governance; exemplifying their implementation not only in living and preaching them, but also in utilising them to solve business dilemmas; and reflecting them in KPIs.

At the top level, this team should be the board of directors, preferably comprising a majority of non-executives, and the top executives of the organisation. Ideally, the non-executives take the leading role and propagate the culture by mentoring top and senior management. In reality, in many organisations it is the top executives and usually the CEO who undertake the leading role, representing the organisation.

Research shows that the effective board and top executive team:

- Are diverse in terms of background, opinion, gender, nationality (especially for international companies), and maturity.
- Exhibit collective wisdom: knowledge, continuous learning, reflection, courage in expressing opinion, humility, lack of arrogance, and willingness to act after consultation.
- Are evidence-led. They continuously assess not only the organisation's reality but also what is happening in its sector, the related technology, the geopolitics, finance, etc.
- Have the wisdom to promptly recognise disruptive trends in technology, in local and international competition, in local and international finances, in the (geo) political environment – in anything that may affect the future of the organisation.
- Are not complacent due to current or past success. They have the wisdom to continuously challenge the current mission of the organisation and revise its vision and, hence, its strategic plans.
- Disrupt or challenge the current mission, whenever necessary, by carrying out frequent zero-based reviews.
- Have the boldness, courage and wisdom to set up a separate organisational structure to implement new business models or create and deliver new products and services, even if they will cannibalise existing successful ones. They pre-empt competitors in doing so (recognising and overcoming the 'innovator's dilemma')

51 Kakabadse A. (2015) *The Success Formula – How Smart Leaders Deliver Outstanding Value.*

or overcome unsurpassable internal problems that do not allow for reengineering – typical for state-owned organisations.

- Have the ability to reflect and refrain from rushed action until the dialogue is exhausted and consensus, alignment, engagement, commitment and ownership are achieved, with due consideration to time.

At the board level, an effective team comprises a good mix of ages. It includes a couple of older individuals, in their late sixties to their eighties, since science has shown that maturity and wisdom come with age, frequently in the role of chairperson and/or lead independent director. These are persons who have excelled as executives with outstanding leadership and management competencies and competences.

These elders, usually with CEO experience, are not only able to bring to the surface the issues and weaknesses hindering the functioning of the board but can also deal with emotions and conflicts and assist in sense-making and sense-breaking. They can mentor the younger persons – especially the executives – on how to control their ego, having experienced the same challenges in the past.

The older directors can help resolve difficult dilemmas facing either teleological (influenced by the opinions of others) or deontological (always acting on their own personal values, and what they consider right or wrong) personalities. They are absolutely necessary, since boards regularly face dilemmas, such as:

- How to negotiate differences in vision, policy and tactics and achieve alignment when dealing with teleological or deontological personalities – substituting animosities with commitment to the team, the organisation and the greater good
- How to face disruptive changes while the organisation is still thriving, forcing passive stakeholders to acknowledge the impending or occurring changes and state what they are willing to do about them
- How to deal with the need to observe the codes of ethics and governance in environments where one only has a chance of competing by deviating from them, especially when customer-facing executives are evaluated and paid on results
- How to resolve differences of opinion or interpretation, eg between non-executive and executive board members or between an entirely non-executive board and the CEO and the top executive team with regard to authority (as is often the case in state-owned organisations)

Executives and executive teams face dilemmas at all levels, and need to resolve these effectively and efficiently while remaining within the boundaries of the organisation's codes of ethics and governance. The guidance of the board and the mentoring of its top executive members in this regard are invaluable.

Successful executives recognise that wisdom is hard-earned through years of experience and that, unlike so much else in life, it becomes more potent with age. It comes from reflection and a willingness to keep learning. It comes from facing difficult situations and dilemmas. Hence, they cultivate a culture of open, sincere discussion and help their team reach widely accepted deductions, conclusions and, ultimately, decisions.

Executives recognise that wisdom resides foremost within wise individuals in the organisation and then, as collective wisdom, within teams. They ensure that hard-earned wisdom is not lost.

In mature, forward-looking societies, successful executives introduce schemes enabling the gradual retirement of wise executives and operatives who undertake the role of part-time internal consultant, supporting the younger – internal or external – people who replace them. In this way, organisations avoid losing valuable knowledge and support the induction of newly appointed executives and operatives to their management and leadership activities. They capitalise on the competences and the competencies of these people to solve outstanding problems and bring about significant improvements or reengineering.

At the same time, they help retiring executives transition gradually from a demanding professional life to a relaxing retirement.

We have repeatedly stressed that organisations exist to realise their *raison d'être*. When they succeed in this, they contribute to their stakeholders' wellbeing and ultimately their happiness. This is true for individuals, too. The Japanese term *ikigai* – reason for being – probably presents this in a better way. We briefly explore this in Chapter Eight, where we discuss the development of executives' leadership and management competencies. Here, suffice it to say that when older people are acknowledged and celebrated, they feel obligated to pass on their wisdom to younger generations. This gives them a new purpose in life outside of themselves, in service to others and their communities.

In summary, successful boards and executive teams are diverse. Of great value are older individuals, having the wisdom to deal with the extremely difficult issues facing organisations in the open business environment of the twenty-first century, characterised by glocalisation* and chaoplexity. These are persons who have the ability to put their Aristotelian wisdom into practice.**

To stand back and reflect, hold back, slow down and rethink before deciding and acting. To give feedback, discuss openly, achieve alignment and never go back. They are people who have impressive passion and professionalism and care about the organisation and its stakeholders.

* www.britannica.com/topic/glocalization

** Horgan J. (1996) *The End of Science: Facing the Limits of Knowledge in the Twilight of the Scientific Age.*

Chaoplexity = chaos + complexity. The convergence of chaos and complexity describes the meta-industrial era in which enterprises are obliged to continually adapt to disruptive changes in a complex and often chaotic environment, and to seek competitive advantage.

Glocalisation = globalisation + localisation/regionalisation. The synthesis of two concurrent trends towards operating in a local environment and competing in an international one – frequently, to the detriment of the national perspective – with the national state proving too big to meet the needs of people in the local environment, and too small to influence international standards and rules (such as WTO, UN, EU and ISO).

Leading the executive's team

In leading their team, successful executives execute specific leadership subprocesses or activities.

They communicate to their people the organisation's purpose and mission, and formulate with their close team the organisation's code of ethics, selecting values that represent the essence of the organisation's purpose and the values of the owners. They present the code to the whole organisational community and fine-tune it based on their feedback, cultivating a climate of open dialogue, ensuring diversity of thought and open discussion until everybody has an in-depth understanding of the organisation's purpose, values and mission. They maintain a climate of free, unhindered expression of sincere dispute until decisions are made based on wide consensus.

They cultivate a culture of trust based on the organisation's code of ethics and ensure that it is cascaded down throughout the organisation. They align their team around the purpose, values, mission and decisions, and achieve engagement and commitment by living, preaching and demonstrating the organisation's values and ensuring that their people do the same.

They ensure that their executive team takes ownership of the productive execution of the organisation's plans by developing, motivating and rewarding them. They maintain a climate of continuous creativity and innovation through visioning, and formulate the organisation's vision for the mid/long term through sincere, open dialogue based on the evolving competences and competencies of the organisation and its people, discoveries, inventions and environmental developments, whether societal, financial, technological, geopolitical, etc.

They ensure that the executive team takes ownership of the effective and efficient execution of the strategic projects that realise the organisation's vision, and that the purpose, code of ethics, and mission of the organisation continually evolve so that they remain contemporary and are propagated throughout the organisation.

Successful executives, as we outline in the next section, exercise the above leadership activities conscientiously, recognising the need to employ effective methods to identify the required leadership competences and competencies, to draw a roadmap for their development, and to continuously develop both themselves and their people.

Extensive research shows that the only way to create and maintain a culture in which executives can successfully perform the above leadership activities – always in parallel with their management activities – is through an extensive network of teams that encompasses the entire organisation, from the top executive team (ideally from the board of directors) to the operational level.

This is the approach that came to be called 'tribal leadership': the creation of tribes of 100–150 people grouped in intertwined teams with shared values, and of the whole organisation (of more than 100–150 people) into a tribe of tribes. Research has shown that it is practically impossible to have a coherent tribe of more than about

120 members abiding by the same set of values under common leadership. Hence the need to build a tribe of tribes, with the deputy leaders of the top tribe leading the next level of tribes, propagating, as far as possible, the top tribe's shared set of values, to the ground floor.

It is evident from the above that successful executives, above all, prepare and develop themselves and build and develop their executive team.

Before embarking on their leadership culture and process at large (encompassing the whole organisation under their jurisdiction), they identify (or conceive, if they are also the founders) and comprehend the organisation's purpose, ie its *raison d'être* and its mission in realising its purpose of creating and delivering value to all its stakeholders. They identify (or conceive, if they are also the founders) and comprehend, at a high level at least, the value streams, the extended organisation's end-to-end processes, and the information entities (their main attributes and especially the KPIs for the processes) and their interdependencies. They also get acquainted with (or conceive, if they are also the founders) the extended organisation's other architectures, assets, enablers and methodologies.

They then select, if they have the right and opportunity to do so, or get acquainted with their close associates and identify their strengths and weaknesses with regard to their competences, competencies, culture and team fit. They place special emphasis on the degree (as a strength or allowable weakness) to which they can collectively play all necessary team roles and on their diversity of thinking. In this way they ensure that their close associates have complementary competences and competencies and will be an effective and efficient team with a common values set.

They work intensely and exhaustively with this group to turn it into an executive team (with the emphasis on the meaning and essence of 'team', as we elaborate later):

- Building a culture of open, frank dialogue with the participation of all members.
- Identifying the prevailing ethical values among the team members and formulating the core of the organisation's code of ethics (to be finalised later with feedback from the whole organisation), if one does not already exist. Or, discuss thoroughly the existing code until it is fully comprehended as applied across the whole of the organisation's governance framework, in the rules governing the value streams and processes, and in tackling practical dilemmas.
- Removing from and replacing in the leadership team any person whose ethical values deviate significantly from the adopted code of ethics, and/or who does not fit with the team culture.

- Discussing exhaustively and in-depth, until thorough comprehension in a common language is achieved:
  - The value streams
  - The extended organisation's end-to-end processes, and the information entities and their interdependencies, not only of the organisation but also its extensions both on the supply chain and in the sales and after-sales chain
  - All other architectures (such as the organisational chart, the post descriptions, their RAEW in relation to the execution of the processes and decision-making) and assets (such as finance, buildings and immovable and movable equipment), and the organisation's management process model (planning, execution, control, review and plan revision) as well as the methodologies used in executing its various subprocesses (as outlined in the previous chapters)
- Planning:
  - For the medium term (three to five-year) horizon, at a high level, the execution of the organisation's mission.
- Via visioning:
  - Mid and short-term improvements, as applicable, to value streams, processes, competences and competencies, equipment, methodologies, knowhow, products, services, and business models
  - For the long term (five to ten or more years) horizon, and formulating (or revising, if it already exists) the organisation's vision and, at a high level, the strategic pillars and projects, and roadmapping their execution to realise the vision
  - For the short term (twelve to eighteen-month) horizon, in detail, the execution of the mission and the improvements and strategic projects falling within this period
- They clarify the boundaries of the work, authority and responsibility of the members of the team, allocating improvement and strategic projects that do not fall clearly into mission-execution jurisdictions.
- They discuss, deduct, reach conclusions, make decisions and achieve alignment, engagement, commitment and ownership of the meaning, the content, and the implementation of the leadership philosophy.
- They discuss and achieve consensus on the modus operandi of the executive team, as a formal or informal management and leadership entity, and the tools it will be using, especially with regard to business intelligence and competitive intelligence.

The members of the top executive team repeat the above, to the maximum applicable degree, with their team of close associates (comprising the next hierarchical level and their staff associates) so that the culture is propagated throughout the organisation.

How successful executives exercise their leadership activities

Successful executives never forget that success is the delivery of value – the creation of value being a *sine qua non* of the successful organisation.

This is our personal conclusion from over sixty years of combined experience. Above all, it is the blunt conclusion of lengthy multi-nation, multi-organisation research, mainly carried out by Professor Andrew Kakabadse, as presented in his 2015 book *The Success Formula – How Smart Leaders Deliver Outstanding Value.*

Value is in the eye of the beholder: an organisation or an individual. Its meaning and its substance differ widely among value recipients and value producers, and evolve constantly with time.

The sole sustainable way of creating value, and hence wealth, is through delivering value that satisfies the organisation's stakeholders. Leaders who seek to create value as they themselves perceive it, and not as specified by the organisation's stakeholders, are doomed to fail. They try to build on a vision detached from reality.

Successful executives follow an organisational modus operandi that dictates:

- The building of a common culture based on an agreed set of values and governance codes
- Alignment around a common understanding of all organisational semantics and entities, based on extreme ownership of the organisation's purpose, mission, methods, plans and targets
- Engagement in whole-hearted participation and collaboration in the execution of the organisation's plans, based on its value streams, processes and rules
- Commitment in executing the processes and projects and achieving the corresponding targets, based on the organisation's plans
- Dedication to continuous self-development, organisational improvement and innovation
- Optimal use of competences, competencies, time and goodwill in creating and delivering value to the organisation's stakeholders

Applying leadership principles

Successful executives apply certain leadership principles.

- They look at the organisation from various perspectives:
  - First, from the perspective of the recipient of the value delivered by the organisation, whether a customer, client, consumer, student, colleague, internal department, patient, member, or citizen.
  - Next, from the perspectives of all other external stakeholder groups, from outside–in, ie from the perspectives of the owner, investor, creditor, partner, supplier, regulator, and community, in terms of the value characteristics each group expects; and from inside–out, ie from the value stream and process perspectives (how value will be created and delivered to stakeholders) and from the perspective of the organisation's people (their competence, competency, working environment, personal growth, performance assessment, reward and work–life balance expectations).
- They formulate the organisation's operational and strategic plans so that they are tightly integrated with both the organisation's processes and the stakeholders' expectations.

- They communicate the organisation's mission and operational plans and its vision and strategic plans so that they achieve clarity and alignment from top to bottom and inspire and achieve engagement, commitment and ownership.
- They plan action around processes engaging all relevant people in analysing the current situation, identifying opportunities, threats and weaknesses; setting targets using external (representing stakeholder expectations) and internal (representing process and people performance) KPIs, critical success factors, and probable inhibitors; visioning the future and formulating actions and projects for achieving critical success factors, surpassing inhibitors, effecting improvement, and achieving innovation.
- They ensure that the organisational architectures are holarchically harmonised to enable optimal process and project execution, by doing what we have outlined in the previous chapters.

Overcoming leadership obstacles

Successful executives surpass certain obstacles.

- **Tradition and inertia:** in maintaining the status quo, resisting change and improvement. Not involving the middle and junior executives and the operatives in the planning process. Or, carrying out the planning exercise once a year instead of regularly reviewing actual results and updating plans.
- **Looking at the organisation from a functional instead of a process perspective:** ignoring the various value streams, mismanaging processes because they are not viewed from an end-to-end perspective, with the usual phenomenon of misaligned handovers and responsibility-jerking. Or, failure to achieve clarity on process parameters, such as inputs, outputs, KPIs, rules and, worst of all, failure to build balanced RAEW into the various work posts at both the management and operative levels.
- **Lack of focus:** setting mismatched targets at the process level, ignoring critical success factors and inhibitors. Or, formulating and undertaking projects beyond the organisation's capability or capacity with regard to knowledge, people expertise, available manpower and other resources, or even regulatory permits.
- **Lack of alignment:** between organisational results and people's performance, expectations and reward systems.

Ensuring diversity of thinking, truthful information and clarity

To create and deliver value, successful executives formulate ambitious but feasible plans, based on sound knowledge of reality. To achieve this, they demand from themselves and their associates constant evidence-gathering and questioning of reality.

Unfortunately, many leaders – chairmen, CEOs, MDs, GMs, divisional and departmental executives – are evidence-averse.

Despite operating in an era of big data, analytics, business and competitive intelligence and thus having the opportunity to challenge and verify data and information, they politicise strategy formulation, without elaborating on what strategy means, and they shut down any executive and non-executive colleagues who dare interrogate their strategy by disincentivising them. In many countries, the stories of the misfortunes of big banks and other public companies are clear examples of situations where CEOs tried to implement faulty strategies that were not interrogated and were not based on hard facts.

The term 'strategy' is of Greek origin. In modern Greek, it means the method of achieving goals. Its ancient roots are *stratos* (στρατός) meaning 'army', and *igeisthai* (ηγείσθαι) meaning 'leading'. It is a noun, not a verb. The derivative verb is to 'strategise', and means to devise a strategy or strategies. As a noun, its true meaning is the way of leading an army; in civil life, it is the method of leading people and ourselves, towards achieving a goal. From the same roots, we get 'stratagem' (στρατήγημα), meaning a specific scheme or method, especially one used to outwit an opponent or achieve an end.

In the management, leadership, and business literature, and in day-to-day language, 'strategy' is used in ambiguous ways and it is abused as a term with widely varying meanings, including:

- The science and art of employing the political, economic, psychological and military forces of a nation or organisation to provide the maximum support to the policies adopted in peace or war
- The science and art of military command exercised to meet the enemy in combat under advantageous conditions
- An action that managers take to attain one or more organisational goals
- A general direction set for the organisation and its various components to achieve a desired state in the future

- Knowledge of the goals, the uncertainty of events, and the need to take into consideration the likely or actual behaviour of others
- The blueprint of decisions in an organisation, which shows its objectives and goals, key policies and plans for achieving these goals, defines its business, the type of economic and human organisation it seeks to be, and the contribution it plans to make to its shareholders, customers and society
- The art and science of planning and marshalling resources for their most efficient and effective use
- A careful plan or method – a clever stratagem
- Integrating organisational activities and utilising and allocating the scarce resources within the organisational environment to meet the present objectives
- The art of devising or employing plans or stratagems towards a goal
- The mission and/or vision of a country or organisation

In the majority of cases, the people listening to bosses speak about *their strategy* do not understand fully what they mean and what their expectations are. That is why, in this book, we use the term 'strategy' sparingly. We prefer to use it in the narrow sense, to mean the way in which an organisation carefully plans its actions over a period of time to improve its position and achieve its mission and vision.

Successful executives demand clarity, of themselves and of their associates. To achieve clarity, they need and use precise definitions, a shared understanding of organisational terms, and a thorough and truthful description of reality.

They not only believe in evidence, but demand it. They base their belief on their real experience, on their successes and failures. They continually demand hard evidence, building around them the right culture.

They build up their team by ensuring that its members exhibit diverse independent thinking. They encourage their stakeholders to raise questions and express their views, opinions and suggestions. They seek to gather both hard (real, objectively collected numbers) and soft (emotional, subjective data) evidence. They assign importance to the quality of evidence. They believe not only that detail is the determinant of quality, but also that detail is the criterion for success. Hence, the methodology for collecting, analysing and interpreting evidence is of crucial significance.

Executives who believe in evidence-led leadership are good listeners. They use hard data to encourage sincere, productive dialogue and, when necessary independent, destructive debate. They do this to the extent of provoking stakeholders to express their views and listen to the rest of the team. They allocate necessary time to exhausting the dialogue, or the debate, when they cannot avoid it. Moreover, they do this in a structured way so that at the end of the discussion, consensus, alignment, engagement, commitment and ownership are achieved.

Research shows that executives, in their role as leaders, fall in one of three types:

1. Those who try to replicate their past success, seeing it as a strategy for value proposition, or even creation and delivery, and who end up failing, discovering sooner or later that the world has changed and the past can no longer be replicated. *They are nostalgic; they live in their past.*
2. Those who formulate a perceived strategy for value proposition and end up failing in their attempts to implement a strategy that is detached from reality. *They are fantasists; they live in their dreams.*
3. Those who strive to create and deliver value implementing the organisation's mission on the basis of hard, thoroughly interrogated evidence. *They are realists and visionaries.*

Successful leaders recognise that their mandate is holistic and acknowledge that managing culture and process and leading people is as important as implementing the corporate mission and vision, always keeping reality (hard evidence) and corporate values in mind.

Executing the leadership subprocesses in the right sequence

Research shows that there are many reasons why executives fail in managing and leading their organisation to create and deliver value in the long term (in many cases even in the mid term), ie in a sustainable way. One of the main reasons is that they do not perform the leadership subprocesses in a natural flow, exercising them in an unnatural, ad hoc manner.

Similar to all other processes, leadership is decomposed into a series of subprocesses, and each subprocess into a series of atomic activities. Certain important subprocesses and activities have strong interdependencies, though this is not as evident as it is in, for example, a manufacturing process. Ignoring their natural flow results in failure, as we shall see.

Alignment-based leadership

Successful executives, recognising that their mission is to satisfy, in a sustainable way, all the organisation's stakeholders by delivering to them the value they expect, align their people and as many of the external stakeholders as possible by cohesively satisfying a series of prerequisites.

1. They achieve a common understanding of what the mission entails and how it can be realised by achieving alignment of thinking and acting (the logic and structure of execution).
2. They win over the majority of stakeholders so that they are engaged (have the desire, willingness and motivation to execute), body and soul, as a coherent team in realising the mission.
3. They enthuse and inspire stakeholders by devising a corporate vision and a strategy for continuous innovation and rediscovery, and by executing strategic projects aiming at maintaining competitive advantage.
4. They create a culture of frequent, prompt, sincere and thorough communication disseminating evidence-based information, open dialogue, free expression of opinion, and exhaustive discussion, guided by the corporate values – the organisation's code of ethics.

For successful executives, alignment is a significant element of the process of creating and delivering value to all stakeholders. Like every other activity, alignment demands the identification of relevant competences (knowhow and dexterities), competencies (personal qualities and characteristics), and tools (specialised, generic and administrative), as well as capability and willingness to use them in conformance with the corporate culture and governance.

Research shows that effective and efficient mission (and, hence, process) execution as well as vision (and, consequently, strategic project) execution demand alignment and (as we shall see) engagement, commitment, ownership and action. In other words, they demand spiritual fitness and willingness, as well as mental and physical competence, competency and capability (ie capacity).

Unfortunately, research also shows that few of top and line executives are aligned in their thinking with the organisational environment in which they operate. The proportion is lower among those recruited from outside the organisation (one in five fail within eighteen months).

Furthermore, it shows that it is essential to recruit people who satisfy the above requirements for the specific environment (culture and team fit) of the organisation, in addition to meeting the typical process-dictated specifications. This significantly increases the chances of achieving a high level of alignment of thinking.

Once alignment of thinking is achieved, organisational structures and operational systems need to be aligned in such a way that engagement is also optimised. Only then can mission-dictated processes and vision-dictated strategic projects be productively executed, and competitive advantage maintained through continuous innovation in value creation and delivery (ie in new and improved business models, products, services, core and support processes, and customer servicing).

Misalignment of thinking, structure and systems, and/or attempts to remedy misalignment of thinking through restructuring are recipes for failure. Similarly, ignoring politics and misalignment, or engagement concerns, and forcing through plans and targets in an authoritative manner (without simultaneously achieving alignment and engagement) will inevitably lead to failure. This, unfortunately, is the rule in the majority of organisations.

It is therefore of paramount importance that the issue of alignment is openly discussed with due attention to the sensitivities that may arise. Once again, values and culture are the foundations for building alignment and then engagement.

Successful executives genuinely believe in the organisation's purpose, mission, structures, assets, and especially its people and their capabilities. They lead their team and all the people of the entity they head, not only in becoming aligned but ultimately in believing in the organisation and its purpose and mission to create and deliver value, and in applying their ability to accomplish this. They are authentic in expressing their true belief in the purpose, mission, vision, and people of the organisation. They believe in the common good and place it above their personal interest.

Lastly, we stress that it is highly improbable that, in an organisation, an executive – and especially a senior executive team – would knowingly choose a course of action that would certainly result in failure. If, however, the executives do not manage to present their chosen course of action clearly to their people, do not explain how it serves the mission, how it will create and deliver value, and do not discuss it until the point where all ambiguities are resolved, questions are answered, and alignment is reached, their people will not believe in it wholeheartedly. The chances for success are diminished. This is especially the case when the decisions need to transcend consecutive hierarchical levels until they reach the people who will execute them.

By contrast, when alignment and belief are achieved, lower-level executives and operatives are empowered, delegation of authority to the level of execution is accomplished, and performance sky rockets.

In summary, successful executives recognise that alignment means speaking the same language, and a deep understanding of the organisation's:

- **Values, architectures and blueprints**
- **Purpose, mission in creating and delivering value, and vision for sustained success**
- **Competences, competencies, strengths and weaknesses**
- **Plans for executing the necessary processes and strategic projects to accomplish its mission and realise its vision**

One of the main reasons executives fail is that they do not follow, or do not manage to apply, the proven formula for success, which dictates that structure and planning should come after alignment and engagement with the corporate purpose and mission are achieved, within a culture based on corporate values. When they try to apply structure and execute plans first, they fail to achieve and integrate alignment and engagement.

Organisational politics and leadership

Another common reason for failure is that executives fail to reign over organisational politics.

Politics (from the Greek *πολιτική*), according to Aristotle (384–322BC), the Greek philosopher who coined the term, is the noblest science because it deals with the affairs of the *polis,* ie the city's commons – vis-à-vis economics *(οικονομική* in Greek), which deals with the affairs of the *oikos,* the household.

In modern times, politics has come to mean making the impossible, possible – dealing with misaligned complexities and diversities and negotiating until compromise achieves alignment – ideally without jeopardising the values and mission of the organisation, enterprise, city, country or nation.

The politics of power, promotion, getting and keeping a new project, and staying as far away from problems as possible, often dominates the time and attention of executives and consumes their energy.

Managing politics is not easy.

In exercising their leadership process, successful executives follow a number of specific steps to navigate varying political agendas to achieve common understanding, alignment, consensus, engagement and commitment (see Figure 6.3).

Figure 6.3: Managing organisational politics

1. They map the various agendas. They identify the influential players and make reasonable efforts to engage them in dialogue.
2. They cultivate close relationships with all stakeholders. They are fair to all, treating people as equals.
3. They communicate and shift mindsets. They recognise each person's sensitivities while building close relationships among them, particularly in triads.
4. They are not stingy, with information. They strive for a golden mean.
5. They network legitimately. They seek support from influential and revered supporters.

6. They are ruthless though respectful to those who cannot blend in with the team, being incapable of alignment even after interrogating and debating exhaustively the various issues, and after the majority of the team has been aligned.
7. They know themselves. They are authentic and consistent and behave with modesty and humility, even when extraordinary cases demand inconsistency.

Successful executives manage politics in a positive way, based on the organisation's ethical values.

EXAMPLE

A typical example is Whirlpool; the organisation's code of ethics[52] states the following values: respect, integrity, diversity and inclusion, teamwork, and spirit of winning. In this company, induction, managerial verbal and body language, and performance management revolve around these values. The company's people are expected to think and act based not only on the *what* (must be achieved) but simultaneously on the *how*. The individuals who get results but do not speak, live, or demonstrate the values are expelled by the system.

Successful executives do not disregard or shy away from organisational politics, recognising that dealing with it is a prerequisite of successful leadership.

They do it discreetly, paying due attention to the sensitivities of each individual until alignment and engagement are achieved – even if they are obliged to fire people who cannot blend in. They deal with politics and build understanding, alignment, consensus, engagement, commitment and ownership, with the values and culture of the organisation as their foundation.

52 http://assets.whirlpoolcorp.com/wp-content/uploads/code_of_ethics.pdf

Engagement, commitment and ownership-based leadership

Another common reason many executives are not successful is that even when they recognise that success requires that structure and planning must follow alignment with the organisation's purpose, mission, plans and targets, or even if they manage to achieve alignment, they fail to achieve engagement. They fail to win the minds and hearts of their immediate team, and then of the great majority of the organisation's people, which is needed if they are to do their utmost in executing the (mission-dictated) processes and the (vision-dictated) strategic projects.

Research shows that between a third and a fifth of top team members in many prosperous countries across the world report fundamental divisions within the top executive team. Also, between a third and four-fifths believe that many serious outstanding issues are not aired and discussed among top teams because they are considered too sensitive.

In an apparent, though not surprising, contradiction, non-executive board members rate their board and themselves highly against numerous hard and soft measures, while executives downrate their non-executive board colleagues by as much as 40%. A similar situation is true for the top executive teams, with regard to how their associates on the next level see them.

In many organisations, there exist poor and untrusting relationships among the board members, between the board and top management, and between successive executive levels. The culture of poor relations starts at the top and spreads down the hierarchy to the operational level. Research shows that external board members have poor insight into the reality of how their organisation operates. Conversely, executives at all levels know what is wrong, but don't dare raise the issues.

There is an obvious result: disengagement.

Disengagement means demotivated people, an unwillingness to go to work, often subversive and damaging behaviour – not only by employees but also by executives – passivity, poor relationships with one's immediate superior and, ultimately, burnout (see Figure 6.4).

Figure 6.4: Disengagement is detrimental

Research shows that only three out of ten employees are fully engaged, while one in four is disengaged.

> **To achieve engagement and commitment, successful executives acknowledge that value for the organisation's stakeholders is created and delivered by people, not technology.**

They recognise (see Figure 6.5) that:

- Engagement is built on dialogue and trust.
- It is the executive's job and duty to create a culture of open and constructive dialogue and sincere interrogation of all issues; to provide intellectual due diligence and search for the best solutions; and to work in-team to improve proposals so that all concerned agree with the conclusion and decision – recognising, at the same time, each individual's view and contribution.
- Executives require resilience and robustness to encourage, listen actively, and endure criticism.
- Trust is essential to achieve transparency and dialogue, and avoid defensive silence and destructive debate.
- Once engagement is achieved, they can inspire commitment and ownership of actions, targets and results.

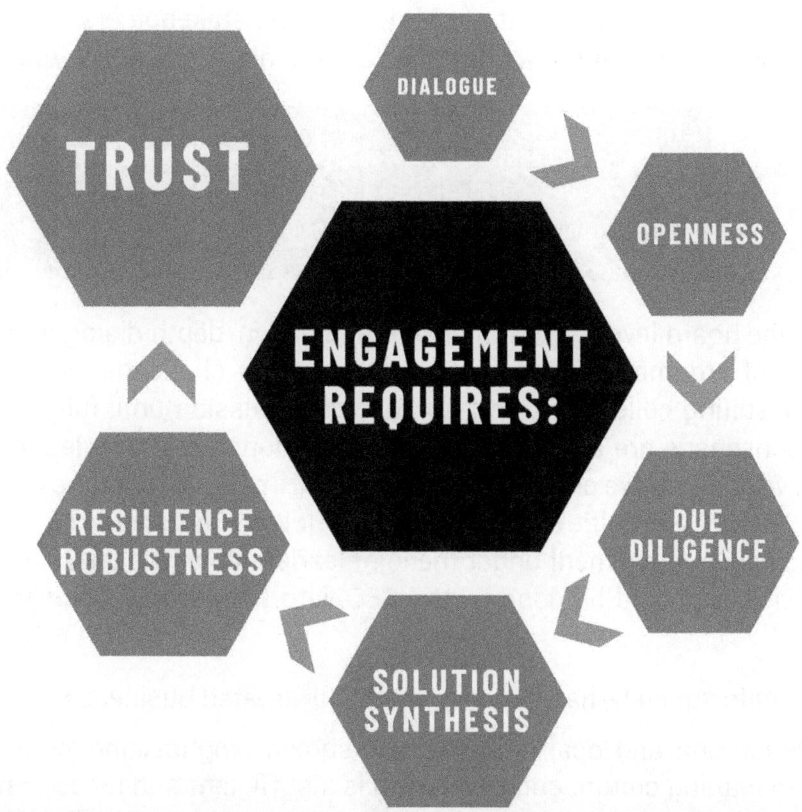

Figure 6.5: Engagement

In summary, successful executives build a positive culture on the basis of the organisation's values, which enable open dialogue, interrogation of all issues, and positive, sincere contributions and proposals. This enables not only common understanding and alignment but also engagement, commitment and ownership.

Dynamic governance-based leadership

As we repeatedly stress in this book, executive success is equal to creation and delivery of value by executing the organisation's mission and realising its vision. Is it, however, adequate for the executive to fulfil the organisation's mission and realise its vision by all means and at any cost?

Global research shows that this is impossible in the mid to long term. It could be possible in the short term, to the detriment of most, if not all, stakeholders, until the organisation later collapses under the weight of its own weaknesses and wrongdoings.

Successful executives create a modus operandi governed by ethical rules and the formal and informal codes of governance, in a culture based on the code of ethics of the organisation.

Similarly, at the board level, governance demands an in-depth dialogue on all issues, interrogation of arguments from various angles, open challenge without prejudice and fear of insulting colleagues, and exhaustive discussion until full understanding and broad consensus are achieved. This must be done under the leadership of the non-executive or executive chairperson with the full involvement of the non-executive members to mentor and guide the executive team. Ideally, this should cover the second level of executive management under the joint leadership of the chairperson and the CEO. Otherwise, it should be done by the CEO with the assistance of the executive committee.

Governance, unfortunately, has become another ill-treated business term.

As many international and local incidents have shown, emphasising monitoring at the expense of managing culture and mentoring is insufficient and leads to mechanical box-ticking and reporting, with grave results. Research shows that many of the big corporate scandals occurred despite exemplary formalities and protocols and full compliance with formal codes of governance, such as those enforced by stock exchange authorities. It also shows that, in many cases, individual board members knew or suspected that something was not right but lacked complete information and preferred to keep silent instead of asking the right questions. Once again, a spirit of pseudo-solidarity, and a 'don't need to know' or 'don't disturb what is working' culture in place of a genuine team culture, prove catastrophic.

Successful executives and organisations acknowledge that:

- **Governance is not synonymous with circumstantial compliance and monitoring, mechanistic questionnaire answering, and belated reporting.**
- **Governance is a two-sided coin: an organisational culture characterised by:**
  - **Open, sincere dialogue, coaching and mentoring, and the personal example set by the executives in living the organisation's codes of ethics and governance.**
  - **Ongoing compliance, monitoring and reporting.**
- **Monitoring comprises actual values of KPIs, internal audit systems, and risk assessment procedures, and aims at providing early warning signals to enable the board and executive management to correct weaknesses and prevent mistakes, bad decisions and wrongdoing.**
- **Applying governance demands a deep understanding of its meaning and its application in difficult situations and dilemmas. It requires inquisitive minds, diversity of thinking, and independence.**
- **Governance should underlie the activities of both the organisation's executives and its board of directors. At the executive level, governance demands the building of a culture of openness, ensuring that:**
  - **All issues are subject to open, sincere dialogue and evidence.**
  - **Proposals are openly and exhaustively challenged with the independent, fearless participation of all concerned, especially all members of formal and informal collective organisational entities, until broad, if not absolute, consensus, alignment, engagement, commitment and ownership is reached and decisions implemented.**
  - **Resulting actions are effectively controlled and monitored, deviations are openly reviewed and discussed, causes analysed, and corrective actions decided upon and implemented.**

The latest trend in tackling the widespread problem of inadequate governance appears to be dynamic governance, and an emphasis on managing the organisational stratification borders. In other words, the hierarchical lines between various levels, such as between board and top executive team, between top executives and general management, and between general management and operational management. It could also be the lines between corporate centre (head office) and national branches or subsidiaries, for international organisations.

According to research, best practice dictates that the board should own the culture while executive management should propagate and cultivate the culture and own the execution of the mission and realisation of the vision. The board should act as the steward of the interests of all stakeholders and hold responsibility for establishing a culture of ethics and governance by adopting and demanding the implementation of a set of rules. It should do this by mentoring the top management (and through them the whole organisation) in observing the values and the rules in executing corporate processes, carrying out strategic projects, and monitoring compliance.

The reality, however, is that many board members are toothless. Instead of scrutinising the issues faced by the business, challenging, arguing, dialoguing (or even debating) and reaching active alignment, they avoid controversy at all costs and leave the organisation on autopilot. They let executive management do as they wish, unchecked and unmonitored. They treat the code as a multiple-choice questionnaire and replicate last year's report with little substance.

What is required is leadership that is capable and willing to create *constructive* conflict. What is needed is a board comprising experienced people with differing opinions, backgrounds and personalities who can work together as a high-performing team.

Where the chairpersons are not able or willing to lead with governance, successful top executives take the initiative and navigate the board of directors towards dynamic governance. When the board proves unable and/or unwilling to follow, successful executives take the initiative and lead the organisation by building a culture based on strong ethical values and a dynamic governance framework.

Research carried out in Europe by Heidrick & Struggles[53] showed a growing demand for dynamic governance based on two main realisations, and came to an important conclusion:

- First, leadership starts at board level.
- Second, governance is a means of enabling and driving business performance.
- All things being equal, well-governed organisations excel.

> **Dynamic governance is not built on defensiveness and bureaucracy, but on the recognition that successful organisations are those which recognise the reality (what's happening) and foresee the future (what's going to happen) within their environment (industry sector, technology, competition, finance, geopolitics, society). It goes beyond compliance. It is about a spirit of governance. In the best organisations, the board governs upfront and monitors afterwards.**

Based on the findings of the study, Heidrick & Struggles identified:

- Four pillars as the foundation of the board and the top executive team's ability to perform:
  - People: continually seek top talent and engage in succession planning
  - Vision: shape and realise a clear vision and strategy with alignment and engagement
  - Leadership: promote a team culture through board leadership
  - Innovation: maximise the team's capacity to assess and innovatively adapt to risk
- Nine drivers for best practice:
  - Balance of competences and competencies
  - Empowered support of committees and teams
  - Regular board and executive committee evaluation
  - Identification and exploitation of board improvement opportunities
  - Balance between executive and non-executive directors
  - Regular board meetings (with frequent second-level management participation)

53 www.heidrick.com/Knowledge-Center/Publication/European-Corporate-Governance-Report-2014-Towards-Dynamic-Governance

    - Explicit criteria for board member replacement
    - Diverse board member mix (gender, nationality, expertise, age, etc)
    - A representative number of genuinely independent directors
- Six characteristics to be developed:
    - Deep business knowledge
    - Diversity of thought
    - Engaged leadership
    - Alignment, engagement and execution
    - Capacity to adapt
    - Leadership talent

Only then can effective mission execution, vision formulation and execution, compliance, and monitoring be achieved.

Dynamic governance requires maturity and deep interaction between board members themselves and with all groups of stakeholders, and, above all, between the board (specifically through the chairperson) and the top executive. Hence it requires more involvement, energy and time. It also demands a more external focus to be able to actively create wealth, jobs and sustainability.

Successful executives ensure that the organisation collects, scrutinises and distributes real and truthful information about the organisation itself and its environment, to both its executives and the board. This information must include the monitoring of compliance with external and internal regulations and rules.

Implementing dynamic governance demands explicit – ideally extreme – ownership of culture, mission, vision, plans and targets, alignment, engagement, and commitment. It requires wisdom and maturity. Above all, it needs leadership capability from both the board chair and the chief executive, as well from the whole hierarchy of executives.

In summary, dynamic governance depends on the effectiveness of the board and the leadership competency of the top executive team. This demands that the board operates as a team, with team and corporate spirit; that it knows and executes effectively its duties (with regard to achieving its purpose, mission, targets and strategic deliverables);

and that it is effectively managed, actively develops itself, and continually measures its performance. The board must shape, manage and own corporate culture; mentor executive management; and exhaustively discuss, interrogate, resolve and decide on (executive-owned) strategic and business issues. It must monitor implementation, compliance and reporting thoroughly and sincerely.

Results-based leadership

> **Successful executives create and deliver value by leading the organisation's people in achieving outstanding results.**

To this end, they satisfy all necessary prerequisites:

1. They establish solid foundations by striving and achieving organisational excellence with respect to all enablers; infrastructure; value streams and processes; people structures; and executives and operatives, suppliers and partners possessing the requisite competences, competencies and cultural fit – as we have elaborated in Part One of this book.
2. They achieve operational excellence by introducing a business excellence model; by building and maintaining continuous improvement and innovation, and cultivating and continuously enhancing the organisation's knowledge; and by formulating and continually updating short, mid and long-term plans and managing all enablers, as we have explored in Chapter Five.
3. They establish and maintain a tribal culture based on a set of broadly adopted shared values and dynamic governance rules and procedures and lead by living the organisation's values; by establishing a network of tribal teams; and by building rapport among team members, based on respect and trust, as we outline in this chapter.
4. They develop their own and their subordinate executives' management and leadership competences and competencies, as we shall see in Chapter Eight.

They acknowledge that all these facets of the executive process are solely focused on the creation and delivery of value and that their effectiveness and quality significantly affects the end result.

Successful executives focus on achieving outstanding results by leading the execution of the agreed plans for creating and delivering value. They lead their people, acknowledging that they are major stakeholders of the organisation. They achieve successful execution of mission-dictated operational plans and vision-dictated strategic projects by empowering and rewarding their people.

Technology, finance, customer demands and globalisation have made organisations complex. Their environment changes fast. Their processes and plans are becoming increasingly complex. In many cases, decisions have to be made in haste and without the luxury of the ample time needed for collecting and validating all necessary information for safe decision-making.

Even the most competent executives can be easily overwhelmed if they try to solve multiple problems or execute many diverse tasks simultaneously. They may confuse their associates and lead their team and organisation to failure.

Successful executives retain their composure, simplify plans, prioritise actions and lead their execution. They manage to do this by staying ahead of real-time problems. They anticipate challenges and needs and plan ahead promptly. Together with their team, they formulate contingency plans so that their deputies are never surprised. In this way, they achieve effective decentralisation and build their leadership competencies and competences.

They avoid micromanagement and keep a high-view picture of the situation, while maintaining effective two-way communication in all directions, so that true and reliable information is continuously collected, scrutinised and propagated. This enables them to respond quickly to shifting priorities and remain focused on executing plans and projects and achieving results satisfying stakeholder needs, sustainably in the long term.

Leading change versus leading the organisation

> **Successful executives manage and lead effectively and efficiently, first, the execution of the organisation's mission of creating and delivering value to its stakeholders and, equally, the realisation of the organisation's vision and, hence, change.**

Many theoreticians claim that successful leaders are those who prioritise the leadership of change (over the execution of the organisation's current mission), exhibit high competency and competence in achieving change, and successfully effect change.

> **Reality shows that successful executives primarily manage and lead their organisation in successfully executing its mission, and that it is only through this that they lead the organisation in formulating its vision for change and innovation. They then realise this vision by implementing the necessary strategic projects, if and when they have the competency to do so.**
>
> **The opposite is rarely true. Executives who have the competency to vision and lead the organisation in continuously effecting change but do not have the competences and competencies and/or the willingness to manage and lead the organisation in realising its (current) mission, cannot achieve long-term success. In many cases, they cannot even achieve mid-term success.**
>
> **Often, they drown their organisation by creating confusion, misalignment, disengagement and disownment due to continuously trying to implement changes. They create a blurred picture of reality.**
>
> **Even in turbulent times, when disruptive changes in the environment endanger the (current) mission, successful executives manage to lead the execution of the mission while increasing their focus on, and dedicating more time, effort and passion to visioning change and innovation, and to managing and leading their implementation.**

Growth-based leadership

> **Successful executives have a growth mindset, nurture a growth-mindset culture, and develop their own and their people growth mindset.**

They recognise that only people with a growth mindset seek and embrace change, self-development and innovation, and that people with a fixed mindset resist them.

They create an environment in which the organisation's people thrive, by:

- Showing that people's capabilities, including their growth mindset and their leadership competencies, can be learnt and continuously developed
- Including in the organisation's code of ethics the value of continuous development with a growth mindset
- Ensuring that executives at all levels give feedback to their people in a way that promotes learning and development
- Nurturing a leadership culture in which executives at all levels are seen and serve as resources for learning – as trainers, coaches and mentors
- Showing that the organisation values talent, not only as a natural quality but as a learnable and developable personal characteristic, and that, above all, it values a mindset of continuous development and growth based on trust and commitment

Team-based leadership

> **Successful executives recognise that an organisation can only be successful when it has a coherent social structure, and that such a culture can only be created and maintained through a network of teams and teamwork, on the basis of a shared set of values.**

They also recognise that to successfully execute complex processes and projects, teams are more effective and efficient than individuals operating independently. They also know that, to be successful, a team needs strong leadership and culture.

Forming successful teams

> **Successful executives appoint and develop effective teams systematically, based on the latest research findings on team composition, team dynamics and team psychology.**

They recognise that an effective leadership team demands:

- Transforming a *group* into a *team*
- Diversity of thinking
- Avoiding destructive debates and establishing constructive dialogues
- Establishing dependence among team members and achieving interdependence with a sense of obligation and solidarity
- Establishing a culture of unhindered open expression of opinion and disagreement
- Establishing a culture where, once a decision is taken, it is accepted and committed to by all
- A set of shared values

> **Successful executives know that it is practically impossible for even the most brilliant individual to know every aspect of every subject and be able to respond to any situation effectively. This includes themselves. Therefore, they create strong teams to attack problems and challenging situations, to design innovative products, processes and business models, and to see businesses through reforms.**

There are three types of team:

1. The most common is the **ad hoc team**, assembled as needed to carry out a project or handle a situation. Once its purpose is fulfilled, the team is dissolved and its members return to their previous routines, or are assigned new tasks and projects. Team members are selected based on the requirements of the assignment, usually based on their knowhow and their strong Belbin role competencies (explained below), to ensure effectiveness, efficiency, quality and completion.
2. Less frequently, teams are **more permanent** – with respect to their composition – and are assigned new projects and tasks as they occur. These are usually first created as ad hoc teams and become permanent after one or more great successes. They may be complemented, as needed, with expert members.

3. **Permanent teams**, which have specific roles:
   - Executive 'teams', such as the executive committee, comprising the CEO and the functional executive officers (CxOs). These are usually based on competence and not competency and, as a result, tend to be groups and not teams. It is the CEO's duty to turn a disparate group into a team.
   - Teams for a specific purpose, such as operational planning and review committees, risk management committees, disciplinary committees and R&D committees.
   - Board of directors sub-committees.

Executives are faced with the question:

Are all teams good, from a business perspective, and are they all able to tackle any assignment?

The answer is: no, they are not.

Many teams are created for a good purpose and are assigned a seemingly straightforward task, yet fail. By understanding what causes team failures, we can determine what teams need to succeed:

- The right mix of people
- A clear and feasible assignment
- Authority to act and to use the required resources

Successful executives satisfy all three preconditions for team success by:

- **Specifying a clear assignment mandate, its members, purpose, the timeframe in which it will operate, whom the team will report to, and anything else that will facilitate its operation**
- **Granting enough authority and clearances for the team to act, and defining the boundaries of this authority**
- **Carefully selecting the team members so that they collectively possess the required technical or specialist skills to successfully carry out the task, while each individual possesses interpersonal team-working skills, such as listening, participating, sharing, respecting, helping, questioning and persuading, and has the capability to make up a cohesive, productive team**

They recognise that individuals with team-working skills are more likely to cooperate and arrive at a positive outcome.

They emphasise still another dimension of teamwork: structure.

- Teams are organisational units, and as such need structure.
- They need just one leader, and people who can take on different functional roles.
- Teams are effective only when their members complement each other in terms of their internal assumed roles.

An individual's role in a team is determined by their tendency to behave, contribute and interrelate with others in a particular way. Specialist organisations have come up with methodologies to determine which role(s) each individual is naturally inclined to assume when in a team environment.

The Belbin Inventory, for instance, scores people on how strongly they express behavioural traits from nine different team roles.[54] A person may, and often does, exhibit strong tendencies toward multiple roles. These people exhibit a strong tendency toward more than one role and are hence flexible. Depending on team dynamics, they successfully undertake one or more different role(s) in a particular team or at a specific project stage. Other people show an extreme tendency toward a single role, in which they are successful. They are, however, inflexible. They should not be pushed to play any other roles, as they will fail themselves, the team, and the project.

The nine Belbin roles are:

1. **Resource investigators**, who use their inquisitive nature to find ideas and specialist knowhow or assistance to bring back to the team. They are outgoing and enthusiastic, explore opportunities and develop contacts. *They might be over-optimistic, and can lose interest once their initial enthusiasm has waned.*
2. **Team workers**, who help the team blend, using their versatility to identify the work required and complete it on behalf of the team. They are cooperative, perceptive and diplomatic. They listen and avert friction. *They can be indecisive, tend to avoid confrontation, and might be hesitant to make unpopular decisions.*
3. **Coordinators**, who focus on the team's objectives, motivate team members, and delegate work appropriately. They are mature and confident. They identify talent and clarify goals. *They can be seen as manipulative and might over-delegate, leaving themselves little work to do.*

54 Belbin M. (2010) *Team Roles at Work.*

4. **Plants**, who tend to be highly creative and good at solving problems in unconventional ways. They are imaginative, free-thinking and innovative. They generate ideas and solve difficult problems. *They may be too preoccupied to communicate effectively.*
5. **Monitors/evaluators**, who provide a logical perspective, making impartial judgements where required and weighing up the team's options in a dispassionate way. They are sober, strategic and discerning. They look at all options and judge accurately. *They sometimes lack the drive and ability to inspire others and can be overly critical and slow to come to decisions.*
6. **Specialists**, who bring in-depth knowledge of a critical area to the team. They are single-minded, self-starting and dedicated. They provide specialist knowledge and skills *but tend to contribute on a narrow front and can dwell on the technicalities. They rarely blend with the rest of the team.*
7. **Shapers**, who provide the necessary drive to ensure that the team keeps moving and does not lose focus or momentum. They challenge, are dynamic and thrive under pressure. They have the drive and courage to overcome obstacles. *They can be prone to provocation and may sometimes offend people, becoming aggressive and bad-humoured in their attempts to get things done.*
8. **Implementers**, who plan a workable strategy and carry it out as efficiently as possible. They are practical, reliable and efficient. They turn ideas into actions and organise the work that needs to be done. *They can be inflexible and slow to respond to new possibilities.*
9. **Completers/finishers**, who are most effectively used at the end of tasks to polish and scrutinise the work for errors, subjecting it to the highest standards of quality control. They are painstaking, conscientious and anxious. They search out errors, polish and perfect. *They can be inclined to worry unduly and reluctant to delegate, and can take their perfectionism to extremes.*

As shown above, each role has both strengths and weaknesses.

> **Successful executives build on the strengths of their team members and contain their weaknesses. They recognise that no two individuals are the same, which is what creates the potential for strong teams.**

They know that:

- Too many coordinators or shapers and a lack of implementers or resource investigators means the job will not get done. On the other hand, in the absence of a coordinator, the team will be indecisive and inefficient.

- A team low on specialists will have a poor idea of what they are doing, whereas a team populated solely by specialists risks endless technical discussions that come to no result.
- A few completers/finishers will make the outcome professional, presentable and low on errors. Too many and they will become bogged down in details, likely missing the point and deadline of the project.

Most of the roles contribute at all stages of a project, while certain ones are more useful at particular stages:

- Shapers, specialists, team workers: throughout the project
- Plants, resource investigators: mostly at the initial ideation phase
- Implementers: during implementation
- Monitors/evaluators: during reviews
- Completers/finishers: during the last stages of the project

Leading teams to success

> **Successful executives acknowledge that teams are formed to tackle difficult situations, find solutions to complex problems, and achieve organisational breakthroughs. They recognise that a balanced mix of competencies, competences and roles is imperative for the team to work effectively, as is a clear mandate.**

How does the team work to achieve its best? As a unit, the team receives its mandate from above and sets out to execute it.

Team leadership

Regardless of the role mix, the team assumes a leader. Sometimes the team leader is appointed officially, sometimes not. In the latter case, the team needs to decide who the leader will be. There may be more than one person in the team with the inclination to lead. These are usually shapers or coordinators in the Belbin Inventory. Usually, the strongest personality or the most senior or experienced person prevails, though not always. People who have successfully led teams before, especially under similar circumstances, have an advantage. Too many strong personalities with leadership skills in a single team often leads to power struggles and conflicts, and should be avoided or managed.

Successful team leaders inspire and motivate the entire team, driving momentum during all phases of the work in progress, resolving conflicts and maintaining the team spirit. They facilitate a decision-making process that is respected by all team members. They cultivate the team culture and keep the team productive continuum through the various phases of their work from initiation to delivering results.

Motivation and inspiration

Once broad consensus is reached on the action to take, and alignment and engagement are achieved around a clearly stated decision, successful executives allocate tasks and projects, delegate sufficient authority, and create commitment and a sense of responsibility, using a push approach. When the specified results are accomplished, there is a great sense of satisfaction.

When it comes to creativity and a decision to strive for improvement and innovation around a new idea for something that has never been done before, or for a cause that may have a dramatic and positive impact, executives inspire their team so that they become excited about the new task or project. This is a *pull* approach. People then exert themselves not because of obligation or accountability but rather out of a personal desire to make a difference. Once again, when the desired results are accomplished, there is a great sense of satisfaction.

Some executives employ the push approach, others pull. Research shows that the push approach is much more effective in driving results than the pull approach of inspiring and motivating without setting deadlines, creating commitment or demanding accountability.

Successful executives know when to use the push and when to use the pull approach.

Adaptability

While roles and tasks should be clearly allocated among team members, the successful team is the adaptable team. As difficulties arise, unpredicted tasks are added, deadlines need to be shortened, and unexpected opportunities arise, the winning team is the one whose members are willing to change plans swiftly and to go beyond their formal duties.

Diversity

By default, most members bring diversity of thought, experience and skills to a team. Successful team leaders embrace diversity, and their teams come up with new and inventive ways to accomplish things. Effective teams listen, share, enrich and question. They are willing to try a new solution to an old problem; are open to new or unusual suggestions; and never dismiss a solution without consideration. The team may seem to stall in its action, but it will scrutinise propositions, throw light on grey areas, stretch knowledge through discussion and sharing of experiences, improve suggestions, and reach conclusions with broad consensus. Its members maintain their alignment and engagement with their values, purpose and plan, and their commitment to realising these.

Effective communication

Productive teams communicate effectively. To this end, formal and informal channels of communication are established. Regular team meetings to assess progress, solve problems, resolve any conflicts and enhance team spirit are essential. In addition, there may be less formal meetings involving fewer team members, those who need to collaborate to accomplish a subtask. Effectiveness in communication is not only affected by the type and frequency of meetings, it is a result of the willingness to listen to others, share knowledge and contribute ideas.

Successful executives are themselves productive team members.

As members of their immediate superior's team and any other permanent or ad hoc team, they:

- Communicate clearly, promptly and practically with both their team and their leading executive. They adopt a delicate and discreet attitude and language.
- Try to understand the dynamics of the hierarchy and their superior's preferences, and use their experience and rapport to influence them positively.
- Exhibit caution and respect.
- Clearly present the situation, the possible threats and obstacles, and suggest suitable actions.
- Strive to thoroughly comprehend what their superior executive communicates to them, and tell them what they intend to do.
- Finally, pass plans and decisions down to their own team(s).

They support their superior, even when they disagree with their decision so that they do not undermine the organisation's culture and capability to create and deliver value and prevail in a highly competitive environment. They will even educate their superiors so that they understand the background to any issues and the prevailing situation, speaking the same language and communicating on the same wavelength.

Communication and tribal leadership

Successful executives communicate frequently with all members of the organisational entity they head, using the most effective channel for each communication purpose.

They acknowledge that:

- Communicating frequently strengthens their relationship with their people, while infrequent communication weakens it.
- Building alignment, motivation, engagement and commitment, and disseminating organisational information requires frequent and effective communication.
- Information must be easily accessible to everyone.
- For communication to be effective it must be bi-directional, and the message from the sender must arrive successfully with the receivers.
- The choice of the specific channels used for communication depends on its objectives.
- Written communication is not the best medium for getting a message across in every situation, and is often not the best way to motivate people.
- The majority of people either never or rarely read anything on the intranet, such as websites, or circulars attached to emails or blogs. They pull information from these sources only when they need it for their work or for their personal affairs as employees.
- A blog is an information-push medium and is usually ignored on an intranet, but not so much on public mass social media.
- The lines between internal and external communication are increasingly blurred.
- Blogs need to be open and accessible to all, whether internal or external stakeholders or the mass media.
- Video clips and podcasts are more effective, enabling communication through body language, passionate voice and imagery, especially when addressed personally to individuals.

Successful executives use various mass media channels to build the organisation's culture; to convey corporate values and stories to internal and external audiences; and to keep the organisation's stakeholders well and promptly informed.

They are effective and efficient communicators:

1. They know that giving a little more information than necessary is far more effective than giving less, belatedly. It is also much safer, since it prevents any fake or distorted information causing damage.
2. They use podcasts and video clips to discuss issues of the day, or have a weekly newscast for employees and/or the mass media.
3. They integrate communication into the daily lives of their people, making it available to them outside their workspace, eg to listen on their way to or from work, or even at home.
4. They use a podcast and video to tell informal stories and create a sense of belonging, which is critical in building a corporate culture, and convey delicate company information through more formal means.
5. They take extra care to ensure that the information they disseminate is thorough, accurate, evidence-based and timely.
6. They use humour and narratives whenever possible, recognising their power to communicate and engage.

Successful executives acknowledge the tremendous power of social networks and public mass media, and assess and mitigate the risks that may arise from their potential misuse.

Simplicity

Life is complex. Organisations are complex. Technology, globalisation, financing and customer demands are complex. People are complex. Organisational processes and plans are complex.

Simplifying as much as possible is crucial for achieving understanding and alignment.

> **Successful executives, as team leaders, present the various issues in a clear and comprehensible manner. They challenge information and arguments, invite questions and provide clarifications in open dialogue. They invite alternative views and opinions, subject them to open scrutiny and adopt them if proven sound. They pursue the various issues until everybody has comprehended them thoroughly. They never discourage their people from disputing or challenging any issue.**

Keeping concepts, structures and plans simple is crucial for the success of the team and, ultimately, of the organisation. It goes without saying that once the discussion is exhausted, a broad consensus is reached and a decision taken, everybody is engaged and committed to its execution.

Team play

The strength of a team lies in the fact that each individual is encouraged to put their talents to work. The team is much better off giving its members space to work in their area of strength, letting them do what they do best. This means letting the specialists work out the technical details, the resource investigators dig out hidden facts, and the completers/finishers fine-tune the deliverables.

> **Successful executives ensure that their team finds balance in working together, complementing each other rather than stepping on each other's feet, contributing rather than competing.**

Complementing and sharing

In a successful team, members need to complement each other. They have different competencies and competences and usually different formal and informal roles. They look after their associates and support and assist them whenever required, whether they are asked to or not. Each member of the team is critical to its success, irrespective of who has the primary and who has the supporting roles.

When success is achieved, everybody shares the benefits. When failure occurs, finger-pointing and blame-placing must be avoided at any cost.

Successful leaders contain this crucial problem. They undertake all responsibility, acknowledging that this cannot be delegated. They lead their team in working together to analyse the reasons for failure, find solutions and corrective actions, reverse the situation, and plan to avoid future failures.

Conflict management and decision-making

Conflict happens. The key is to build a strong team culture, where conflicts are instead seen as different views on the same subject that have the potential to teach everybody something new. As such, they can be discussed constructively by all involved and there is no reason why differing opinions should be discouraged. It is well known that the most innovative ideas have been born through challenging the norm and deviating from the established. Free, unrestrained discussion is the foundation of democracy and a natural human tendency, but it is not productive as the deadline approaches.

Successful executives, as team leaders, establish from the outset a mechanism through which decisions can be made without discussions becoming endless.

This is one of the few teamwork methods they formalise to avoid misunderstandings and be efficient and productive. Decisions may be taken by consensus or majority voting, or by the leader, or by the specialist, depending on the nature of the issue. The rule doesn't matter, provided the team members accept it.

Successful team leaders formalise the teamwork to a reasonable level. Above all, they cultivate team spirit.

Authenticity

Hypocrisy is a recipe for disaster. It destroys every effort for alignment, engagement, commitment, solidarity and sacrifice.

As leaders, successful executives are authentic.

They not only preach the values of the organisation and demand that all team members are aligned around them and their mission, they genuinely live the values and are always authentic in their attitude and behaviour.

Humility

Ego clouds and disrupts everything: objectivity, judgement, respect for others and their opinion, constructive criticism, planning, review and revision activities, even self-preservation.

Everybody has an ego. Ego is necessary and useful because it drives ambition for success, but it must be controlled. It must always be subordinate to the organisation's values and the common and greater good.

> **Successful executives exhibit humility.**

They feed their ego with the silent respect, admiration and, above all, the belief and love of their associates, as well as ultimately of the organisation's stakeholders, who enjoy the value that is delivered to them. When they exhibit extreme ownership of failure and submit and even sacrifice their own good to the common good, they enjoy gratitude.

Prioritise and execute

Value streams, end-to-end processes, supply and delivery chains, market developments, customer demands, plans, and, above all, people are complex. The environment in which modern organisations operate changes rapidly. Disruptive technology and market changes are common. Executives are overwhelmed with information, frequently contradictory, and feel obliged to change plans and decisions on the fly. This often results in confusion and tends to blow away alignment and engagement in plans and commitment to results, diminishing team spirit and tearing teams apart.

In their roles as leaders, successful executives:

- **Simplify challenges, problems, weaknesses and threats by breaking them into manageable chunks and identifying priorities**
- **Present, in a comprehensible manner, the top priority action within the big picture**
- **Develop and discuss a solution within their team, using clear, concise language until everybody understands it thoroughly and consensus is reached**
- **Plan, in-team, the implementation of the chosen solution, utilising the competencies of specific team members**
- **Lead the execution of the priority plan, either directly or indirectly via the heads of lower-level specialised subteams**
- **Review results and next priorities, keeping all concerned informed, and move to the next top priority**
- **Do not fixate on a single issue, but maintain a view of the big picture, ready to (re)act when priorities change**

Decisiveness and uncertainty

Executives and their teams formulate plans and make decisions based on the available information. This information is seldom absolutely correct, especially when it comes to competitive intelligence.

Successful executives feel comfortable with uncertainty and make all necessary decisions promptly.

They continue collecting and validating information and are ready to adjust plans so that they continue to reflect reality. They give ample leeway to their deputies to adjust plan details swiftly within agreed boundaries.

Discipline versus freedom

Executives frequently walk a fine line between exhibiting and demanding discipline and giving ample freedom to themselves and their team members. Unfortunately, the majority veer too much toward one of the two extremes, with detrimental consequences for team spirit and performance.

Successful executives balance discipline in values, rules and previous decisions with freedom to make decisions in view of new realities. This capability makes for high leadership competency in contrast to mechanistic management competence. They balance opposing forces and even their own opposing traits and feelings.

They know how to:

- Win and lose
- Have the last word but listen to subordinates who may have a better solution
- Be aggressive, defensive or reserved
- Be detached or emotional
- Be confident but not over-confident
- Be close to their associates but not too close
- Exhibit ownership and delegate authority
- Be leaders and followers
- Demand commitment, loyalty and subordination to the common cause
- Serve their followers

Avoiding personal evaluation frustration

The secret to leading a team is the relationship between the manager and the members. Nothing can destroy this relationship faster than a flawed performance review.

The catalyst to a doomed relationship can be as simple as poorly communicated and informal feedback, causing employees to think that the executive is not taking their review seriously. In addition, showing blatant leniency in ratings, using 'average' or 'satisfactory', solely to avoid having difficult direct conversations has the same detrimental results.

Good employees know their strengths and weaknesses. They are aware of their downfalls and will more than likely be expecting a conversation about them. To gloss over those shortcomings will cause more harm than good. The employee will be frustrated because, as hard as it can be to receive feedback, that is what people crave. They want to know how, in their boss's opinion, they are performing.

Successful organisations have effective performance review systems and tools, with the aim of making life easier, less painful and more rewarding for both the assessors and the assessed. The system guidelines include:

- What to do, what to say, and what to avoid
- A step-by-step checklist
- Sample written reviews

Successful executives speak to their people about their successes, failures or mistakes as near as possible to the event, praising or reprimanding them, together with the required advice, and maintain a critical incidents diary, which they use during formal evaluation sessions. They carry out formal evaluation reviews on a quarterly basis, even if the official review is annual, evaluate formal and informal personal development during performance reviews, and formulate or update personal development plans. They know that performance evaluation is a vital subprocess of the leadership process and exercise it continually.

The art of delegation

Executives are continuously faced with the conundrum of finding an equilibrium between macro and micromanagement, as we will see in Chapter Eight. In doing so, it is not only their time and stamina that are challenged but also, and more critically, the culture of the organisation and the development and performance of successive hierarchical levels, since their style sets the example.

Micro and macromanagement are two extreme executive styles that, in general, have adverse effects on the people and the organisation. Their key difference is the extent to which the executives delegate authority to their team members and enable them to delegate further down when appropriate.

Delegation is the assignment of authority to another person, generally from an executive holding an executive post in the organisational hierarchy to a subordinate, who may hold either an executive or a purely operative post, to carry out specific activities and make relevant decisions. Delegation is entrusting a subordinate to carry out part of the executive's job.

Successful executives clearly define the extent of delegation for all three of its elements: authority, accountability and responsibility.

When executives delegate, they assign a particular person to executing a task or making a decision. That person should be entrusted with the relevant authority and expected to assume, under certain conditions, the respective responsibility. The assignment must be accompanied by a description of the task, the expected result, the deadline, all relevant parameters, specifications and interfaces. This is the starting point of the delegation process: the need to get the task or project executed, the choice of who will accomplish it, and the communication and, where applicable, the acceptance of the assignment.

Unfortunately, many executives assign the task or project without delegating the necessary authority for the assignee to be empowered to perform optimally. In the worst cases, they even demand that the person assumes the responsibility, forgetting that responsibility cannot be delegated, and should never be demanded, unless specific important prerequisites are satisfied.

Successful executives recognise that to execute the task or project, responsibility must be accompanied by the required authority to utilise assets, including financial, and manage and lead others, not only further down the hierarchy but, in many cases, peers. They acknowledge that without authority, it may not be possible to complete the assignment.

Therefore, they make arrangements so that the assignee has the power necessary to get the job done. Authority usually stems from one's positioning on the organisational chart, which might mean placing the person in a suitable position in the organisational structure (based on a predefined scope). They acknowledge that delegating responsibility without ensuring adequate authority leads to confusion and misunderstandings in the organisation, dissatisfaction of the assignee, ineffectiveness and inefficiency with respect to the execution of the assignment, and a high risk of failure.

Accountability

Successful executives demand accountability from the assignee by agreeing on clear budgets, KPIs, targets and/or deliverables and milestones, as well as any applicable rules and restrictions.

They know that ultimate responsibility and accountability cannot be delegated and that, while they may be free to pass down some authority, they remain accountable and responsible for the outcome of the delegated work. Accountability means being liable for the end result. It arises from responsibility. No matter how much there is, and how far down the organisational structure delegation goes, the executive is still accountable for the final result. Even though their subordinates are responsible for their own part of the work, the executive is accountable for the result as a whole. They are also accountable for their choice of delegate, for the effectiveness and quality of their guidance, for the frequency of their reviews, for the effectiveness of their problem-solving, and for recognising promptly any danger of failure and taking corrective action.

Delegation is good and necessary. Executives, as single individuals, are not in a position to do everything themselves, and are not supposed to. Therefore, they are expected to empower their subordinates to execute tasks and make decisions, acting on their behalf. This action entails shifting the decision-making authority to lower organisational levels. Delegation improves the efficiency and effectiveness of the organisation, and saves time and money. It helps people build skills and motivates them. It gives executives more time to focus on non-routine, strategic issues.

Low or lack of delegation is a common characteristic of micromanagement. Micromanaging executives do not trust their subordinates and are reluctant to delegate authority to them in case they misuse it, and/or due to fear of failure. As a result, they are over-burdened, spend valuable time on trivial issues and inadequate time on important ones, while subordinates are inefficient and frustrated by the lack of trust.

In the case of over-delegation, a characteristic of macromanagement, executives give away too much of their authority, under the illusion of having also delegated responsibility. As a result, they appear to their people as incompetent or indifferent. They are not only rendering the organisation vulnerable to failure, they also risk losing people's respect.

In summary, to achieve successful delegation, executives:

- **Assign activities or tasks.** The clearer the description of the assignment, the definition of the end result, and the time schedule, the better.
- **Grant authority.** The authority granted should be relevant to the task and sufficient to facilitate its completion.
- **Create responsibility.** The assignment should be linked with the requirement to deliver and own the specified results.
- **Show accountability.** Accept overall ownership, praise or blame for the end result and the decisions made, passing to their team the praise.

Successful executives are well aware of the abilities of their subordinates and make their delegation decisions based on the knowledge, experience, ability and workload of their staff. They provide guidance, obtain frequent feedback, assess results and revise plans as needed.

The miracle of empowerment

We talked about delegation and the benefits of assigning authority and, to some extent, responsibility, down the hierarchy to increase organisational effectiveness and efficiency. Delegation can only lead to success when it genuinely empowers people.

Empowerment means the release of power to lower levels in the hierarchy. Our experience and research show that this can develop, strengthen, motivate and satisfy people to the highest degree. They also show that few organisations manage to empower their employees successfully. Why? What does it require that so many executives fail to do? Empowerment begins with a culture of sharing, trusting, appreciating and believing in people's potential. When projected onto the team, it creates incredible momentum.

The success of empowerment is that, for the people involved, it creates a shift away from a deficit-oriented toward a strength-oriented perception. This has profound and lasting results, enabling people at any level to overcome a sense of powerlessness and lack of influence, to recognise their abilities and put them to use. People learn to cope with their work-related challenges more independently and confidently.

Empowerment can be both a management and a leadership practice. Both aim at driving employees to take initiative, make decisions and improve their own and the organisation's performance. It can lead to better information-sharing and higher rewards.

Successful executives empower their people by:

- Vesting them with more authority – more discretion in decision-making and increased liberty in the use of resources, while demanding respectively higher responsibility, retaining for themselves the ultimate responsibility
- Developing and enhancing any necessary competences and competencies in their people
- Sharing management information, such as the results of the organisation's targets, plans, and budgets
- Seeking greater participation of their people in the decision-making process
- Flattening hierarchies and establishing autonomous, self-managed teams
- Adopting people's suggestions, even if they carry some risk, and then assigning to them their implementation, strengthening their empowerment
- Giving team members opportunities to act, create, develop, learn, interact and shine
- Introducing self-evaluation procedures
- Supporting the development of their competences, competencies and growth mindset through training, coaching, mentoring, providing constructive feedback and matching the role of each person to their capabilities and preferences, where feasible

They acknowledge that empowered people take initiative, are creative, exceed expectations, are happier, need less control, achieve better results across the board, are proud and make their leader proud.

Many executives question whether empowerment works, and do not allow it because they are afraid that it might backfire.

Successful executives are aware of the dangers and exercise empowerment carefully.

They recognise that:

- There are circumstances under which empowerment efforts will lead to a dead end, or even to failure.
- When a team is exceptionally dissatisfied or if the management and/or leadership style thus far has been controlling or autocratic, then an abrupt shift to an empowerment model may not sit well with the majority.
- In some instances, abrupt empowerment may cause suspicion or confusion regarding how senior management wants to deal with people. People may simply find it difficult to respond to such a change.
- Though empowerment is bliss, it needs to be applied when the culture is ready to accept it.
- They need to assess the effectiveness of empowerment and take corrective actions as needed, acknowledging that certain tactics may be more appropriate than others, depending on the type of business, culture and individual characteristics.
- No matter how well intended, empowerment should not be left to chance. It must be structured and assessed.

Successful executives acknowledge that, if delegation can bring improvements, empowerment can work miracles.

Extreme ownership

The team leader's success emanates from extreme ownership.

> **On any team, in any organisation, all responsibility for success and failure rests with the executives in their role as leaders. They must own everything in their world. There is no one else to blame. They must acknowledge mistakes and admit failures, take ownership of them and develop a plan to succeed.**

Successful executives do not take passive responsibility for their mission. They take extreme ownership of everything that impacts their mission.

- They do not blame their team members, if and when any of them do not do what they should.
- They bear the responsibility for having gone through (or not) all leadership activities that should have enabled their people to successfully execute their process, activity or project, and to create and deliver value.
- They take responsibility, if any team member underperforms, for developing their competences and/or competencies through training, coaching or mentoring until their performance reaches a satisfactory level.
- They remain loyal to the mission, the team and the organisation above the individual team members. Whenever any team member continually underperforms or fails to meet standards and targets, they replace them by transferring them to another post where their capabilities, with or without retraining, indicate that they can perform well, otherwise terminating their service with appropriate compensation.

Successful executives, taking extreme ownership of their organisation/team's mission and vision, problems and failures, look at them through the objective lens of reality, with emotional detachment from agendas, plans and people.

They set aside their ego, accept responsibility, roll up their sleeves, face failures, weaknesses and problems, analyse the reasons for deviations between actual and targeted performance, plan corrective action, and lead execution. They do not take credit for success but bestow it on their people. They coach and mentor them to do the same in leading their own teams. Above all, they cultivate a value-based team culture. Once this culture is entrenched in their team and then cascades down to the whole organisation, it performs well and continuously improves. In such a culture, performance increases exponentially.

> **Successful executives develop the executive competencies and competences of their team members so that they can deputise them whenever necessary without jeopardising performance. They not only exhibit extreme ownership but instil the same noble spirit in their people through their own example.**

Successful executives are never satisfied

> **Successful executives strive relentlessly for improvement and innovation.**

They instil in their team's culture, and subsequently in the organisation's culture, the spirit of creativity and the thirst for continuous improvement, innovation and growth. Everybody in their team looks for work-related weaknesses and opportunities and puts them on the table so that all have the chance to seek and propose solutions. By openly discussing weaknesses, problems, threats and opportunities, the culture is strengthened and becomes more innovative, flexible and resilient, thus promoting sustainability.

The decision-making process

One of the most challenging tasks of an executive in any organisation is decision-making. Decisions are made every day, at all organisational levels, just as in all aspects of life. Some are subconsciously made and some require conscious thought. Some are trivial and some carry great significance. In any case, persons in executive positions will be required at some point in their career to make some tough or critical decisions.

Why are decisions difficult? Decisions are difficult by default, simply because there is always more than one possible route to take at every junction. For every problem raised, there is more than one solution, and executives are required to choose among them. Since no one can guarantee the outcomes and consequences of every possible scenario, it is impossible for executives to predict the best choice in every situation. Decisions may have severe implications for the wellbeing of the organisation, and they may affect the feelings of individuals, too. As such, decision-making responsibility is often a burden.

Decision-making ability varies from person to person. Whereas some find it easy to make seemingly difficult decisions, others struggle with an apparently straightforward choice. This depends on the personality of the individual, their clarity of thinking, and ability to choose with assertiveness.

How can the decision-making process be facilitated?

> **Successful executives facilitate decision-making through gathering evidence-based information and assessing alternative lines of action, in a structured way.**

- **They model information.** They ensure that information related to the processes of the extended organisation (ie to the processes of the supply and sales chains) is thoroughly modelled in parallel with modelling the processes; that this information includes KPIs, targets and actual results; and that it covers rules and restrictions in a decision-making model to enhance effectiveness, efficiency, quality and compliance.
- **They focus on the decision to be made.** They clarify the key question to be answered and distinguish it from secondary questions. They acknowledge that clarity on priorities is crucial.
- **They seek and systematically collect facts, data and information.** They establish relevance, accuracy, completeness, quality and quantity to make informed decisions. They demand that external data be collected from the source, or as close to the source as is legally and ethically possible. They give due consideration to internal information, understanding that it may be specific to individual competencies, such as risk attitude, risk tolerance and assertiveness.
- **They identify and assess the alternatives.** They consider all available paths to resolve a problem.
- **They recognise that a decision must be made even when facing the dilemma of doing something or nothing.** When the decision is critical, they list their options and run a cost-benefit analysis for each, acknowledging that even though there are no guarantees, this exercise will likely rule out some options and make the final decision easier. At this stage, they determine which of the alternatives have higher implementability. An option may seem to be the best solution but have a slim chance of being implemented due to factors that can't be controlled. They prioritise their options based on the likelihood of a successful outcome and of successful implementation, either formally (on paper) or informally (in their mind).

- **They discuss and interrogate the issue in open, exhaustive dialogue with their team and, depending on the subject, invite specialists to contribute.**
- **They make a choice.** They do not shy away from making a decision. They weigh all available facts – numbers, data, information, probabilities, statistical analysis and associates' opinions – together with judgement: instinct, experience, emotions and intuition. They remember that time is of essence.
- **They communicate.** They inform their team and all other affected stakeholders about their decision, the result that is expected from it, and the possible consequences of failure. They give their people discretion to handle unforeseen challenges that demand urgent action.
- **They act.** They put the decision into action. They put aside the choices not made and move forward in implementing the chosen path.
- **They assess the result.** Once the related actions have been concluded, they evaluate the result in-team, asking relevant questions. Has the original problem been solved? Was this done effectively? Efficiently? Were there any unwanted consequences? If the desired result was not achieved, should the decision-making process be repeated?
- **They learn from experience.** They revisit, after some time, a choice made or not made, as part of their own and their associates' learning process. They recognise that they may not be able to correct a poor decision, but valuable lessons could be learnt from mistakes and every experience can be useful in future decision-making situations.

Successful executives recognise that, while they may try to formalise the decision-making process, the human factor plays an important role that cannot be overlooked. There may be many right choices, and as many wrong ones, in any given scenario. They isolate the problem, use hard data and facts but also trust their gut and their associates. They put their leadership ability to good use, making critical decisions, having conscientiously considered the collective wisdom.

Decision-making is often stressful

The relationship between pressure and performance is a subtle one. When executives experience the right amount of pressure, they do their best work. Too much or too little pressure and performance can suffer.

Successful executives recognise that, in reality, the point of equilibrium depends on the situation and the individual person.

They take into consideration all four of the main influencers of each individual's decision-making capability: skill level, personality, trait anxiety, and task complexity.

Research shows that experience, self-discipline and a sense of professionalism help people avoid performance issues. Their training and experience support them in controlling their stress related to decision-making, although there is a point at which even experienced professionals may become so overwhelmed that their work suffers.

Successful executives acknowledge the high importance of maintaining a balanced specification of expertise, workload, authority and responsibility (RAEW) for the majority, if not all, of the organisational posts, and staff them with people who meet, to the highest possible degree, the post requirements.

They also recognise that a person's competences and competencies are not sufficient for success; they must also fit with the organisation's culture and, where applicable, the team personality mix, and be able and willing to put their capabilities to good use, considering internal pressures (eg concerns about their role and prospects in the organisation) and external pressures (eg personal, family or health problems) they may be already experiencing. They also acknowledge that they will not be able to balance all influences in all situations, and thus ensure that they know how to develop their people's competencies so that they are able to perform in all situations.

They do not confuse *pressure* with *stress*, which is where people feel out of control and, hence, is an overwhelmingly negative emotion. They know that by increasing people's stress, rather than increasing positive pressure, they will create an unhappy, under-performing work environment.

Successful executives know that managing pressure and stress ultimately boils down to culture, and that nurturing a culture based on shared high values is their primary duty as leaders.

They train and coach their people to manage pressure and stress and align themselves within a uniform organisational culture governed by the same set of values. If needed, they use external expert services capable of covering the whole leadership process holistically.

Dealing with complexities in executive decision-making

Extensive multinational research shows that decision-making in all kinds of organisations has enormous room for improvement in terms of effectiveness, efficiency and quality.

Successful executives recognise that above all they must effectively exercise the management and leadership aspects of decision-making, by focusing on certain broad areas.

They clarify:

- What the mission actually means in terms of creating and delivering value to the organisation's stakeholders
- Which are the core value streams and end-to-end processes that create and deliver value
- Which are the KPIs that reveal the degree to which the created and delivered value satisfies the stakeholders' needs

They formulate a vision for the organisation's mid to long-term future based on hard, high-quality information – on business intelligence (BI) and on competitive intelligence (CI).

They collect, filter and verify the data needed for decision-making by optimally exploiting modern technology, for example:

- Automating processes productively following process management or reengineering where appropriate
- Managing core and support process KPIs
- Using analytics effectively
- Building and using dashboards
- Building and using business and competitive intelligence applications

Successful executives' main strength is their leadership competency: they understand how human beings fit into the organisational structures, and how they perform processes. In particular, they understand the decision-making activity on the basis of which they achieve alignment, engagement, commitment, ownership, execution willingness and capability, and, ultimately, outstanding results.

They know that:

- The best technology in the world will not help an organisation if its people, particularly their executive colleagues, do not trust the technology, find it difficult to use, or for some other reason are disinclined to use it.
- There is an inevitable tension between formalising processes and trying to benefit from intuition and gain a significant competitive edge by understanding the uses and limits of both.
- Decision-making is at the core of all organisational activity, as executives at all levels manage and lead mission-dictated operations and vision-dictated strategic projects by weighing up a vast array of factors to arrive at the desired balance of risk and reward.

It is alarming that executives themselves perceive the quality of decision-making in their organisations to be mixed at best.

International research[55] shows that:

- Well over half of the executives surveyed – three-quarters in large organisations – characterised decision-making at their organisations as moderately efficient or worse.
- Nearly one in five executives thinks that management frequently gets its decisions wrong.

This may result in part from the greater challenges of running an organisation in a period of rapid growth or difficulties. It also reveals deeper problems.

55 Economist Intelligence Unit (2007) *In Search of Clarity: Unravelling the complexities of executive decision-making.* A report from the Economist Intelligence Unit sponsored by Business Objects, http://graphics.eiu.com/upload/EIU_In_search_of_clarity.pdf

Major conclusions of the research:

1. Poor data leads to poor decisions.
    - Fewer than one in ten executives receive information when they need it, and nearly half assert that the sieving of vast volumes of data impedes decision-making.
    - Worse still, more than half are often concerned about making poor choices because of faulty, inaccurate or incomplete data.
2. Culture plays a critical role in decision-making.
3. Approaches to decision-making vary across the world. There are distinct geographic differences in how executives make decisions and in their reliance on technology in doing so. For example:
    - Asian executives are more likely to trust their own intuition and judgement, while Europeans are more guided by the opinions of their peers.
    - Asian executives make greater use of technology to support decision-making.

> **Successful executives take cultural differences into account as they seek to improve decision-making tools and processes in multinational organisations. They recognise that detailed, uniform decision-making processes may be hard to apply across different cultures, and that broad frameworks describing values, mission and vision may be more appropriate.**

4. Approaches to decision-making vary depending on the nature of the organisation and the status of the executives.
    - There are distinct differences in how decisions are made between private, public and state-owned organisations.
    - There is also a difference between profit-making and non-profit-making organisations.
    - Risk-aversion grows moving from the higher to the lower-level executives. It also increases moving from internally promoted, to appointed, and to elected executives.
5. The size of the organisation also plays a part, with the challenge increasing as organisations grow.
    - Executives in smaller organisations are more confident in their decision-making than their peers at larger organisations. They are more reliant on people over process, more consultative and less worried about data overload.

- This is an advantage to being small. The ability to retain these qualities is a vital executive challenge for organisations, especially in rapid growth periods.

6. Too much art, not enough science?
    - Senior management decision-making at more than half of organisations proved to be largely informal and unstructured, with executives consulting others mostly on an ad hoc basis.
    - Most executives seem comfortable with these arrangements: only one in four thought that poor decision-making structures are a common cause of bad choices.
    - This reflects a view expressed by several executives that strategic decisions always require a significant element of intuition or judgement.
7. Selected decision-support tools need to be easier to use.
    - Executives believed that technology can play a crucial role in improving decision-making by making it quicker and easier to access and organise large amounts of information.
    - This is hugely important as organisations become larger and more complex, and as the volume of available data increases.
    - Too many executives did not feel comfortable using dashboards and other IT tools that could sharpen their decision-making.
    - Organisations, therefore, need to introduce or develop decision-making tools that are sufficiently reliable and user-friendly to appeal to even the less technology-savvy members of the management team and broader workforce.
    - Intelligence applications can make a big difference.

To us, it is clear that if top-level executives want their organisations to be successful, they need to acknowledge the discouraging research findings summarised above. They must develop the leadership and management competencies and competences of their executives and empower them to build and nurture sound organisational architectures and systems, and a people-centric value-delivering culture based on ethical values. By doing so, they will be able to manage and lead their people successfully in creating and delivering value to their stakeholders and in achieving sustainability.

In summary

Successful executives exhibit outstanding performance in carrying out their mandate by:

- Acknowledging that business success is creating and delivering value to the satisfaction – ideally to the delight – of the organisation's stakeholders.
- Recognising that their mandate covers, holarchically, the management process (see Figure 5.3) and the leadership process (see Figure 6.6, read bottom–up) plus any core, support or staff process (subprocess or activity) that may be delegated to them, and devoting the necessary time, effort and passion to each, in a balanced way.
- Ensuring that their leadership process covers, holistically, all subprocesses listed in Figure 6.6 and ensuring that they are all executed with due diligence.
- Leading the people of the organisational entity they head effectively and efficiently, as the most critical enabler within an integrated system comprising, in a harmonious whole, its various enablers. Building and nurturing a value-based growth-mindset culture of:
  - Clear and truthful evidence-based communication
  - Deep comprehension of the organisation's mission, value streams, enterprise business architectures (eg the value stream, process, data, information system, and post-process RAEW architectures), its organisational chart, operational business plans, vision, and strategic plans and projects
  - Univocal alignment around the organisation's mission and targets, and its vision and strategic deliverables
  - Sincere engagement
  - Results-oriented commitment
  - Extreme ownership
  - Continuous development and improvement
  - Creative innovation of products, services, processes and business models
  - Productive action
- Achieving high productivity and outstanding results, delighting the organisation's stakeholders with the value delivered to them.

<table>
<tr><td rowspan="11">Leading the People (Tribes/Teams/Individuals)</td><td>In Realising the Vision (Strategic Projects)</td></tr>
<tr><td>In Executing the Mission (Operations)</td></tr>
<tr><td>Improvement and Innovation</td></tr>
<tr><td>Visioning</td></tr>
<tr><td>Coaching and Mentoring</td></tr>
<tr><td>Ownership</td></tr>
<tr><td>Commitment</td></tr>
<tr><td>Engagement</td></tr>
<tr><td>Alignment</td></tr>
<tr><td>Communication – Comprehension – Conceptualisation (Architectures, Models, Mission, Knowledge, Targets, Plans, Projects, Actuals, Deliverables)</td></tr>
<tr><td>Tribal/Team Leadership</td></tr>
<tr><td colspan="2">Leading Stakeholder Relations</td></tr>
<tr><td colspan="2">Leading Staffing and People Development</td></tr>
<tr><td rowspan="5">Leading the Organisation</td><td>Wisdom Leadership</td></tr>
<tr><td>Excellence Leadership</td></tr>
<tr><td>Governance Leadership</td></tr>
<tr><td>Value Leadership</td></tr>
<tr><td>Culture Leadership</td></tr>
<tr><td colspan="2">Spiritual Leadership (Rapport)</td></tr>
<tr><td colspan="2">The Executive as Leader</td></tr>
</table>

Figure 6.6: The executive's leadership process

Vital questions

1. Do you acknowledge that an executive's process must cover the management process, as exposed in the previous chapter, and the leadership process, as exposed in this chapter, plus any other activities that may be delegated to them, and which may belong to any core, support or staff process?
2. Do you recognise the need to not only *mechanically manage* the organisation, as outlined in previous chapters, but to also *lead* its people to excel in executing their processes and projects, creating and delivering outstanding value to the delight of the organisation's stakeholders?
3. Do you recognise the difference between management and leadership?
4. Do you know which activities make up the leadership process?
5. Do you recognise the importance of ensuring that:
    - A culture is built and nurtured based on a consistent set of ethical values adopted by the vast majority of its people, who should not only know them but also preach and live by them, following your own example?
    - All information exchanged between the organisation's stakeholders is evidence-based, truthful and as complete as possible?
    - Sincere communication is achieved in open dialogue?
    - All issues are challenged openly, and all people feel able to speak out?
    - You lead the discussion until widely accepted deductions and conclusions are reached?
    - You cultivate a culture of visioning, inspiring people to seek continuous improvement, be creative and innovate in conceiving new products, services, processes and business models, ie a culture of growth mindset at both the personal and the organisational level?
    - You achieve alignment around decisions, targets, operational and strategic plans, with broad consensus?
    - You inspire the organisation's people so that they are sincerely engaged and committed to achieving results?
    - You inspire extreme ownership of processes and projects by empowering people so that they can execute their tasks devoting their best selves to producing outstanding results?
    - You delight the organisation's customers (consumers, clients, students, patients, etc) and its other stakeholders by delivering value that satisfies their needs?

6. Do you recognise that delivering value that delights stakeholders is ultimately the only thing that matters?
7. Do you acknowledge that leadership activities and competencies can be learnt, developed and taught, and that it is the duty of executives to develop their own skills and ensure that the leadership competencies of their subordinates are developed through training, coaching and mentoring?
8. Do you recognise and comprehend the various leadership subprocesses and activities comprising the leadership process, as presented in the above table?
9. What is the formal view, if any, of your organisation on the above questions?
10. Does your organisation include in its executive post specifications explicit descriptions of the management and the leadership processes? Does it specify any other processes or activities? Does it have any relevant, comprehensive training programmes for executives?
11. How would other executives in your organisation respond to the above questions?
12. What is your view on the modern philosophical approach to how an executive should carry out their leadership activities and duties as it is presented in the previous chapter?
13. Does the culture of your organisation enhance clear and truthful communication, deep and univocal understanding, full alignment, genuine engagement, results-oriented commitment, extreme ownership, continuous improvement, creative innovation and productive action?
14. Are you evaluated for development and for reward purposes on the basis of KPIs explicitly related to your management and leadership competencies and competences, and the results of your implementing them?

CHAPTER SEVEN

THE EXECUTIVE: MANAGER OR LEADER?

Directing and conducting a symbiotic orchestra demands outstanding execution of both management and leadership. Management without leadership is a recipe for mediocrity, whereas leadership without management is a recipe for disaster.

Standing outside the Vienna State Opera, as a music lover, you admire the Neo-Renaissance style building of 1869 for a few minutes. You enter, showing the expensive ticket you purchased electronically months earlier. You take your seat in the auditorium half an hour before the concert begins and you look around, taking in the view of the beautiful theatre, letting your mind wonder and your thoughts wander. You are thinking that an orchestra performance is probably the best example of leadership and management working together to produce an awesome result. You have always admired orchestra directors and conductors. Today, you give yourself permission to step into the conductor's shoes for a while, even if only in a daydream...

Conductors typically act both as managers and leaders. As orchestra directors, they manage organisational affairs, such as planning the concert season, scheduling rehearsals, usually a year in advance, holding auditions and selecting musicians and soloists, and promoting the programme in the media. They choose the works to be performed and study the scores, making adjustments regarding tempo, articulation, phrasing, repetitions, and prepare the conducting gestures. Then, of course, they conduct.

What competences do they require?

Conducting requires a deep understanding of all elements of musical expression. They definitely need a broad education in the history of music, music theory, instrumentation and musical notation, and expertise in at least one instrument, preferably the piano, which helps them analyse scores and try them out. They must understand the major languages used in choral music (Italian, French, German, and Latin) and must know their correct diction in the context of a score.

What about competencies?

In selecting the works to perform, conductors need to study them in detail, and also have a feel for the audience's expectations and tolerances, as well as an understanding of the abilities of the ensemble. In planning the season and the rehearsals, they need planning and logistics skills. In selecting members, they must be able to assess the standard of performance for every instrument, even if they don't know how to play it themselves. They need to assess the fit within the ensemble of each auditioned candidate. Is the candidate likely to complement the rest of the members, or are they likely to try to overpower others or overplay? They therefore need to understand group dynamics on top of music-related technicalities.

When actually conducting, they need to communicate effectively with their ensemble. They must be able to inspire, empower, and make each member feel important – because they are. They all have their role, their piece to play. Conductors need to maintain eye contact and rapport; they need to dialogue with their performers, contain them or encourage them.

The conductor is fully aware that the show is not all about them. It's a group effort that should honour the composer, be pleasurable to the audience and fulfilling to the orchestra, and put cash in the till so that the orchestra is in business for the next season, too. Exceptional directors/conductors do not micromanage. They plan, they schedule, they select, and they provide direction. They delegate. They know that they should invest in their first violinist and entrust them to lead the rest, under their instructions. They imagine every performer watching them, checking in with them, seeking out any subtleties of interpretation not indicated in the score, looking to be pushed forward or guided toward a different articulation or sound quality. They try to rebalance the instruments so that a particular orchestral voice is heard. They acknowledge that to achieve this, they must help each performer develop their competencies on the job through coaching and mentoring. They need strong people skills.

Once everyone is ready, their job is to unify the orchestra, set the tempo and shape the sound of the ensemble. Prior to the public performance, they prepare the orchestra by coordinating rehearsals, in which they provide instructions to the musicians on their interpretation of the music to be performed. In an orchestra, as in any organisational entity, it is imperative that everyone plays their part in such a way that a harmonious whole is achieved, in this case heard, by those on the outside. Everyone is important. Everyone has their role and if they don't feel trusted and valued, there is a risk of monotony or poor performance. The musicians, the people of this ensemble, may come from different nations, cultures, and walks of life. Each has potential and they all want to showcase it. It is the conductor's task to bring out the best in them all.

As you continue to daydream, you think about the fact that, just as organisations are broken down into divisions or departments, orchestras are divided into sections: woodwind, brass, percussion, string, solo instruments, soloists and choir. Each section has its lead player – first violinist, first clarinettist – just as the organisation has its division or departmental executives. As the conductor of the orchestra, they will be your executive team.

The composer's score is your raw material – the input information and knowledge – and the musical instruments are some of your assets, significant enablers. Instruments need to meet strict specifications, be of high quality and correctly tuned. The ensemble are the organisation's people – its most important enabler. Each of them develops his or her competence – the hundreds of hours they attend a conservatory, the thousands of hours they practise and the hundreds of hours they play in public performances before they are judged skilled enough to play in an orchestra such as the one you have travelled so far to enjoy. You contemplate the competencies they need to develop, so that each cooperate within an orchestra and follow the directions of the conductor to become coordinated. They need to learn to listen attentively, perform precisely and feel involved in the music-making process. Learning the notation, bowings, dynamics and articulations indicated in the score is only the beginning of the orchestral experience, and is done before even the first rehearsal. Good musicians learn their score well enough so that they can focus on following the conductor's directions, watching bows and bowings, listening for and following solo and accompaniment voices and, sometimes, leading. All at the same time. Only then can they become artists, contributing to and participating in the symbiotic symphony orchestra.

The first bell wakes you out of your reverie. You look around and realise that you are the main stakeholder of the orchestra: the client. You have paid for your ticket to enjoy the concert.

You wonder: is it enough to have music written by an accomplished composer, excellently constructed instruments, an experienced, renowned conductor, and well-trained and rehearsed musicians?

You realise that no, this is not enough. You also need the appropriate infrastructure. The chamber, with its acoustics, lighting, ventilation, air-conditioning, and fire-detection and fighting. Its safety, security and its ancillary spaces – for the musicians, the audience, the administrators and the technical staff – need to be correctly architected, designed and constructed with regard to space, furniture, materials, and internal and external aesthetics. Only then will the orchestra be able to deliver a complete music experience.

As the second bell rings, you begin to appreciate how much effort is required in the planning of each performance, and how much work is accomplished for you to enjoy the 100 minutes of the concert.

The third bell marks the beginning of the performance, and a warm voice welcomes you and requests that you switch off your personal devices. You tense, as you anticipate the first gestures of the conductor. The concert commences and soon, you let go. You relax and lose yourself in the melody. You know that if any instrument falls out of concord, is too quick or slow by a few milliseconds, the harmony will be spoiled. Nothing of the kind happens. Everything is smooth, perfect, and you find yourself contemplating your new job as the chief executive of a medium-sized organisation of 500 people. You think of its purpose, its mission, its business model and its products, and how they are positioned in the market. You wonder how you should approach your duties as the CEO and compare your challenges with those of the white-haired conductor in front of you.

You acknowledge that it is imperative to learn quickly how your organisation is set up: its various architectures, value streams, processes, data, KPIs, track record, and its short-term plans. To get acquainted with its people – their strengths and weaknesses. You recognise that you need to exercise your management activities effectively and efficiently, and wonder whether this is enough and, above all, safe.

You remind yourself that successful executives sometimes act as technocrats, striving for organisational excellence, sometimes as managers, executing management activities, and sometimes as leaders, executing leadership activities. Most of the time they function as both managers and leaders, performing management and leadership activities simultaneously, producing a harmonious concert (see Figure 7.1 and Figure 7.2, read bottom–up; rows do not correspond).

Your thoughts return to the music. You contemplate on what distinguishes the few famous philharmonic orchestras from the many that are mediocre; the few immortal composers from the many that remained anonymous; and the few eponymous conductors from all others. You acknowledge that the difference is that the outstanding ones excel not only in managing the various enablers that need to work together to create and deliver what you are currently enjoying (working hard to learn and master the necessary knowledge – the music composition, the instruments, the directing techniques, the chamber, etc – getting acquainted with your musicians and performers, and planning the various actions, from preparing the orchestra to delivering the symphony) but also in leading the musicians in playing their part, both individually and collectively. In aligning, engaging and committing them so that each owns both their part and also the whole composition, devoting their best self to the task at hand.

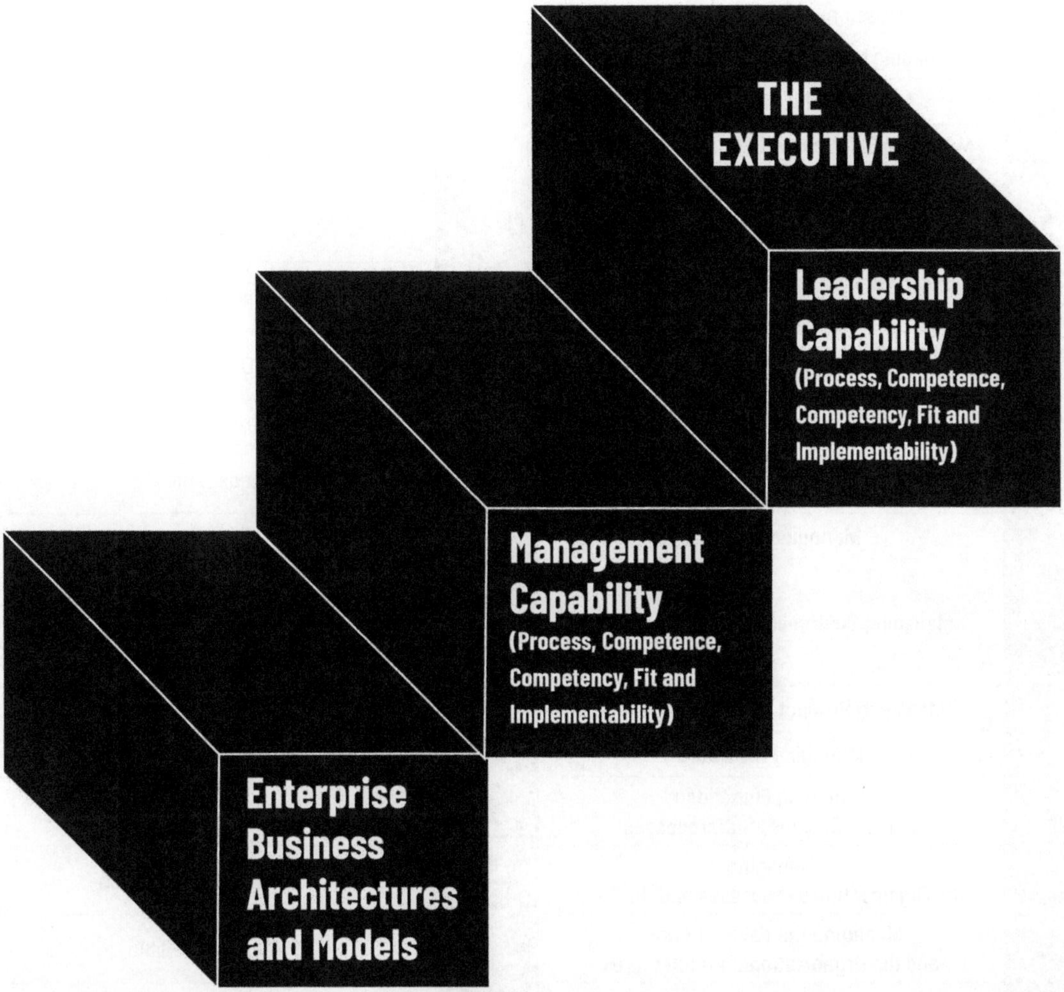

Figure 7.1: The successful executive

	Managing Strategic Projects (Vision Execution)		Leading the People in Realising the Vision (in Executing Strategic Projects)
	Managing Operations (Mission Execution)		Leading the People in Executing the Mission (in Executing Processes)
	Managing Non-Human Resource		Leading Stakeholder Relations
Managing Stake-holders	Managing the Human Resource		Leading Staffing and People Development
	Managing Relations with Partners, Suppliers and Sellers	Leading the People (Tribes/Teams/Individuals)	Improvement and Innovation
	Managing Relations with the State (Regulators, etc)		Visioning
	Managing Relations with the Chairperson and the BoD		Coaching and Mentoring
Managing the Organisation as a System	Managing Relations and Value Delivered to Stakeholders		Ownership
	Managing Information, Knowledge and Wisdom		Commitment
	Managing Improvement, Creativity and Innova-tion		Engagement
	Managing Finances		Alignment
	Managing Customer Lifecycle and Value		Communication – Comprehension Conceptualisation (Architectures, Models, Mission, Knowledge, Targets, Plans, Projects, Actuals, Deliverables)
	Managing Product Lifecycle and Value		Tribal/Team Leadership
	Managing the Brand	Leading the Organisation	Wisdom Leadership
	Managing Embedded Generic Business Subprocesses		Excellence Leadership
	Managing the Organisation's Processes and the Data		Governance Leadership
	Managing the Value Streams and the Organisational Architectures		Value Leadership
	Managing the Culture		Culture Leadership
	Managing Ethics, Governance, Policies and Compliance		Spiritual Leadership (Achieving Rapport)
	The Executive as a Manager		The Executive as Leader
	The Executive		

Figure 7.2: The successful executive's management and leadership process

Even then, the best performances are those in which the conductor establishes a spiritual rapport with each and every performer, helping channel their musical energy toward achieving the end result. The conductor's challenge is to turn all these individuals into a cohesive team and lead them within a common culture of shared values and enthusiasm, to deliver an extraordinary performance.

You realise, at the same time, that leading is not enough. You need to be leading something worthwhile. Without high-quality, well-tuned instruments, profound knowledge of the score, well-trained musicians who rehearse until they all function as a cohesive team; without meticulously planning and managing all enablers and actions from your appointment to the staging of the performance; without directing and coordinating all preparatory actions, the resulting performance will be mediocre or poor. Making the right movements with your baton will not save the day.

You return to consciously enjoying the music, feeling that you know what you have to do to be a successful executive. The concert comes to an end and receives a standing ovation. You walk out with a sense of exhilaration, feeling that you have enjoyed what you had hoped and paid for.

You are ready for your new duties. You have confidence in your capabilities, having worked hard to develop your organisational, management and leadership competence and competency, and having succeeded at lower executive posts. You know how to go about creating and delivering value in a sustainable way, and how to continue developing yourself (Chapter Eight).

Strolling towards a well-earned dinner, the need to innovate pops into your restless mind. Your thoughts return once more to the orchestra conductor. Do conductors innovate? Yes, they do. They set the tempo, the articulation, the phrasing, the feel of each performance. That's how successful conductors differentiate their performances, within the limits of the score. You smile. They could always choose to conduct a jazz ensemble, if they wanted to improvise, to bring a radical change to their audience...

You relax. You acknowledge that in both private and professional life, success and happiness demand balance. Balance between mission and vision, between management and leadership.

PART III

MANAGEMENT AND LEADERSHIP COMPETENCIES AND COMPETENCES

CHAPTER EIGHT

THE SUCCESSFUL EXECUTIVE'S COMPETENCIES AND COMPETENCES

Successful executives continuously develop their management and leadership competences and competencies, with special emphasis on living their values and cultivating their interpersonal skills. They learn through study, training, coaching and mentoring, but mainly on the job, executing conscientiously their management and leadership activities, as well as developing, coaching and mentoring their people. They trust and respect their people; they empower and support them.

They lead by authentic personal example, exhibiting humility, accessibility, decisiveness, ownership, responsibility and accountability, nurturing a culture of values, results, innovation and growth.

Successful executives sometimes act as technocrats architecting, building and improving the organisation they head, sometimes act as managers, executing management activities, and sometimes as leaders, executing leadership activities. Most of the time they act as managers-cum-leaders, performing management and leadership processes simultaneously, as summarised in Figure 7.2. In addition, many executives devote some of their time to executing core, support or staff activities delegated to them.

The successful execution of the management process demands specific competences (knowhow) and, to a lesser degree, specific competencies (personal qualities and capabilities). Conversely, the successful execution of the leadership process demands specific competencies (personal qualities and capabilities) and, to a lesser extent, specific competences (knowhow).

The competences demanded by the management process were exposed in the first five chapters of this book. Those required by leadership are different, and concern human nature at both the individual and collective levels, as we have seen in Chapter Six and will explore further in this chapter. Many of the competencies required by the leadership activities are also required for management activities, though in many cases to a lesser degree.

The competences (knowhow) demanded for the activities of architecting, building and maintaining the organisation, as an effective and efficient static and dynamic holarchical system, were exposed in Part One of this book. Executives do not need to possess them in depth. They should, however, have a good general knowledge of each one and of their relationships and ensure that the organisation has at its disposal the necessary technocrats who possess them in a holistic way, be them employees, partners or consultants, and who can work as a coherent productive team.

Lastly, the successful execution of any core, support or staff activities, delegated to or undertaken by executives, demands relevant specific competences. These relate to the executive's academic and vocational background and experience, the development of which lies outside the scope of this book. Any competencies required by these activities are a subset of those required by the management and leadership processes.

The competences required by the management process are taught at management schools and institutes, at the undergraduate level for generalists, and usually at the postgraduate level for specialists, as part of a scientific management syllabus in parallel with teaching classical management functions, such as finance and marketing. They are extensively covered in these courses and seminars because they have been well researched, studied and comprehended by academics and professional educators, and are extensively covered in the literature. As a result, we discuss them here only briefly.

The competencies required for successful execution of the management processes, and especially the leadership processes, are only partially and rather poorly explicated in most management courses and seminars. The main reasons for this deficiency are that:

- They had not been extensively researched and analysed until very recently.
- They are not understood in depth by many academic and professional educators.
- Most of the people endeavouring to teach them do not possess them themselves, and have not been, or have not had the opportunity to be, successful managers or (and in particular) leaders in their professional life.

- Competencies are based on personality traits and, as such, they can be enhanced to various degrees only when there is a minimum level of predisposition, a starting point.
- Competencies are primarily self-developed, mainly on the job with the assistance of coaching, mentoring and by example, and, to a lesser degree, by classroom teaching.

In this book, we do not cover explicitly the competences (the knowhow) required by the leadership activities, since there are hundreds of books and articles discussing these and they are well taught in management schools and institutions. They are implicitly covered in our in-depth presentation of the competencies required for management and leadership processes.

In Table 8.1, we list the competences and competencies demanded by the management and leadership processes. In this table, the significance of each competence and competency for the productive execution of the management activities is shown in the M column, and for the leadership activities in the L column, with degree of significance indicated by the darker shade of the tick sign ✔.

In an ideal world, all these competencies are necessary for success. In real life, no person possesses, exhibits and utilises all of these competencies at a high level. For an executive to succeed, though, it is essential that they have many and a good mix of these competencies at a high level, know their weaknesses, and try, on one hand, to develop themselves and, on the other hand, to complement their deficiencies with the competencies of close associates. Clearly, this is possible only for specific competencies and competences.

Table 8.1: The successful executive's leadership and management competencies and competences

S/N	The Successful Executive's Leadership and Management Competencies and Competences	M	L
1	Has high **ethical values**, believes in them, preaches them in every relevant organisational context, lives them, demonstrates them and demands them from all their people. Exhibits character and consistency.	✔	✔
2	Builds an **all-around leadership team** believing in the same ethical values, and propagating them throughout the organisation by their example, thus building a uniform culture based on the same set of ethical values. They are complemented by their team members, who also complement each other.	✔	✔
3	Manages **relations with all stakeholder groups** and builds a **network** propagating the organisational values and slogans, collecting, cross-checking and distributing complete, sound and true information (ie business and competitive intelligence).	✔	✔
4	Has a high **IQ** and puts it to productive use to quickly comprehend complex issues and conceive solutions.	✔	✔
5	Quickly **conceptualises** the organisational architectures, strengths, weaknesses, problems, challenges, opportunities and threats, and **conceives scenarios, roadmaps and plans for action**.	✔	✔
6	Has clear **thought** and clear, enlightening, convincing **words,** achieving **belief in the organisation's values, purpose, mission and vision**.	✔	✔
7	Is **authentic, stable** and **consistent,** and builds **credibility**.	✔	✔
8	**Leads the discussion,** builds an atmosphere of **open dialogue, influences** the direction of the dialogue, maintains **focus, acknowledges** and **summarises** the various opinions, **persuades, advises, develops** convincing **guidelines,** and reaches widely accepted **conclusions**. Achieves **consensus and alignment**.	✔	✔
9	Is **decisive**.	✔	✔
10	Has a high **EQ** and builds **trust around a productive tribal culture**.	✔	✔
11	Builds **team spirit** and achieves **engagement, commitment** and **ownership** to accomplish **results,** always within the **common culture**.		✔
12	Exhibits and builds **discipline** in honouring values and commitments.	✔	✔
13	**Promptly feeds back adequate information,** maintaining credibility, trust, belief and ownership of the mission, vision, organisation, people, targets and plans, and exhibits sincere and full accountability.	✔	✔
14	Achieves **spiritual rapport** building trust, engagement, commitment, devotion and ownership, and inspires the people to exert themselves in producing results and working wonders.		✔
15	**Delegates** with confidence and **empowers, supports** and **rewards** their people.	✔	✔

S/N	The Successful Executive's Leadership and Management Competencies and Competences	M	L
16	Has a **growth mindset, nurtures a culture of development** and **develops the people growth mindset**.	✔	✔
17	Continually develops themselves, and develops leadership talent at all levels.	✔	✔
18	**Coaches** and **mentors** their people, especially in developing their leadership and other soft competencies.	✔	✔
19	Fosters **creativity,** encourages and rewards **innovation,** and **celebrates both success and failure**.	✔	✔
20	Devotes time to and leads team **visioning** for short-term improvements.	✔	✔
21	Devotes time to formulating, reviewing and revising the organisation's **vision** and to designing and planning the **strategic projects** which will realise the vision.	✔	✔
22	Ensures that **strategic wins** and victories are embedded in the organisation's architectures.	✔	✔
23	Ensures that the organisation's mission is reviewed, revised and kept contemporary, ensuring **sustainability**.	✔	✔
24	Achieves high **personal productivity** by maintaining a **thorough portfolio of activities,** both as a manager and as a leader, and prioritises and devotes adequate time to each activity.	✔	✔
25	**Leads change** without sacrificing the execution of the (current) mission	✔	✔
26	**Checks their ego and operates with humility and empathy.**	✔	✔
27	**Exhibits respect, honesty, sincerity, integrity, perseverance and loyalty.**	✔	✔
28	**Strives for the happiness of their people and themselves in a holistic way, optimally balancing their work and life.**	✔	✔
29	**Masters the Scientific Management process** (planning, coordinating, directing and controlling, acting, reviewing and revising plans) at an adequate level.	✔	✔
30	**Masters the main classical management functions** (finance, HR, marketing, sales, supply chain, CRM, logistics, etc) and their KPIs at an adequate level.	✔	✔
31	**Masters the generic managerial subprocesses** (risk, environment, health, and safety management, etc) at a reasonable level, ensures they are embedded in the organisational processes and monitors their execution via suitable KPIs.	✔	✔
32	**Masters the core processes of the organisation** (which realise its purpose and its mission).	✔	✔
33	**Masters organisational and operational excellence modelling.**	✔	✔
34	**Leads execution.**	✔	✔
35	**Exhibits extreme ownership, ultimate responsibility and thorough, sincere accountability.**	✔	✔

Leadership competencies

Research and experience show that successful executives possess and develop the leadership competencies shown in Table 8.1. These are the competencies that enable them to exercise effectively and efficiently their leadership activities and achieve business success. We expand on these in this section.

Many of these competencies are employed, to various degrees, by successful executives in exercising their management activities, employing simultaneously their management competences (their knowhow), which we will expand briefly on in a later section.

Some of these competencies and competences are put to good use by professionals before becoming executives, while acting as operatives in charge of a big or small team or project. These enable operatives to successfully complete their atomic activities and/or their projects, individually or as members of a team, in core, support or staff posts without subordinates.

To be promoted or recruited to an executive post, professionals need to possess and employ leadership and management competencies and competences. Executives need to get a small or large number of people to successfully create and deliver value by executing a variety of processes and projects, while continuing to perform themselves the leadership and management processes described in this book, and perhaps certain operational processes related to their technical expertise.

Successful executives know that:

- **To get the job done, management must focus on organising the processes and the other enablers; on optimising supply lines, production lines and sales and delivery chains; on planning, budgeting, staffing, and allocating assignments; on coordinating and controlling people; and on predicting the evolution of their environment.**
- **Leadership, by contrast, is about communication, creating consensus, alignment, inspiration, engagement, motivation, commitment, loyalty, and ownership, responding to change, creativity, innovation, sacrifice, and building spiritual rapport.**

[continued]

- **Management and leadership are complementary modes of executive action in any formal or informal executive role.**
- **Successful executives employ management and leadership competencies and competences selectively to optimise the creation and delivery of value to their organisation's stakeholders.**
- **These competencies are intellectual and interpersonal skills and can be learnt and developed.**
- **Each person has a different underlying disposition and, consequently, will learn and integrate these competencies in a different way.**

We recommend that you use Table 8.1 to:

- Identify which competencies characterise the executives you admire, and which are lacking in the ones you do not.
- Think about how you would like others to see you.
- Identify which competencies you already possess and employ successfully.
- Identify which you would like to improve in your current or new role, or in the role you aspire to have in the future.
- Study the relevant sections of the present guide and other sources, draft a roadmap for applying these competencies formally or informally depending on your circumstances, frequently review your progress and plan how to develop them further.

Do not forget to consider the emotional challenges of moving from a purely operational role to an executive one, such as lack of or over-confidence, confusion, anxiety, frustration, resignation, regret, unhappiness and work–life imbalance. Deal consciously with any challenges you face, decide whether you need help in the form of coaching or mentoring, and seek a suitable person to discuss the issue and, if necessary, to help you overcome the emotional turmoil. Alternatively, they might direct you to a suitable mentor. We touch briefly on these issues in a later section of this chapter.

Creating trust based on values, character, consistency and integrity

Successful executives have high ethical values, believe in them, preach them in every relevant organisational context, demonstrate them, live them, and demand them from all their people.

They never forget that:

- The foundation of leadership is trust.
- Trust cannot be bought or sold; it cannot be granted, it can only be won.
- Trust is won by character and performance – competence, competency and consistency in action and behaviour.
- Subordinates ask you, silently or loudly:
  - On what values will you act when encountering difficult dilemmas?
  - Is it safe for us to open up and express our disagreement with you?
  - Do you actually want to hear our opinion?
  - How much do you value us?
  - How will you react when we make a mistake, or when our project fails?
  - Will you stand up for us in a difficult situation and take responsibility outside of our team?
  - Will you give us credit when we succeed?
- Subordinates evaluate and judge you, as their boss, at every moment. They are ready to idealise or condemn you. They are strict because humans are social animals. By nature, they want to rely on the leader of their tribe, whether a small team, a department or division, an organisation or a nation. They, as members of the tribe, want to feel their leader as one of them, their equal, but at the same time as someone a little wiser.
- Subordinates want and expect their executive, their leader, to:
  - Have high values
  - Be consistent
  - Exhibit absolute integrity
  - Strive for the creation and delivery of value in a balanced way
  - Control their emotions

- Behave well – be polite, friendly, and not detached
- Be interested in and concerned about them – their work progress, their development, their problems, their concerns, their successes and their failures, their ideas, even about their personal and family life
- Seek their opinion, views, feedback
- Explain policies, rules, decisions and higher-level plans and ask their opinion
- Always be one step ahead and know their processes and the related general information
- Quickly grasp situations – the problems, challenges, and weaknesses
- Confront even the toughest issues and surpass hurdles and inhibitors
- Be honest, sincere and thorough
- Evaluate and contain risks and plan for business continuity
- Attribute success to the team but take responsibility for failures
- Invite them to criticise their leaders' actions.

Successful executives are authentic. They do not pretend. They know who they are and what drives them. They cultivate their self-awareness and their support network.

They maintain their physical, mental, intellectual and spiritual health. They maintain a work–life balance and encourage their people to do the same, restricting the occasions of strenuous overtime to what is absolutely essential.

Ultimately, they create trust and credibility by not only preaching a consistent set of ethical values but by living them and demanding them from all internal stakeholders and close partners: suppliers, associates, wholesalers and retailers.

Understanding team dynamics and building team spirit

Successful executives build a well-rounded leadership team that believes in the same ethical values, propagates their common values throughout the organisation through their personal example, and cultivates a uniform culture based on those values. Their team members complement not only each other but also their leader – their executive.

They know that a well-rounded, effective and efficient team needs people who:

- Can play collectively all necessary roles without rivalries
- Have, collectively, all competencies and competences required for the productive execution of the processes and projects allocated to the team
- Fit with one another – especially important when newcomers join an existing team
- Adopt the organisation's code of ethics
- Develop and lead them as a coherent team, cultivating a winning team spirit with a growth mindset

Cultivating and maintaining an extensive network of associates

Successful executives establish and sustain fruitful relations with all the organisation's stakeholder groups and build a network propagating the organisational values and slogans, collecting, cross-checking and distributing sound and true information.

They recognise the importance and usefulness of maintaining an extensive network of associates who support them and to whom they provide support. They base their relations on their code of ethics; they are consistent, have integrity and are available for support, listening and cooperation.

Productively using high IQ

Successful executives quickly understand complex issues, conceptualise them and present them in a clear, comprehensible manner.

They cultivate their mental competencies and their knowledge of a broad spectrum of issues. They understand that success is the creation and delivery of value to the organisation's stakeholders and they translate this convincingly to their people – whether that's a small team, a big department or a whole organisation – in conceptual and practical terms, in: value streams, end-to-end processes, KPIs, targets and deliverables, quality and excellence, continuous improvement and innovation, sustainability, operational and strategic plans, and productive execution with outstanding outcomes.

They keep themselves and their people well informed, and review and revise plans promptly.

Successful executives see their role and their people's roles in the big picture of the organisation and its architectures, and present this to them clearly to achieve their alignment, engagement, commitment and ownership.

Having strong analytical and conceptualisation capabilities

Successful executives conceptualise the organisational architectures, issues, challenges, opportunities and threats, and conceive solution scenarios, roadmaps and plans for action.

They keep themselves up to date on business models and tools, on the economy at large, on the technological and market developments of their business sector, and leadership and management developments. They analyse and conceptualise them, and use them in conceiving scenarios for action, roadmaps and plans.

Being eloquent and convincing

Successful executives have clear thought and clear, enlightening, compelling and inspiring words, achieving belief in the organisation's values, purpose, mission and vision.

They develop their language, their wording and their tone, and adapt their speech to the audience, speaking *their* language at *their* wavelength and pace.

Successful executives achieve and maintain rapport with their audience, winning them over by promptly presenting accurate, sincere and complete information.

They continuously cultivate their language and their wording. They seek feedback and take into serious consideration the comments, criticisms and suggestions of the organisation's stakeholders.

Successful executives are convincing.

They develop their persuasion competency by:

- Listening more than talking
- Being more open-minded
- Having a growth rather than a fixed mindset
- Being tactical (mission-driven) and strategic (vision-driven) in a balanced way
- Cooperating more than competing
- Resolving rather than creating conflict
- Delivering conclusions, proposals and decisions with clarity and precision
- *Pulling* (inspiring) more than *pushing* (hard-driving)

Research shows that three out of four executives are rated higher on their ability to push, ie to drive results, than their ability to pull, ie to inspire and motivate, and that pushing often produces, in the short term, better results, though to the detriment of engagement and commitment.

Successful executives are effective at inspiring and thus achieving engagement, commitment and compliance, creating enthusiasm and energy in their people, and succeeding in aligning their people around the organisation's mission and vision. They acknowledge that people act and make changes because they believe in them and they want to, rather than out of obligation.

Being authentic, stable and consistent and building credibility

Successful executives are authentic. They are good-natured and this presents itself naturally. They do not need pretension and fake language.

They passionately believe in the organisation's values, purpose and vision and their importance for the creation and delivery of value to the organisation's stakeholders. They win over their people with their credibility, consistency and commitment to their values. They care for their people, their needs and their sensitivities.

Successful executives, being authentic leaders, build on their life experience, their long exhibition of their ethical values and their consistency in living them.

People with the ambition of climbing to the executive level should remember that they will carry with them their behaviour, their actions, their successes and failures – their history. They cannot exhibit authenticity out of the blue.

Building a climate of constructive, open dialogue and achieving consensus around conclusions

Successful executives lead the discussion, build an atmosphere of open dialogue, influence the direction of that dialogue, maintain focus, acknowledge and summarise the various opinions and suggestions of their team members and other interested parties, develop convincing guidelines, reach conclusions and make decisions ensuring high levels of consensus, alignment and ownership.

They set the framework for constructive dialogue. They present the various issues with compelling evidence and position them within the organisation's architectures, plans, targets and actual performance, as well as the relevant market situation, and invite comments, opinions, advice and disputes in a climate of open discussion.

They lead the discussion so that everybody feels comfortable in voicing their views, opinions, questions, and disputes, and seeking clarification on ambiguities. They allocate enough (though not unlimited) time to the discussion, while maintaining focus until widely accepted conclusions are reached. They positively influence the discussion and the opinions of their associates, without manipulating them.

Successful executives win the hearts and spirit of their people by being sincere, authentic and consistent.

Being decisive and making sound decisions

> **Successful executives do not procrastinate. They make decisions promptly, and continue moving forward even when faced with uncertainty. They balance reflection with decisiveness. They reach sound decisions based on real-life, evidence-based information, and a mixture of analysis, wisdom, experience and judgement.**

They develop their decisiveness and their competency to reach sound decisions by:

- Collecting, interrogating and analysing internal and external evidence-based information
- Taking risks
- Communicating, aligning and engaging
- Exhibiting a growth mindset and nurturing an environment of the same
- Visioning and presenting strategic perspectives
- Mastering the organisation's core processes, information and knowledge
- Cultivating an open, creative, innovative, courageous culture
- Inspiring and motivating
- Driving results, in a balanced way

Achieving consensus in decision-making

> **Successful executives make decisions ensuring a high level of consensus, alignment and ownership.**

Having led an exhaustive, though not interminable, open dialogue on each issue, they manage to align their people around the conclusion of the discussion, always within the framework of the organisation's values and key targets. They make decisions based on which they build engagement, commitment, ownership and enthusiasm for productive execution.

Having high emotional quotient (EQ) and building a productive tribal culture

> **Successful executives have a high emotional quotient, ie high capability to accurately perceive and manage their own and others' emotions; understand the emotional signals surrounding relationships and feelings; and exhibit genuine empathy.**

- They recognise and understand the emotions, moods and desires of themselves and their people, exhibiting self-confidence, self-evaluation and a sense of humour.
- They control their emotions, moods and tendencies; maintain their judgement and poise before acting; exhibit credibility, consistency and integrity, and openness to change and innovation; and build trust.
- They show passion for the creation and delivery of value to all the organisation's stakeholders, personal drive and persistence, self-motivation, optimism, and commitment, and motivate the achievement of outstanding results.
- They feel, understand, respect and take into consideration the emotions of internal and external stakeholders; exhibit due sensitivity; develop their people; and work to create and deliver value to the organisation's customers and all other stakeholders.
- They exhibit effective interpersonal skills; present common values and interests; build strong relationships and networks and coherent teams with a tribal spirit; convince and align their people on values, purpose, targets, improvement and innovation; and achieve engagement, commitment and extreme ownership.
- They are able to adapt their attitude according to the EQ of each member of their team, since different people need different approaches and treatment – always within the common code of ethics.

> **Successful executives exhibit strong self-awareness, self-control, self-drive, empathy, and interpersonal skills. They have a growth mindset, a positive attitude, and are adaptable to change. They don't procrastinate, and do not exhibit denial, aggressiveness against others, or defensiveness in regard to their own failures or poor decisions.**

They acknowledge reality even when this is adverse, control their stress and help their people to also control theirs. They defend their people, take responsibility for failures, and recognise and contain any adverse impact on their people.

Successful executives continuously develop their own and their people's skills.

Building teams and achieving engagement, commitment and ownership within the common culture

Successful executives build well-rounded productive teams and lead them into reaching evidence-based conclusions resulting in sound decisions that win broad consensus, alignment, engagement, commitment and ownership.

They understand what it takes to build a productive team and, in particular, that:

- The team mix must include persons who are able to play collectively all necessary roles (such as Belbin), resulting in high productivity (effectiveness and efficiency) and quality.
- The team mix must include a wide diversity of minds and skills.
- To be able to collaborate and avoid detrimental rivalries, the team members must fit together.
- The team members must believe in the same ethical code.

They lead their teams by:

- Explaining in clear, convincing language the organisation's values, purpose and mission
- Clarifying that success is equal to the creation and delivery of value to the organisation's stakeholders
- Eloquently presenting the organisation's architectures and explaining how the team can and should contribute towards realising the plans and projects for the creation and delivery of value in a sustainable way
- Setting the framework and rules for the team's operation
- Building relationships among the team members in both formal and informal ways
- Presenting the various issues and higher-level targets in comprehensible language, while inviting questions and providing clarification

- Encouraging open, sincere dialogue and the expression of views, opinions, doubts, suggestions, and advice by all members – especially the more silent, introverted ones
- Listening carefully and recapitalising
- Maintaining focus
- Intervening discreetly when necessary
- Identifying the persons who cannot, or simply do not want to, merge into the team and who endanger team spirit, and either isolating or removing them
- Identifying biases and conflicts and resolving them
- Reaching widely adopted conclusions
- Making broadly supported decisions, striving, within available time limits, for consensus
- Leading the execution of the decisions by delegating tasks and projects and the leadership of lower-level organisational entities or subteams, ensuring that the necessary assets are made available, and entrusting to incumbents the required authority that ensures they can accomplish their part
- Keeping themselves and the team fully informed of progress
- Providing prompt feedback from sources outside of the team
- Reviewing in-team interim results and revising plans whenever necessary
- Reviewing in-team final results, awarding praise where due
- Drawing in-team improvement lessons for the future

Successful executives create an enthusiastic, productive and creative team spirit. They help members recognise that the team's success depends on them collaborating and complementing each other, and that the team performance can and should be higher than the sum performance of each individual member.

They encourage innovation, inviting members to openly express radical suggestions for improvement and reengineering of processes, rules, methods, technology, products, services and business models. They discuss all proposals within the team, adopt those that are judged feasible and fruitful, and delegate their realisation.

They develop the competences and competencies of each team member and of the team collectively.

Successful executives inspire and motivate their people to achieve outstanding results by:

- Cultivating a culture of visioning and being visionary themselves, presenting their vision for the future with clarity
- Nurturing a growth-mindset environment
- Creating excellent relationships and emotional connections between their people using the triad method
- Driving focused alignment, engagement and pursuit of outstanding outcomes
- Consistently employing the organisation's values and principles
- Being energetic, enthusiastic and passionate about creating and delivering value through action
- Being knowledgeable and providing clear direction

Successful executives exhibit the capability to use productively the above approaches and develop their competencies to inspire and motivate – in particular, building deep belief in and adherence to shared values, authenticity, consistency and self-discipline.

Research shows that developing leadership competencies through study, coaching, mentoring and practising on the job is possible and does not require charisma.

Exhibiting and building discipline

Successful executives exhibit themselves and build, demand, inspire and instil discipline in honouring values and commitments.

They recognise that people often look for a shortcut, and that this is unsustainable. Shortcuts are wrong, and never lead to long-lasting success – in most cases, not even to short-term success. A shortcut is an excuse, a lie.

They know that accomplishing goals and objectives, achieving targets, realising critical success factors, removing inhibitors and overcoming obstacles does not happen by itself. It never happens by cutting corners, taking shortcuts, looking for the easy way, or through firefighting.

Successful executives acknowledge that success (the creation and delivery of value) demands:

- **Continuous intensive study, learning and comprehension, in a holistic way**
- **Diversity of thought and thinking outside the box**
- **Open discussion, listening and interrogating all issues until clarity of thought is reached**
- **Late night work and contemplation**
- **Early morning planning, review and action**
- **Overcoming stress, frustration and fear**
- **Patience and perseverance**
- **Engagement, commitment, ownership**
- **Above all: self-discipline**

They know that self-discipline:

- Is the root of all good competencies (ie good personal qualities)
- Is the driver for:
  - Continuous self-development
  - Being well informed, motivated and proactive
  - Open discussion and sound conclusions
  - Decisiveness
  - Alignment around decisions and plans
  - Engagement and commitment
  - Extreme ownership of processes, assets, plans and targets, projects and deliverables, responsibilities, and failures
  - Effective and efficient execution and outstanding outcomes
- Overcomes weakness, hesitation, procrastination, indecision, jerking, even stress and fear
- Helps stick to beliefs and values, and face dilemmas
- Helps maintain excellent physical, emotional, mental and spiritual health

Successful executives exhibit strong self-discipline.

They know that this discipline comes from within, it is an internal force for living one's values, for success – for self-actualisation.

They do not impose it, because they know that imposed discipline is fake discipline, which dissipates as soon as the people lose their leader, or when the leader looks the other way.

They demand it from their people, coaching them and setting an example, by:

- Persuading them that self-discipline is necessary for success
- Building long-lasting relationships with them based on shared values
- Keeping them well informed, with clarity and thoroughness
- Holding open and sincere discussions with them
- Finding common ground, bridging different views and opinions and, where necessary, compromising on tactics and strategy, but never on values
- Reaching conclusions and decisions with consensus, or at least wide acceptance
- Delegating actions and authority
- Leading and supporting execution – always in a disciplined way

Successful executives build discipline in their close associates, and then downwards to the bottom level, through their own example of extreme self-discipline.

Exhibiting prompt, thorough and sincere accountability

Successful executives promptly feed back to each stakeholder group adequate, true and relevant information, building and maintaining credibility, trust, belief and ownership in the organisation's values, mission, vision, people, plans, targets and results.

They believe in transparency and prompt, thorough and sincere accountability.

They have strong ethical values and live by and exhibit them in all their organisational activities.

Successful executives believe that plans, decisions, actions and relations with their stakeholders must always be based on hard evidence. They believe that informed people stay aligned, engaged, committed and loyal to the organisation and their mandate, and exhibit strong ownership.

They ensure that the organisation collects, scrutinises and stores all data that describes its assets and its people; the technology and market relevant to the organisation's products, services and processes; and the organisation's processes, plans and projects, their execution, and their actual results.

They keep every stakeholder group informed about their interests in the organisation and the organisation's results, using appropriate KPIs so that they are promptly given a thorough, truthful picture, while taking the necessary care to avoid leaking sensitive information to competitors.

They keep their people fully informed at all times on the general standing of the organisation so that they remain aligned, engaged and committed, as well as loyal to the organisation, its values and purpose.

They regularly communicate, in person, all vital information to their close associates and, when appropriate, to wider audiences, within the framework of the organisation's values, purpose, mission and vision. They do this to maintain rapport with their people and other stakeholders, not only verbally but also with body language, recognising and making good use of its strong communicative power.

Successful executives demand accountability from all the organisation's people by embedding this requirement in all process specifications and post descriptions, and by setting an example. They adhere to legislation and externally imposed and internally adopted governance rules with regard to accountability and disclosure.

Achieving spiritual rapport

Successful executives achieve spiritual rapport, and motivate and inspire their people to exert themselves in achieving extraordinary results and working wonders.

The most successful executives transcend value-based and culture-based leadership and achieve spiritual rapport with their people and other stakeholders. Through their personal example, their actions, wording, and body language, their consistent authenticity and genuine passion, they build trust and credibility and align and engage their people around the organisation's values, purpose, mission and vision at large, and in their specific targets.

They exhibit and build commitment, devotion and ownership, resulting in their people presenting their best selves and putting their talent to productive use.

Delegating and empowering people

Successful executives delegate with confidence, and empower, support and reward their people.

They lead the organisation's people by effectively delegating tasks and projects that do not fall within the formal duties of the incumbents of the organisation's posts.

Successful executives, having formulated the post descriptions based on a balanced RAEW (specified expertise, allocated workload, delegated authority, and anticipated responsibility) and staffed the posts with people with competences and competencies that match, as closely as is feasible, the specified expertise, delegate to their people extraordinary tasks and projects, with due consideration to their competences, competencies and workload.

They avoid firefighting, delegating firefighting, and undermining the hierarchy of the organisation.

They delegate by:

- Selecting the most suitable person(s), considering their expertise, availability, leadership and management capability, motivation, and time availability
- Explaining clearly, though discreetly, their delegation decision
- Clarifying the mandate: its purpose, expected deliverables and milestones
- Agreeing the processes and interfaces with the executive in charge of the delegated project
- Communicating the project discreetly to the organisation's stakeholders
- Providing all necessary support: resources, coaching, mentoring and staff
- Avoiding close involvement, ie micromanagement, or undertaking any of the duties of the project leader
- Assisting in realising the project's critical success factors and removing its inhibitors
- Continuously furnishing the project leader with all thorough and true information concerning the project
- Providing continuous reinforcement

Successful executives build and nurture a culture in which authority and responsibility are allocated to the people executing the respective activities and their immediate hierarchy, maintaining a lean and agile organisation.

Developing growth mindset and leadership talent at all levels

Successful executives have a growth mindset. They nurture a culture of continuous development, developing both their own and their people's growth mindset and leadership competencies.

They recognise the importance of nurturing a growth mindset and leadership competencies at all levels of the organisation. They systematise assessment, and scientifically assess the leadership capabilities of the organisation's lower-level executives. They formalise the planning, and plan the development of each and every executive and junior talent, on a personal and collective basis, carry out the plans, assess each person's progress, and take corrective action.

Successful executives pave the way by exhibiting self-knowledge and sincere self-development.

Coaching and mentoring

Successful executives coach and mentor their people, especially in developing their leadership and other soft competencies.

They acknowledge the importance of coaching and mentoring in developing the competencies of the organisation's people. They lead by personal example, encourage – and themselves provide – energetic coaching to develop the soft competencies of both executives and operatives, and encourage energetic mentoring to develop the leadership competencies of the organisation's executives at all levels, from crew leaders to the top executive level. They themselves act as mentors when appropriate and feasible.

Successful executives nurture a culture in which people seek coaching and mentoring to develop their competencies and competences, and in which these are promptly and amply offered by executives and competent colleagues.

Fostering creativity, encouraging and rewarding innovation, and celebrating failure

Successful executives promote creativity and innovation through the continuous cultivation of a creative culture, which encourages all kinds of creative improvement and innovation.

They acknowledge that true creativity involves:

- Incremental improvements in processes, methods, procedures, technology and automation
- Radical reengineering of processes and digital transformation
- Product and service improvement

- Incremental and radical improvement in customer service
- Incremental and radical improvement to the supply chain
- Incremental and radical improvement in the wholesale and retail sales chain
- New innovative products, services, processes and business models
- Disruptive technological inventions

Successful executives use modern, effective methods and tools to foster and achieve creative improvement and innovation.

They include creativity and innovation within the organisation's values set. They create and cultivate a growth mindset, and a culture of open, sincere dialogue and free expression of ideas and opinions. They introduce mechanisms for creativity and innovation with appropriate rules of conduct, and encourage universal participation in proposing ideas and in creativity and innovation activities.

They use convergent and divergent tools for creativity: classic, imaginary and reverse brainstorming, visioning, biomimicry, mind-mapping, catchballing, and experimenting. They overcome negativity and resistance to change, establish reward schemes for creativity and innovation, and stage celebrations honouring outstanding contributions to improvement and innovation.

EXAMPLE FROM NICOS' PERSONAL EXPERIENCE

During the second decade of my career (1986–1995) as an executive, I headed the reengineering and computerisation of all core and many support processes of my organisation, achieving a significant productivity increase in executing its mission. To achieve this I, together with a handful of young graduates, a bunch of 'power users' and consultants, built architectures of the organisation's processes and its data and information systems. We implemented a single integrated database for the entire organisation and designed and constructed the necessary integrated online systems using an integrated computer-aided software engineering (ICASE) tool. Our bold, experimental approach and methodology were acclaimed not only by our European sister organisations but also by some of the biggest USA ones – which still had diverse, 'bolted-on' systems operating on partial databases. Heading the systems development teams (especially in the analysis, design,implementation and transition phases), helped me comprehend holistically and holarchically the entire organisation: its value streams, its processes, its data, its functions, its strengths, its weaknesses, its people, all executives, and many of its operatives. I had gained an invaluable benefit.

My knowledge of the organisation and the success of the programme got me promoted to assistant, and soon afterwards deputy general manager (or executive vice president), in charge of telecommunications and information technology – the equivalent of chief technology and information officer (CTO/CIO). In parallel to heading all technical divisions, I headed the holistic business reengineering of the organisation, introducing a process-centric structure (1996–1997), KPIs for all core processes, and a rudimentary business intelligence system feeding actual results to the front-line customer agents. We accomplished unheard of improvement in customer and employee satisfaction.

After being promoted to CEO (in 1998), I introduced 'tribal' leadership using a set of carefully chosen values in an effort to align and engage the staff. During the 1990s our ICT (information and communications technology) sector was characterised by continual technological disruptions. In addition, the world was undergoing a wave of market liberalisation, severely impacting the state-owned incumbent telecommunications organisations. Responding to the threatening challenges, my executive team managed to align, engage and commit the great majority of the 2500 people of the organisation and increase their loyalty and ownership to unprecedented heights, not only for the standards of Cyprus but also for Europe. The result was that the organisation 'attracted the interest' of the National Commission for the Protection of Competition (CPC). The profits of the organisation were so high that it was penalised, with proportionally the highest fines in the European Union – a decision revoked a couple of years later by the Supreme Court. Meanwhile, responding to the CPC's decision, we lowered our tariffs to the level of the average European cost of capital and became so competitive that the interest of foreign competitors in participating in the ensuing public auction for mobile/cellular communications frequencies was diminished.

Despite the improvement in productivity, customer satisfaction, loyalty and retention, I felt that the organisation was not quick enough in introducing new products and improvements. We held an in-house competition to develop a system encouraging our people to propose ideas for improvements and new products and services. We developed an innovative system covering the whole lifecycle, from proposing ideas to screening them, adopting the feasible ones, developing and introducing them, and rewarding the proposers. We tested and fine-tuned the online system. We decided to introduce it at the annual gathering of 500 executives, which I would hold once a year at a conference centre (in parallel with the four huge meetings of the organisation's 2000 operatives) and try to turn around the change-averse attitude of our people who were, in essence, civil servants.

We presented the excellent results of the previous fiscal year and the ambitious plans for the current one. Our invited consultant, Dimis Michaelides, then gave an inspiring keynote speech on creativity and innovation and performed a couple of magic tricks, being an excellent performer. I followed, introducing our ideation system. To convince our people that we had to think outside of the box if we wanted not only to survive but to thrive, in a liberalised market, I swapped my formal neck tie for a yellow bow tie with two blinking LED lights (a radical move and an extreme accessory at the time). The result was amazing. For months, everyone was talking about the 'chief' who wore a blinking bow tie before 500 executives, from field foremen to senior managers. The LED bow tie had served its purpose: ideas and suggestions poured in by the hundreds. Many were truly innovative, and were implemented.

Devoting time to and leading the team in visioning for short-term improvements

Successful executives formulate, review and revise the organisation's mission, and design and plan the short-term projects that will improve the performance of their organisation. They devote the necessary time to reviewing all proposals for short-term improvement and innovation, and the progress of ongoing relevant projects, for brainstorming, discussion and revision.

They encourage their teams and all people in the organisation to propose small and big improvements. They welcome all ideas, evaluate them, and implement all those judged applicable and feasible.

Successful executives cultivate a culture of continuous improvement. They nurture suitable systems, such as quality circles and excellence models, with appropriate KPIs and targets, and then monitor and evaluate the actual results.

Devoting time to and leading visioning for strategic planning

Successful executives formulate, review and revise the organisation's vision, and design and plan the strategic projects that will realise the vision. They devote the necessary time to reviewing the current vision and the progress of ongoing strategic projects, for brainstorming, discussion and revision of the vision and the strategic planning.

They devote time to:

- Discussing strategic issues
- Reviewing the results of (internal and external) strategic projects
- Following the evolution of technology and competition, as well as of customer expectations and demands
- Visioning where the various stakeholder groups would like the organisation to be in the mid to long term
- Conceiving multiple vision scenarios
- Evaluating the feasibility of the various scenarios and selecting the most ambitious and (probably) feasible vision, evolving or even replacing the current one
- Formulating strategic projects for its realisation
- Assigning the projects to appropriate executives and/or departments, or even setting up new internal or external entities, allocating the necessary assets and delegating the required authorities

They regularly review the progress of ongoing projects and revise the strategic project plan as needed. They revisit the organisation's vision and strategic planning annually, as well as whenever disruptive internal or external changes appear to potentially threaten the plan or offer new opportunities. They systematise the strategic planning process and the selection, analysis and presentation of all relevant internal data in the business intelligence (BI) system and external data in the competitive intelligence (CI) system.

Successful executives cultivate their visioning and strategic planning competencies and nurture a culture of visioning and love for innovation and change.

Ensuring that strategic wins are embedded in the organisation's architectures

Successful executives update the organisation's architectures and structures by incorporating strategic wins, gained through small and big improvements, and the realisation of the organisation's vision by successfully executing its strategic projects.

They review regularly, usually yearly, the organisation's architectures (such as value streams, end-to-end processes, production and R&D equipment, and supply and sales chains) and incorporate the deliverables of the strategic projects derived from its vision, taking into consideration existing, improved and new products and services:

- New, reengineered processes and in/outsourced processes
- New and updated process automation and disruptive technologies
- New and updated value streams
- New business models
- New knowledge and methodologies
- New competences and competencies
- New strategic and tactical partners

Successful executives keep the architectures of the organisation contemporary, contributing to its sustainability.

They are bold enough to ditch technologies and even processes reaching the end of their lifecycle and replace them with new, innovative alternatives.

Contemporising the organisation's mission

Successful executives update the organisation's mission by incorporating strategic wins, gained through the realisation of the organisation's vision by successfully executing its strategic projects.

They review regularly, usually yearly, the organisation's mission (ie the creation and delivery of value to its stakeholders, and its product and service portfolio) and incorporate the deliverables of the strategic projects derived from its vision.

Successful executives keep the mission of the organisation contemporary, ensuring its sustainability.

They are bold enough to ditch products, services and even markets reaching the end of their lifecycle and replace them with new, improved or innovative alternatives.

Successful executives do not sacrifice the sustainability of their organisation for short-term gains. On the contrary, they look at the big picture and seek a healthy balance of short and long-term goals and targets.

Achieving high personal performance

Successful executives achieve high personal productivity by maintaining a thorough portfolio of activities both as managers and as leaders, and by prioritising and devoting adequate time to each management and leadership activity, or combination of activities.

They know that their mandate is to create and deliver value and they recognise that to achieve this, they must not only focus on executing the (current) mission of the organisation (ie on implementing its operational plans) but must, at the same time, devote time and effort to:

- Building and maintaining a productive and innovative culture based on values
- Managing the assets and the processes of the (extended) organisation so that they are always at the optimum productivity level
- Leading their people so that they are always devoting their best selves to productively and competitively creating and delivering outstanding value
- Developing themselves and their people with regard to their competences and competencies

They execute their rich and complex portfolio of activities by:

- Avoiding both micro and macromanagement
- Delegating wisely, implementing balanced RAEW for both the formal posts and for ad hoc task and project allocation, giving due consideration not only to the capabilities (competences, competencies and fit) of their people but also to their personal circumstances
- Being accessible but also detached, timeboxing their personal schedule and retaining focus
- Knowing when and how to say no
- Managing and leading their close associates and their space

- Managing their network and their relationships with authenticity, sincerity and openness so that they are not overwhelmed, ensuring their support
- Keeping themselves well informed about both the internal affairs of the organisation and its technological, financial, market and competitive environment
- Developing themselves and managing their careers – maintaining objective self-knowledge and identifying their own weaknesses
- Keeping their body, mind and spirit healthy
- Managing their life so that they maintain a positive work–life balance, feel comfortable and can manage their (at times, inevitable) stress
- Being a good example, by living the organisation's values, keeping their promises, and responding promptly to demands from their people and other stakeholders for both routine activities, such as clearing their in-tray and their inbox, and more demanding ones, such as preparing progress reports and proposals for action

To achieve all these activities, successful executives develop their time-management competency.

- **They manage their time in a balanced, conscientious way. They cultivate a culture in which executives and operatives are time-conscious. They acknowledge that time is crucial to process and project productivity and manage their time productively.**
- **They attain high personal performance, and demand it from their team and, through them, from everybody.**

Leading change

Successful executives lead change without sacrificing the execution of the (current) mission.

In modern life, disruptive technology, market, financial, political and other changes that affect the environment in which the organisation operates are abound. In addition, disruptive changes occur, usually infrequently, within the organisations themselves, in the form of radical inventions, severe financial problems, take-overs and mergers.

Disruptive changes dictate radical organisational change and transformation. The implementation of these changes is undertaken by executives at various levels, and is usually delegated down the hierarchy. Unfortunately, in most cases, they fail.

In many of the few cases in which they succeed, it is to the detriment of the organisation. In very few cases, they succeed without disrupting the execution of the mission of the organisation.

Why?

The reason is that successful executives have already:

- **Created and are maintaining a culture of high performance and growth under various conditions**
- **Aligned, committed and engaged their people in executing the organisation's mission of creating and delivering outstanding value**
- **Established and maintained an environment of continuous visioning for ongoing improvement and, hence, frequent small changes, and for large strategic projects and programmes for drastic change**
- **Formulated and communicated, clearly and convincingly, a vision for the organisation**
- **Prepared their people for abrupt, unexpected change before the need for radical action arises**
- **Led the execution of strategic programmes and projects that brought about dramatic change**

They succeed in leading change by:

- **Creating a sense of urgency** – by projecting either the issue as it is, or an exaggeration of the issue and its potential positive or negative consequences
- **Creating a critical mass** in favour of change by clarifying and stressing the relationship between the issue and the organisation's vision through open, sincere, in-depth dialogue and discussion with representative *power* stakeholders associated, directly or indirectly, with the issue at hand
- **Translating the necessary change into specific projects** – identifying and analysing the probable critical success factors and inhibitors, detailing adequately the plans and defining intermediate deliverables and milestones

- **Aligning and engaging the people** who will be directly involved in executing the change
- **Creating enthusiasm, commitment and ownership** among the project team(s) members
- **Keeping informed the whole organisation** and, where necessary and useful, the external stakeholders of the organisation, of any significant change, at the right time, clearly and adequately, with due attention to sensitivity and confidentiality
- **Realising all critical success factors and removing any inhibitors**
- **Leading the project team(s) in productively effecting the required change**
- **Accomplishing, presenting and celebrating intermediate deliverables – maintaining and intensifying momentum**
- **Reviewing progress and revising plans and schedules** so that they remain ambitious but feasible
- **Avoiding the creation of false prospects and premature success**
- **Embedding all successful changes** in the organisation's architectures and structures, products and service portfolio and plans
- **Modifying, as appropriate, the organisation's mission**

> **Successful executives continue to lead, with the same zeal, the execution of the (current) mission, creating and delivering value, while also leading change.**

Controlling ego and emotions

> **Successful executives check their ego and their emotions and operate with humility and empathy.**

They regularly take inventory of their own emotional intelligence competencies, keeping a diary of critical incidents, in a way similar to the best personnel assessment methods, and draw up a roadmap for self-development, seeking out suitable:

- In-class training
- Experiential workshops
- Coaching
- Mentoring

They trace and analyse:

- Their emotions: anger, sadness, pessimism, optimism, irony, joy, happiness, and empathy
- Their language and gestures
- What was the cause of each emotion, eg someone's repeated misbehaviour
- Why each emotion occurred, eg because of stress or fatigue
- What was the frequency and intensity of each emotion
- Whether they exhibited adequate, inadequate or too much self-control
- Whether each emotion showed improvement or deterioration
- Whether each had a positive or negative effect on their leadership
- How it affected and was received by others

> **Successful executives continuously improve their attitude and interpersonal skills.**

Exhibiting humane attitudes

> **Successful executives exhibit gratitude, respect, honesty, sincerity, integrity and loyalty.**

They acknowledge that being a successful executive means serving your people in addition to leading them in devoting their best selves to the creation and delivery of value. They know that to be an exceptionally successful executive, you need to be there for your people as much as they are there for you.

> **Successful executives serve their people: they respect them, listen to them actively and support, teach, coach, mentor and reward them. They express their gratitude and are loyal. They exhibit empathy and passion. They win the hearts of their people and establish rapport by allowing, sometimes, their own vulnerability to surface.**

Striving for the happiness of the organisation's stakeholders

> **Successful executives strive for the happiness of themselves and their people in a holistic way, balancing their work and personal life. They acknowledge that what matters most is the happiness of the organisation's stakeholders and, especially, its people.**

They strive for:

- Their welfare, measured as relative purchasing power
- Balanced work and responsibility in terms of expertise, authority, cultural and team fit, and personal preferences
- The maximisation of positive feelings, such as elation after successes, pleasure in the work environment, and joy from positive cooperation
- The minimisation of negative emotions, such as sadness, anger, pessimism and anxiety

> **Successful executives strive to contribute to the happiness of the organisation's stakeholders by creating and delivering balanced value in the context of the purpose and mission of the organisation.**

Management competences

> **Research and our experience show that, to succeed, executives need not only to possess, develop and implement their executive competencies but also develop and put to productive use their management competences, ie their knowledge and dexterity, in executing productively the management process as presented in Chapters One to Five.**

Many of these competences are employed, to various degrees, by successful executives in exercising their leadership activities while they concurrently carry out management activities, such as in formulating business plans.

We briefly outline in this section the management competences, methods and tools.

Mastering the scientific management process

Successful executives recognise that they need to have profound knowledge of and experience in all management subprocesses and activities, and ensure that these are put to good use at all levels.

- They have excellent knowledge of the organisation's architectures – value streams, end-to-end processes, supply and sales chains, KPIs, and tolerance levels – its assets, and its people and their capabilities.
- They translate the organisation's purpose and mission, the expectations of its stakeholders, and the market status, into short-term targets.
- They formulate plans aiming at achieving the predefined targets.
- They identify the critical success factors and the inhibitors that must be removed to significantly increase the probability of successfully executing the plan and meeting the targets.
- They identify any gaps in the competences and competencies of the organisation's people, and plan their bridging.
- They direct the execution of plans and projects by issuing appropriate and timely instructions.
- They coordinate the execution of plans and projects.
- They monitor and review progress and results.
- They revise plans as needed so that they remain realistic.

Mastering management methods and tools

Successful executives have good knowledge of the most modern and effective methods and tools for the design, planning and execution activities, such as:

External environment assessment

- Market
- Technology
- Customer

- Competitor
- Organisation's stakeholders
- PESTLE (political, economic, social, technological, legal, environmental) analysis
- SWOT (strengths, weaknesses, opportunities and threats) analysis
- Identification and assessment of external critical success factors and inhibitors
- Scenario planning

Organisational assessment and design

- Organisational architectures (value streams, extended organisation end-to-end process architecture, data architecture, fixed assets, internal technology, organisational structure)
- Organisational knowledge
- Internal financials
- People's capability (competences, competencies)
- Operations
- Cost analysis (cost centres, cost drivers, cost allocation)
- Profit analysis (profit centres, profit drivers)
- Culture, management and leadership capability
- Risk and business continuity

Planning and reviewing

- Review of the organisation's mission and value creation, and its delivery portfolio
- Review of the organisation's vision and strategic plans and projects
- Short to medium-term operational and improvement plan formulation, including setting broad and KPI-related targets
- Medium to long-term strategic plan formulation, including setting deliverables and strategic targets
- Plan execution control
- Monitoring and review of internal actual operating results and strategic deliverables, and external environment
- Plan revision
- Annual review and revision (as needed) of business architectures, mission and vision

Formulating thorough business plans

- Critical success factors and inhibitors (as derived from PESTLE and SWOT analysis)
- Medium to long-term, high-level strategic plan and deliverables
- Medium-term high-level operational plan and targets
- Short-term detailed plan covering operations for the creation and delivery of value with specific targets and KPI values, projects for short-term improvement with specific deliverables, and strategic projects (scheduled for the short term) with targets and deliverables, including:
  - Product and service lifecycle analysis, and short-term production, marketing and sales plan and cost analysis
  - Customer lifecycle analysis and short-term sales and revenue plan
  - Strategic project cost analysis
  - Capital expenditures plan
  - Staffing and training plan
  - Operational expenses and cost analysis
  - Cash flow analysis
  - Financial planning
  - Short-term budget (preferably three years, analysed in quarters)
  - Profit and loss analysis and balance sheet

Targets for KPIs, such as:

- Customer KPIs
  - Customer value lifecycle
  - Customer engagement index
  - Customer complaints index
  - Customer satisfaction index
  - Customer promoter score
  - Customer retention rate
  - Customer turnover rate
  - Customer profitability index
- Marketing and sales KPIs

- Market growth rate
- Market share
- Conversion rate
- Cost per lead
- Advertising campaign success index
- Sales campaign success index
- Word of mouth referral index
- Cross and up-sales rates

- Operational KPIs
  - Order fulfilment indices
  - Capacity utilisation index
  - Process waste index
  - Sales, after-sales and SLA commitment satisfaction rate
  - Inventory management indices
  - Production cost variance and analysis in cost component (material, labour, services, asset) variances
  - Project schedule and cost variances
  - First-pass repair and rework effectiveness and efficiency indices
  - Quality indices
  - Complaint handling indices
  - Improvement (Kaizen) and innovation indices
- Technology KPIs
  - Production downtime indices
  - Production and repair lines effectiveness indices
  - Comparative technology effectiveness indices
- People KPIs
  - People alignment index
  - People engagement and commitment index
  - People satisfaction index
  - Revenue and cost per person

  - People churn rate
  - Competency, competence and cultural fit index
  - Training return on investment
  - Absenteeism index
  - Emoluments competitiveness index
  - Recruitment indices (interest, fit, time-to-hire, turnover)
- Culture, governance and compliance KPIs
  - Tribal leadership culture stage
  - Product and waste recycling indices
  - Environmental (carbon dioxide, water, energy, waste, chemical) footprints
  - GRC (governance, risk, compliance) indices
  - CR (corporate responsibility, including social responsibility) indices
- Financial KPIs
  - Gross profit margins
  - Operating profit margins
  - Net profit margin
  - Net profit
  - Revenue growth
  - EBIDTA
  - Return on investment (ROI)
  - Return on capital employed (ROCE)
  - Return on assets (ROA)
  - Return on equity (ROE)
  - Debt/equity ratio
  - Leverage ratio
  - Working capital ratio
  - Operating expense ratio
  - Capex to sales ratio
  - Cash conversion cycle
  - Price/earnings ratio

    - Economic value added
    - Total shareholder return
- Value KPIs
    - Economic value added
    - Stakeholder (owner, investor, creditor, employee, community/society, etc) value added and satisfaction indices
    - Knowledge enrichment index (papers, patents)

Managing the execution

- Directing and coordinating
- Controlling
- Monitoring and reviewing internal actual operating results, strategic deliverables and external environment, and revising plans
- Disseminating thorough, true and timely information to the organisation's stakeholders on a need-to-know basis

Mastering the classical management functions

> **Successful executives master the classical management functions: financing, human resource management, marketing, sales, supply chain, customer relationships, logistics, etc, and their KPIs.**

- They recognise the content of the various functions, understand their jargon and respective processes, and comprehend how each function/organisational unit correlates with the various processes.
- They acknowledge the position of each function in the various value streams and know how their performance is measured by utilising suitable indices and their respective process KPIs.
- They recognise the handovers between various functions as probable fault lines, and make every effort to automate all processes that transcend them to eliminate, or at least minimise, errors and delays.
- They acknowledge the dynamics between various functions and know how to handle possible rivalries.

Mastering the generic management subprocesses and embedding them in the organisational processes

> **Successful executives master the generic managerial subprocesses, such as risk, environment, and health and safety management and ensure they are embedded in the organisational processes.**

They acknowledge the importance and the contribution of the various generic subprocesses that modern organisations embed in their core, support and staff processes, such as those presented in Chapter Four.

Mastering the core processes of the organisation

> **Successful executives have good knowledge of the core, support and staff processes of the organisation.**

With the exception of when professional operatives or executives are promoted within the organisation, all other executives, once appointed, must learn within a short time (not more than a few months) the core processes of the organisational entity they are mandated to head, plus all interfacing processes and respective KPIs.

> **Successful executives undertaking a new executive post, having already mastered the management and leadership processes, the traditional management functions and the generic subprocesses, devote the necessary time and focus to learning the specific core processes of their new organisation and to getting acquainted with the process owners and the organisational structure.**

They accomplish this within the (usually short) time tolerated by the organisation's stakeholders, becoming promptly effective in executing the organisation's mission, creating and delivering outstanding value, and in pursuing the realisation of the organisation's vision.

Mastering excellence modelling

Successful executives have good knowledge of business excellence modelling (BEM) and introduce one of the proven excellence models, such as the European Foundation of Quality Management (EFQM) Business Excellence Model or the Malcolm Baldrige National Quality Award (MBNQA) model.

They not only use BEM to guide the operations of the organisation but also apply a variety of suitable management tools and techniques in its operation, as outlined previously, besides using specific mechanisms, programmes and KPIs to cultivate the organisational culture towards excellence.

Successful executives pay due attention to pursuing excellence by adopting suitable organisational architectures and KPIs.

They do it by setting respective targets, monitoring actual results, and continuously adapting the organisation's plans for:

1. The enablers of the creation and delivery of value:
    - Culture, leadership and management
    - Architectures, processes, information, knowledge and policies
    - People and partners, competences, competencies, and cultural fit
    - Physical assets and intellectual property
    - Learning and innovation
    - Execution performance
2. The outcomes, in terms of:
    - Delivered value realising the organisation's purpose and mission in economic, product, service and social value indices
    - Customer or principal stakeholder (to whom products/services are delivered) satisfaction indices
    - People (active executives and operatives) satisfaction indices
    - Society (communities and regions directly or indirectly affected by the organisation's operations, products and services)
    - Organisation's health and sustainability

They carry out periodic self-assessment and third-party assessment and then take actions to address the weaknesses and problems identified. They participate in national and international quality award programmes, such as the EFQM Global Excellence Award, the Malcolm Baldrige National Quality Award, the ESPRIX Swiss Award for Excellence, the Japanese Deming Prize, and the Dutch Quality Assessment, thus creating internal enthusiasm, challenge and momentum for improvement and excellence.

Overcoming emotional challenges

Transiting from a professional operative post or a simple team member role to an executive post presents a significant emotional challenge. Transiting persons experience various emotions, such as insecurity, anxiety, excitement, pride, arrogance, regret, loss and loneliness, and may face a lack of cooperation, and resentment and/or enmity from ex-peers who become subordinates.

Mastering both negative and positive feelings helps turn the newly appointed/promoted professional operative into a successful executive. Conversely, when such emotions are left unchecked, they can easily lead to failure and catastrophe.

Unfortunately, schools and organisations rarely prepare people for this transition and, in many cases, instead of helping them they condemn them to failure. This is to the detriment of both the organisation and the incumbents' professional and personal life.

Successful executives master their emotions and overcome emotional challenges.

There are many techniques for dealing with negative emotions, either as self-help tools or administered by professionals. These fall outside the scope of this book. We simply stress that newly appointed executives should employ the leadership techniques mentioned previously in the context of leadership activities and self-development, such as:

- Allocating time for emotional self-reflection and self-awareness
- Seeking solutions
- Looking at the big picture and finding perspective
- Seeking discreet assistance and coaching from their immediate superior, or mentoring from a senior executive they admire and with whom they have previously established rapport

- Learning relaxation techniques, such as meditation or yoga
- Being methodical, engaged, consistent and trustworthy
- Quickly learning and comprehending the core processes, information and knowledge related to the new post by:
  - Reading relevant material and public literature
  - Speaking with superiors and consulting subordinates and associates during one-to-one acquaintance meetings, and current conditions review and planning meetings
  - Speaking with peers in parallel with internal supplier and customer organisational units
- Establishing strategic relationships with close associates and subordinates while maintaining a level of detachment
- Supporting associates and subordinates promptly whenever they need help, by either teaching, coaching and mentoring them or seeking external support if they lack the necessary knowhow
- Avoiding isolation
- Keeping to the ethical values of the organisation, or introducing them if they are absent

Leading execution

Successful executives focus on execution first and strategy planning second. They acknowledge that success means creation and delivery of value through the execution of the organisation's plans.

They acknowledge that organisations succeed when they execute their plans, and not by having excellent strategies and plans on paper.

Research shows that execution is critical. A value-based culture, effective and efficient processes; well-structured, accurate data; people with the required competences, competencies and fit; elaborate plans with suitable targets; promising strategic projects with specific deliverables; and availability of the necessary assets and resources are all critical success factors. They can only take the organisation up to a point, though. Execution makes the difference.

Successful executives lead their organisations to outstanding execution, outperforming their competitors by accelerating the organisation's metabolic rate, which research shows directly affects the organisation's performance.

The metabolic rate of an organisation is characterised by:

- **Its speed of mobilisation** across the whole executive process, from reviewing past performance and current situation and formulating plans to creating and delivering value: focus, alignment, engagement, commitment and ownership for execution, overcoming uncertainty, ambiguity and confusion
- **Its execution efficiency and quality**, despite complexity, inevitable unclear authority and accountability, as well as competency and competence gaps
- **Its transformation capability, willingness and speed**, overcoming the fear of failure, jerking, complacency and competition
- **Its agility in promptly finding answers, thinking outside the box, and exploiting retrospection without being bogged down by:**
  - Hindsight: always seeking in the past answers to current problems
  - Immunity: avoiding acknowledging and learning from mistakes
  - Indecisiveness: avoiding failure at any cost
  - Inflexibility: resisting change
  - Fragility: lack of resilience, being unable to recover from failures

Successful executives accentuate the organisation's metabolism.

They do it by:

- Placing the best people in the posts that have the potential for the most significant outcomes in:
  - Creating and delivering value
  - Transforming the organisation
  - Innovating for sustainability
- Leading their team and the organisation in sifting through conflicting priorities and selecting those that make the most difference
- Promptly ditching products, services, markets, customers, and business lines and models that have exhausted their potential and are getting close to dropping below their break-even point

- Keeping the organisation and its business intelligence (its executive information) lean and healthy
- Keeping their people healthy – physically, emotionally and spiritually

> **Successful executives focus on four implementation imperatives:**
> - **Question everything**
> - **Inform everyone, then empower champions**
> - **Keep relationships tight and rules loose**
> - **Modify quickly**

Extreme ownership and ultimate responsibility

> **Successful executives do not take passive responsibility for their mission. They take extreme ownership of everything that impacts their mission.**

They acknowledge that on any team, in any organisation, all responsibility for success and failure rests with the leaders.

> **Successful executives own everything in their world.**

Successful executives are never satisfied. They strive relentlessly for improvement and innovation. They instil in their team's culture and, through it, in the organisation's culture, a spirit of creativity and a thirst for outstanding results, continuous improvement, innovation and growth. In their organisation, everybody seeks out weaknesses and opportunities and puts them on the table so that solutions can be proposed. By openly discussing weaknesses, problems, threats and opportunities, the culture is strengthened and becomes more innovative, flexible and resilient, thus safeguarding sustainability.

> **By exhibiting extreme ownership, successful executives cultivate a culture in which most, if not all, of their people feel and show extreme ownership and commitment to their mandates and their world.**

Developing the executive's competencies and competences

> **Successful executives exhibit strong and sincere self-awareness and evaluate their competencies and competences both through self-assessment and through formal methods, such as 360-degree assessment. They become role models and set a good example by submitting themselves to periodic formal psychometric assessment and interpretation by expert assessors using recognised tools, such as the Myers–Briggs and other personality tests.**

They have a growth mindset, develop it in themselves and others, and nurture a culture that values the continuous development of this mindset. They continuously strive to develop their competencies and competences by exploiting various appropriate formal and informal methods and by employing them conscientiously on the job. They exhibit humility and admit any mistakes and misbehaviour. They promptly apologise for and rectify any wrongdoing.

Developing leadership competencies

Until recently, competencies were thought to be inherited, and therefore it was considered impossible to improve on weaknesses. Research has since shown that they can be taught and developed to a level that ensures success in executive positions. The main prerequisite for developing most of the competencies and soft skills is an above average emotional quotient (EQ). A high intelligence quotient (IQ) helps in improving competencies.

Leadership competencies are mainly self-developed, with perseverance, via self-study and on-the-job practice, observing good and bad examples, recognising mistakes, seeking and exploiting sincere assessment, and coaching and mentoring. In this regard, **neuroplasticity**, the ability to reshape our brains (especially in response to learning) and, therefore, change our personal traits, promises extraordinary results.

Developing management competences

Competences (ie knowhow, dexterities and experience) can be developed through study, training, coaching, and on-the-job practice. They are easier and quicker to acquire and develop with a high IQ and a broad academic background, such as a general first university degree and a specialised postgraduate degree. A postgraduate degree, ideally acquired after at least medium-term professional experience, is helpful in developing management competences, especially those that have not been acquired through academic study and professional training.

IQ and EQ

Our experience and research show the impact of the level of EQ and IQ on personal development:

- **Intelligence quotient**

  An above average IQ and an academic and/or professional background means that leadership competencies can be employed in leading people and organisational entities in parallel with effectively employing the necessary management competences.

- **Emotional quotient**

  An above average EQ is also a prerequisite, because many, if not all, leadership competencies are based on the personal capability to establish trust, creditworthiness and rapport, nurturing sound interpersonal relations and exhibiting genuine empathy.

> **High IQ and low EQ may make a good manager, but not a good leader – as a rule, this executive will remain at a low-level managerial position. These people can thrive in autocratic organisations, where they will not be admired or loved by their people.**
>
> **High EQ and low IQ may make a popular leader, who may lead people and organisational entities for some time, but will not, as a rule, result in long-term business success and sustainability. The only possible, though rare, exception is people with high self-awareness who select as close associates, and especially as their deputies, people with high IQ and high EQ who complement their own weaknesses.**

It goes without saying that organisational culture, personal development process and drive play significant roles in the development of leadership competencies and management competences.

Prerequisites for personal success and flexibility

Successful executives recognise that the major prerequisites for employability, for success in any executive position, and for flexibility in moving between organisations with different purposes and missions is mastering:

- **The leadership competencies**
- **The management competences**
- **The generic subprocesses**
- **Excellence modelling**

They make it a life goal to continuously develop their competencies and competences and to employ them in creating and delivering value in whichever organisation and post they find themselves. They exploit the most appropriate methods and tools for each post/organisation: in-class, through self-study, and by seeking coaching and mentoring, but mostly on the job.

Having acquired, as early as possible, a holistic executive capability, they become productive and successful within the (usually short) probation period in any new organisation and/or executive post. They do this by devoting the necessary time and effort to learning, quickly, the specific core processes and knowhow of their new organisation.

The other prerequisites for success are:

- The adoption of and deep belief in a broad set of ethical values
- Personal ethos, integrity and consistency
- Flexibility in fitting into diverse cultures and teams, maintaining a set of values that closely overlap with their own values
- Belief and enthusiasm in creating and delivering value

Successful executives develop these personal attitudes by actively exhibiting them in their verbal and body language, and in their professional and personal life.

Unfortunately, the majority of executives neglect one or more of the above components of executive capability, and either fail or plateau.

Achieving wisdom – Ikigai

We have stressed repeatedly that organisations exist to realise their *raison d'être*: to create and deliver specific value to their stakeholders. When they do this successfully, they contribute to their stakeholders' welfare, wellbeing and, ultimately, their happiness. This is also true for individuals. The Japanese term *ikigai* ('reason for being') encapsulates this well.

Ikigai is the convergence of four primary elements:

1. What you love (your passion)
2. What the world needs (your mission)
3. What you are good at (your vocation)
4. What you can get paid for (your profession)

Figure 8.1 shows the relationship between these elements.

Figure 8.1: Ikigai: a Japanese concept meaning a reason for being

The Japanese believe that discovering your own *ikigai* will bring you fulfilment, happiness and longevity.

If you want to find your *ikigai*, ask yourself these four questions:

1. What do I love?
2. What am I good at?
3. What can I be paid for, now or in the future?
4. What does the world need?

Try to define your passion, your vocation, your profession and your mission, and compare them to where you currently are and where you want to be in the future.

EXAMPLE FROM KORALIA'S PERSONAL EXPERIENCE

Being a management consultant in a big consulting firm was overall a very rewarding experience for me. For most of the years, I had a really good time and was producing great results, delighted clients and revenue. I spent the second half of my twenties as well as my thirties expanding my knowledge, person-skills and resourcefulness. I met a lot of people and organisations and did quite a lot (mostly inland) travelling. I had the freedom to make my own day-to-day work schedule and handle my clients in person. I had enough autonomy and the consulting job as such was rewarding. I was happy. As the years passed, I grew tired. Regardless of promotions, I was doing essentially the same job for a decade and a half. I was increasingly feeling that I was not growing any more. I wasn't expanding my knowledge or skills as I would have liked and despite the envious title on my business card, I felt stagnant. In my mind, internal procedures became bureaucratic and meaningless, and I was finding myself caught up in pointless meetings, reviews and forms to be filled. It felt like I was missing the point of making real and big impact. I was suffocating.

The aggressive client-securing approach of the sector did not fit my introvert nature either. I prefer cooperation rather than competition and it was becoming clear to me that this attribute of my character was neither helping me sell the firm's services nor myself as a person internally in the organization. Other people thrive in highly competitive environments but I definitely don't. On the other hand, I had strong feelings on the technical part of my job and wouldn't tolerate anything less than perfect. This resulted in my work-done versus work-invoiced KPIs to drop dramatically. I couldn't decide at that point whether it was I who was "wrong" or everybody else. Neither was the case. I was just at the wrong place at the wrong time. I was unhappy and my implementability suffered as well. This made my boss unhappy too. I had a problem and I was also creating a problem to the team. I had to move on and I did. Since then I came to realise that this was a straightforward case of cultural mis-fit. I didn't fit into the corporate culture and environment. It was competitive and I was cooperative. It was aggressive and I was placid. It was fast and I wanted to finally slow down. It was formal and I wanted to be relaxed and cosy. It was distant and I wanted to be approachable. We didn't fit together and it was hurting both sides.

I also acknowledge that whereas I was happy in that same workplace until a few years back, it wasn't necessarily a bad thing that I wasn't anymore. Both my employer company and I had grown. We had changed, but in opposite directions. It is sometimes natural that this happens and it's ok.

I am happier now as an author, as a trainer in executive excellence and as an Intuitive Life Coach and Rapid Transformation Facilitator. I hope that I have found my ikigai.

If you want to be a successful executive, identify your strengths and weaknesses vis-à-vis the leadership and management competencies and competences we present in this book. Make a conscientious and systematic effort to improve yourself and to put your capability to good use within an environment in which you fit well.

In summary

Successful executives have the personal characteristics summarised in Table 8.2.

Table 8.2: The successful executive's personal characteristics

S/N	Successful Executive's Personal Characteristics
1	Has high ethical values, believes in them, preaches them in every relevant organisational context, lives them, demonstrates them and demands them from all their people. Exhibits character and consistency.
2	Manages relations with all stakeholder groups and builds a network propagating the organisational values and slogans, collecting, cross-checking and distributing sound and true information (BI & CI).
3	Has high IQ and uses it productively to quickly comprehend complex issues and conceive solutions.
4	Quickly conceptualises the organisational architectures, strengths, weaknesses, problems, challenges, opportunities and threats, and conceives scenarios, roadmaps and plans for action.
5	Has clear thought and clear, enlightening, convincing words, achieving belief in the organisation's values, purpose, mission and vision.
6	Is authentic, stable and consistent and builds credibility.
7	Is decisive.
8	Achieves consensus and alignment.
9	Has high EQ and builds trust around a productive tribal culture.
10	Exhibits discipline in honouring values and commitments.
11	Promptly feeds back adequate information maintaining credibility, trust, belief and ownership in the mission, the vision, the people, the targets and the plans, and exhibits sincere and full accountability.
12	Achieves spiritual rapport, building trust, engagement, commitment, devotion and ownership, and inspires people to exert themselves in producing results and working wonders.
13	Delegates with confidence, and empowers, supports and rewards their people.
14	Develops his/herself continually and coaches and mentors his/her people, especially in developing their growth mindset and their leadership and other soft competencies.
15	Devotes time to and leads team visioning for short-term improvements.
16	Devotes time to formulating, reviewing and revising the organisation's vision and to designing and planning the strategic projects that will realise the vision.
17	Achieves high personal productivity by maintaining a thorough portfolio of activities, both as a manager and as a leader, and prioritises and devotes adequate time to each activity.
18	Checks his/her ego and operates with humility and empathy.
19	Exhibits gratitude, respect, honesty, sincerity, integrity, perseverance and loyalty.
20	Exhibits extreme ownership and ultimate responsibility.

Extensive international research shows that it is a myth that successful executives are born with these characteristics and that, on the contrary, these can be acquired, developed and cultivated through training, coaching, mentoring and, most effectively, through practice.

It is true that upbringing and a genetic predisposition can help by offering the incumbent a solid foundation on which to build their competencies and competences to acquire these characteristics. This is a double-edged sword. On one hand, it decreases the effort needed, while on the other, it may create a false sense of self-sufficiency, diminishing the drive for self-development.

Successful executives acknowledge that to successfully execute their management activities they must acquire the specific competences summarised in Table 8.3. They also recognise the importance of their continuous development.

Table 8.3: The successful executive's management competences

S/N	Successful Executive's Management Competences
1	Masters the scientific management process (plan, coordinate, direct and control, act, review and revise plans) to an adequate level.
2	Masters the main classical management functions (finance, HR, marketing, sales, supply chain, CRM, logistics, etc) and their KPIs to an adequate level.
3	Masters the generic management subprocesses (such as risk, environment, health and safety management) at a good level and ensures they are embedded in the organisational processes.
4	Masters the core processes of the organisation (which realise its purpose and its mission) in depth.
5	Masters excellence modelling.

They strive to acquire and develop these competences mostly through education and training, by attending management schools, courses and seminars, by following the relevant literature, and by employing them in their day-to-day work.

Table 8.4: The successful executive's leadership competencies

S/N	Successful Executive's Leadership Competencies
1	Builds an all-round leadership team believing in the same ethical values, propagating them throughout the organisation by their own example, thus building a uniform culture based on those ethical values. Is complemented by their team members, who also complement each other.
2	Manages relations with all stakeholder groups and builds a network propagating the organisational values and slogans, collecting, cross-checking and distributing complete, sound and evidence-based information (ie business and competitive intelligence).
3	Leads the discussion, builds an atmosphere of open dialogue, influences the direction of the dialogue, maintains focus, acknowledges and summarises the various opinions, persuades and advises, deduces convincing guidelines, and reaches conclusions.
4	Achieves consensus and alignment.
5	Builds team spirit and achieves engagement, commitment and ownership to produce results within the common culture.
6	Exhibits and builds discipline in honouring values and commitments.
7	Promptly feeds back adequate information, maintaining credibility, trust, belief and ownership in the mission, the vision, the organisation, the people, the targets and the plans, and exhibits sincere and full accountability.
8	Achieves spiritual rapport, building trust, engagement, commitment, devotion and ownership, and inspires people to exert themselves in producing results and working wonders.
9	Delegates with confidence, and empowers, supports and rewards his/her people.
10	Continually develops leadership talent at all levels.
11	Coaches and mentors his/her people, especially in developing their leadership and other soft competencies.
12	Fosters creativity, encourages and rewards innovation, and celebrates failure.
13	Devotes time to and leads team visioning for short-term improvements.
15	Devotes time to formulating, reviewing and revising the organisation's vision and to designing and planning the strategic projects that will realise the vision.
16	Ensures that strategic wins (victories) are embedded in the organisation's architectures.
17	Ensures that the organisation's mission is reviewed, revised and kept contemporary, thus ensuring sustainability.
18	Leads change without sacrificing the execution of the (current) mission.
19	Strives for the happiness of their people and themselves in a holistic way, balancing work and personal life.
20	Leads execution.

Successful executives recognise that to be successful leaders, they need to acquire and hone the specific competencies summarised in Table 8.4. They also recognise the importance of their development and of putting them to productive use.

They devote time, effort and enthusiasm to acquiring and developing these competencies through education and training and, most effectively, through on-the-job-practice. They acknowledge that most management schools and seminars focus on, and are more effective in teaching, management rather than leadership.

They recognise that what makes the difference is strong ethical values; living by them, setting an example, preaching and demonstrating them. They build a culture around them, ie a code of ethics, and lead their people within this culture to achieve business success in creating and delivering value that delights the organisation's customers and other stakeholders. Finally, they continuously develop their leadership competencies and the leadership talent of their people.

They also recognise that nobody exhibits to a high degree all of the necessary leadership competencies, and that success requires profound self-knowledge, effective employment of one's strengths, and overcoming one's weaknesses through teamwork and complementary associates, superiors, peers or subordinates. While further developing their strengths, they compensate for their shortcomings by delegating related activities to associates exhibiting the necessary strengths.

Vital questions

1. Do you recognise the difference between management and leadership?
2. Do you acknowledge that (in a realistic, though seemingly artificial sense):
   - Management is equal to:
     - Designing, planning, acting, coordinating, monitoring and revising the designs and plans of the organisation's value streams and their subordinate architectures, enablers and resources; and realising the value streams, as processes, data, production lines, supply and sales chains, work posts, competences, competencies, RAEW, KPIs, and rewards?
     - Planning, coordinating, monitoring and revising the plans for the production and delivery of value to the organisation's customers and other stakeholders?

- Leadership is equal to:
  - Communicating with, and achieving deep common understanding, alignment, inspiration, engagement and commitment from, the organisation's people for productive and competitive action?
  - Leading the people in executing their activities (processes or subprocesses) and projects to produce outstanding results and deliver value to the satisfaction and delight of the organisation's customers and other stakeholders?

3. Do you acknowledge that to successfully execute your mandate as an executive you need to exercise, *in parallel*, management and leadership activities, and hence to acquire and develop the competences demanded by the management process and the competencies demanded by the leadership process, as presented in this book?
4. Are you aware of your strengths and weaknesses? Have you been evaluated by any experts (for example, a Myers–Briggs test) to gain an objective picture of your strengths and weaknesses?
5. Does your organisation evaluate your management competences and your leadership competencies? If yes:
   - Have you ever been evaluated and put on a personal development plan aiming at bridging any identified gaps?
   - Do you think that your competencies and competences have improved?
   - Do your colleagues – superiors, peers and subordinates – think that your competencies and competences have improved?
   - Do you think that your performance has improved?
6. Does your organisation have a 360-degree evaluation scheme? If yes, does it include questions about management competences and leadership competencies, and does it lead to personal development plans and action?
7. Do you follow any self-development plan to hone your management competences and your leadership competencies?

EPILOGUE

> **Successful executives are seldom born with charisma. They are self-made through hard work, continuous learning, perseverance and self-discipline. By knowing themselves, being flexible, planning for and welcoming change; by defeating arrogance, over-confidence and lack of confidence.**

Many organisations fail. They fail in the private sector; they fail in the public sector; they fail in the state-owned realm. In some instances, they take down with them entire communities, or even states.

A look at the Fortune 100 or Fortune 500 lists over the last fifty years proves that many legendary corporations no longer exist. The majority of the airlines that operated in the USA and Europe in the 1980s have vanished. The same is true for information technology companies.

What is the most significant reason for their failure?

Poor executive capability. In many cases, this is a lack of management competence and competency. In many others, it's poor leadership competency. In most cases, it's a combination of the two.

Business failure boils down to executive failure and presents itself in many forms:

- **In failure to contemporise the organisation's mission:** incapability of the executives to formulate and execute a sound vision and to incorporate strategic wins in the current mission
- **In failure to assess correctly and promptly disruptive changes, and to adjust the organisation's architectures, business model, product portfolio, customer experience or operational and strategic plans:** inability of the executives to collect evidence-based information, assess it correctly, and adapt to what it suggests; to reach sound conclusions; and to convince, align, inspire and engage close colleagues and the wider organisation in designing and planning change and in leading change execution

- **In unproductive operations:** incapability of the executives to achieve mission execution, or inability to outperform the competition

EXAMPLE FROM NICOS' PERSONAL EXPERIENCE

As I mentioned in Chapter Two, I served for a decade as the CIO of a major technological organisation. In formulating its process reengineering and automation strategic plan, we built a number of interrelated architectures. Prominent among these was the Information Technology architecture comprising a high-speed wide and local area network, a major central computer centre, a relational database management system and ancillary software systems, a remote back-up data centre, several hundred networked personal computers, several tens of network printers, and a suite of personal productivity software applications. After a tedious multi-month international tender procedure, the multi-million dollar contract was awarded to Digital Equipment Corporation (DEC), USA.

The decision came as a big surprise since everybody had been expecting that one of the well-established mainframe computer manufacturers, such as IBM and NCR, would win. DEC, however, had received a higher score in the combination of technical and financial evaluation criteria.

Our experience with DEC proved excellent in all respects. Its equipment was excellent and its service outstanding. We continued ordering equipment and services from DEC and its successors for many years and we built the biggest and most complicated computer system in the country, which enabled the automation of practically all core and support processes of the organisation, the provision of outstanding service to our customers, and an unheard of productivity increase.

I continued following DEC's development even after I was promoted to the post of CEO not only due to the close relation of our organisation with such a major supplier and my background and interest in IT, but also because I was impressed with DEC's culture which was characterised by a values-based leadership founded on the co-founder and CEO Ken Olsen's belief:

- In rational problem-solving
- In active problem-solving
- That giving people freedom will make them responsible
- That responsibility means being on top of one's job
- That you must own your own problems
- In "truth through conflict" and getting "buy-in"

- In internal competition and "let the market decide"
- That work should be fun and enjoyable
- In management by passion
- In benign manipulation of controlled chaos
- In perpetual learning
- In loyalty and lifetime employment

DEC was an exemplary enterprise in product innovation and rapid growth and drew the interest of famous academics and researchers. Its troubles helped inspire Harvard Business School professor Clayton Christensen[56] to develop his well-known ideas about disruptive innovation.[57] According to an article in Strategy+Business, watching the problems of Digital and other minicomputer companies in the late 1980s got Christensen thinking about disruptive technology.

Edgar Schein, professor of management emeritus, senior lecturer at the Sloan School at MIT and fellow of the American Psychological Association and the Academy of Management, researched and wrote the story[58] of DEC as one of a dramatic rise and fall.

DEC was an entrepreneurial computer company that grew to $14 billion in sales and employed more than 100,000 people worldwide at its zenith. They invented the minicomputer, which displaced quite a few mainframe computer manufacturers that failed to move promptly into the era of minicomputers: Honeywell, Amdahl, Burroughs, NEC, NCR.

However, DEC itself failed to adapt successfully, and the personal computer eroded its minicomputer market. It proved that even a 'culture of innovation' can become dysfunctional as market conditions change. DEC continued to technologically innovate by inventing what was at the time the most powerful microprocessor, the heart of microcomputers, but it failed to also invent a new business model, when competitors did. Compaq Computer Corporation bought out DEC but then also failed to adjust to the market disruption caused by microcomputers and was acquired by Hewlett-Packard a little later.

DEC had microprocessor technology, but its business model meant it could not profitably sell a computer for less than $50,000. It failed to innovate its processes.

---

56 www.sloanreview.mit.edu/article/lessons-from-ken-olsen-and-digital-equipment-corp; https://www.strategy-business.com/article/14501?gko=ca7ad

57 Christensen C. (1997) The Innovator's Dilemma – *When New Technologies Cause Great Firms to Fail.*

58 Schein E. with DeLisi P., Kampas P., and Sonduck M. (2003) *DEC is Dead, Long Live DEC: The Lasting Legacy of Digital Equipment Corporation.*

Its technology, trapped in a high-cost business model, had no impact on the market and the world. This ultimately killed the company. By contrast, IBM Corp, with similar processors at its disposal, set up a different business model that could make a profit at a $2,000 price with 20% gross margins – and changed the world.

DEC continues to be acclaimed as one of the most innovative and entrepreneurial organisations of the twentieth century and a text book case. Its co-founder and for most of its life CEO, Ken Olsen, who passed away in 2011, was considered by many "...a titan in the computer industry. But ...also a personal titan to most of the employees... They knew Olsen for his humility and the culture of fun and excitement he created."

I recall with fond memories my visits to DEC's research labs and my discussions, even disputes with DEC's engineers and executives, when I insisted that they deliver to us 'intelligent user terminals', ie personal computers, instead of 'dumb' ones, as they used to until then (the beginning of the 1990s).

DEC's demise saddened me, because I admired its culture, innovations and rapid growth.

I believe that it set the example on how a culture based on sound values and authentic, inspiring leadership can help achieve continuous innovation and growth. It also, however, taught us that it is not enough to invent new products. Successful executives manage and lead the transition from the old product portfolio to the new one: they reengineer, in parallel, the organisation's business model and its production and delivery processes, reinventing, in essence, its mission. Only so, do they create a disruptive change and thus a temporary monopoly in the market. DEC accomplished it with its minicomputer and had a dramatic rise. It then failed miserably with the microcomputer despite the invention of the most powerful microprocessor.

We managed to avoid DEC's fatal mistake by successfully adjusting the organisation's business model and processes twice. Firstly, in the late 1990s, we slashed international telephone voice service tariffs by more than 90% within a few years, so that it became affordable to the average business individual. It was widely used by travel agents and export/import merchants and parents having children studying abroad, as most were doing at the time. Secondly, at the beginning of the 2000s with digital mobile (cellular) communications, we changed the business model by turning it quickly into a mass market product at an affordable price of cost plus cost of capital, ie with a profit of 10–12 % – the lowest price in Europe at the time. At the same time, we reengineered our delivery process cutting provisioning time down to twenty minutes and simplifying it by introducing 'a general service agreement' covering all services contracted by a residential or business customer.

- **In failure to build a growth culture**

  Incapability of the executives to conceive, build and cultivate a culture of strong moral values, sound governance and productive individual and collective learning, visioning and innovating.

- **In failure to satisfy stakeholders by delivering to them the value they envisage**

  Incapability of the executives to conceive what value the various stakeholder groups expect and are willing to pay for:

  > Customers, in price

  > Employees, in aligned, engaged, committed, wholehearted effort and results

  > Investors and creditors, in risking their money

  > The community, in supporting the organisation

  and to create and deliver it to them in a competitive way.

The list goes on.

In the great majority of cases, failure could have been avoided if executives had better competences and competencies, and had put them to productive use. Could the executives of the failed organisations have developed their capability and taken prompt action to avoid failure?

Yes. Extensive research and our long experience show that this is indeed possible. What is holding back executive development?

The main reasons are:

1. Incapability of the board of directors to identify or recognise the executive inefficiencies of the CEO and their executive team, or to take prompt corrective action
2. Incapability of the chief executives to identify or recognise their own inefficiencies and the inefficiencies of their executive team and take prompt corrective action
3. Incapability of the organisation to introduce evaluation methods that reveal executive capability inefficiencies
4. Incapability of the organisation to develop the competences and competencies of their executives, even when they identify inefficiencies

The consequence of organisational failure is that all stakeholders suffer, and in most cases the executives themselves.

The mission of this book is to inform our readers what the essence of successful executives is; what their job, in the sense of executive activities, must be; and which competences (knowhow) and competencies (personal traits, qualities and characteristics) they should have to successfully execute their roles as managers and leaders; and to encourage them to identify and develop those that need improvement.

We want to remind board members, CEOs, human resource managers and, above all, our readers aspiring to be successful executives, that the biggest enemies of self-improvement (Figure 9.1, where the vertical axis shows *actual* competence and competency for the solid curve and *perceived* ones for the other two curves) are:

- Lack of self-knowledge
- Lack of self-confidence
- Over-confidence

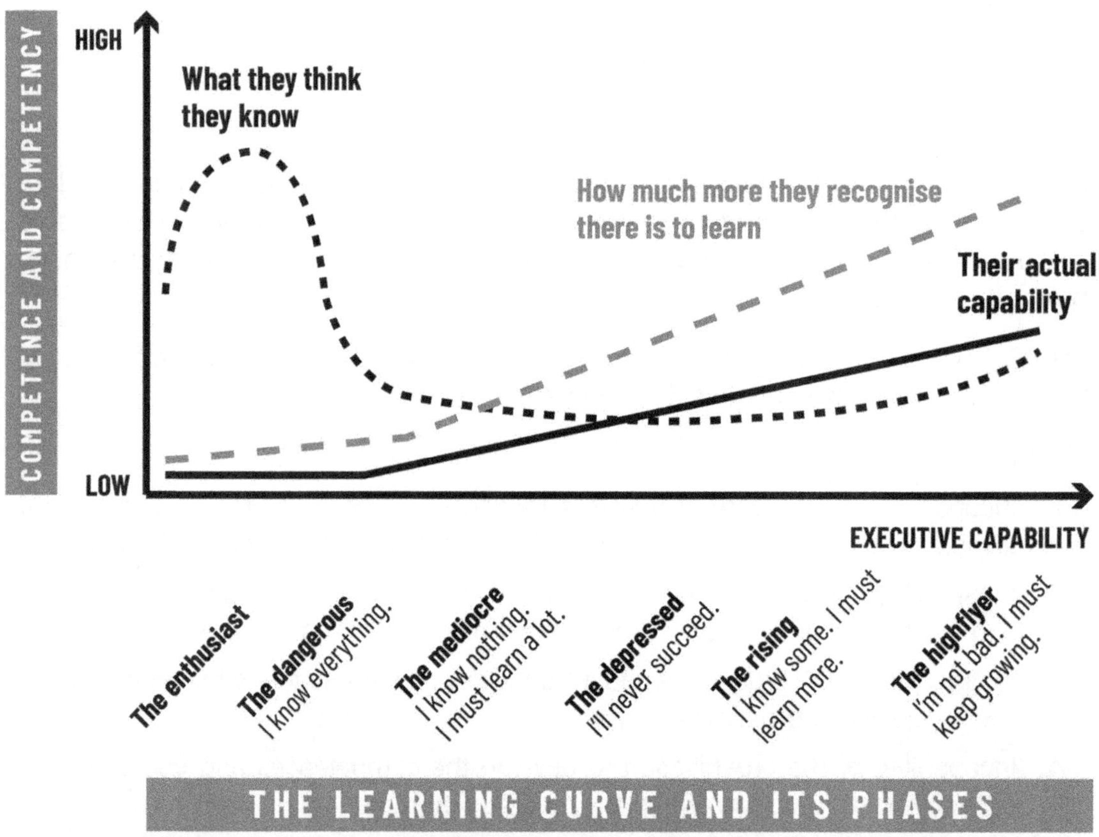

Figure 9.1: The danger of over-confidence, lack of self-knowledge, and lack of self-confidence

Occasionally, it is useful to remember:

- The law of unintended consequences:
  - How to expect the unexpected, and to manage it
  - How to vision the need for change, plan for it, and act on it
- A famous quote from the Greek philosopher, Socrates: 'I know that I know nothing.'

The Dunning–Kruger effect[59]

The more we learn about our processes, our competences, our competencies, and our business, the more we realise how little we know. When we begin to learn about a new topic or new skill, we might overestimate our competence and competency, as we haven't yet discovered all the things we don't know or haven't mastered. As we learn more about what we don't know or haven't mastered, our confidence tends to diminish. When we continue to learn, our confidence increases again being more educated (Figure 9.2).

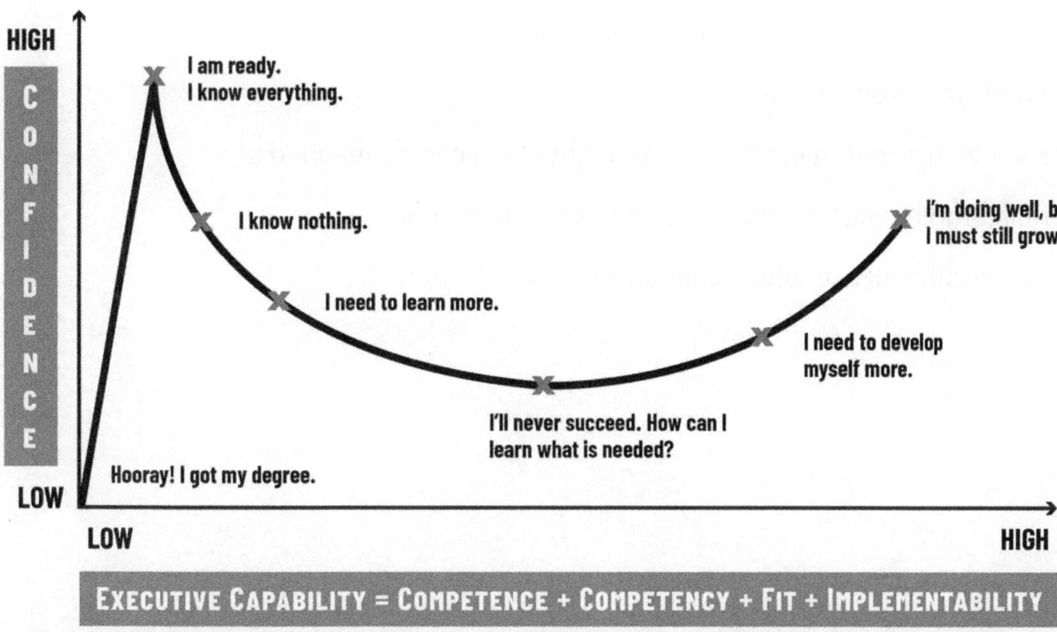

Figure 9.2: The Dunning–Kruger effect

59 Kruger J. and Dunning D. (1999) *Unskilled and Unaware of It: How Difficulties in Recognizing One's Own Incompetence Lead to Inflated Self-Assessments.*

In this book, we give you the necessary framework for developing your management and leadership competences and competencies, as the distillation of our sixty-five combined years of successful executive and consultancy work, our own research and extensive meta-research.

We also give you an extensive bibliography for each chapter, indicating the significance of these works to the content of this book. Some of the listed works present research supporting our views, others discuss in more detail certain of the issues we cover here, while the rest can serve as tools for the development of the various competencies and competences and as guides for what is essential and what should be avoided. Don't be surprised if you notice diverse views – they do exist.

Our mission in writing this book is to help our readers to realise their dream of a successful executive career, and organisations to develop the executive competencies and competences of their people and, through them, achieve success and sustainability.

Our wish and vision is to witness organisations thrive to the benefit of all their stakeholders, including wider society and the environment, on a local and a global scale.

Now, the ball is in your court. Play the game!

We wish you every success.

We would love your feedback and thoughts, and can be reached at:

koralia.timotheou@strategic-change-consultants.com

nicos.timotheou@strategic-change-consultants.com

AFTERWORD

I, Nicos, have followed a half-century-long successful engineering and executive career that culminated in heading, as its CEO, CYTA, the state-owned telecommunications operator of Cyprus, one of the country's larger and most technologically advanced organisations and probably the most diverse and complicated operator in Europe. After my early retirement, I followed a successful and rewarding consultancy career.

In this book, Koralia and I claim that to be a successful executive, one must satisfy three prerequisites:

- Have profound comprehension of the organisational entity one is appointed to head
- Master the management process and have the competency to execute it productively, ie effectively, efficiently and at the specified operational and outcome quality
- Understand well human nature, master the leadership process, and develop and implement the competency and willingness to lead the people of the organisation in creating and delivering value in a sustainable way

I was lucky to three times go through the learning process of satisfying these prerequisites, at increasing levels.

As a teenager, I helped my self-made father operate, maintain and repair his small factory staffed by five seasonal workers. I got acquainted – the hard way, getting my hands dirty – with the engineering infrastructure of three production systems (an olive mill, an olive-kernel oil production plant and a soap production plant). I learnt how to plan production and sales and to manage and lead a small bicommunal team of workers in exerting themselves in adverse conditions. I also learnt a few essential support activities, such as purchasing, stock control, book-keeping and accounting. In this way, I laid the foundation for an executive career and became interested in engineering.

I went on to study at and graduate from the National Technical University of Athens, Greece as a Diplomate Electrical and Mechanical Engineer. Over the course of my five-year studies, in addition to the many engineering subjects, I took elective courses in production management, operational research, and investment theories and methods. I became genuinely interested in management and leadership.

In my professional life, I combined my job with two of my hobbies: information and communications engineering, and management and leadership. In my private life, I indulged my third and fourth hobbies, mechanical and civil engineering and, later, sailing. In addition, I have always been an avid reader.

At the beginning of my career as a young engineer, I headed technical teams installing telecommunications systems. In parallel, I attended an evening postgraduate course leading to a Diploma in Scientific Industrial Management. In this way, I continued developing my theoretical management competence while, at work, I was practising the management techniques I was learning at college and the leadership competencies I had acquired at my father's factory, broadened at cadet school and honed as a young officer during my fourteen-month military service. I was awarded the Diploma in Scientific Industrial Management having submitted a thesis on management techniques with an emphasis on organisation and methods (O&M). Later, during my telecoms engineering work, I completed a one-year professional postgraduate course in Germany where, in parallel to the technical syllabus, I was taught the German systematic approach to management and problem-solving. During this phase of my career, I had the good fortune to work for a few months in Japan with one of the big telecoms manufacturers and studied the Japanese teamwork and attention to quality.

Over the course of my ten-year (1973–1982) telecoms engineering career leading technical teams and managing projects, I developed a deep understanding of the telecommunications infrastructure and systems and headed many installation projects all over the country. I honed my leadership competency while implementing the latest management techniques and leadership approaches, achieving an extraordinary increase in effectiveness and efficiency that cut project duration and labour consumption by as much as 50%. I discovered that empowering my people through training, coaching and delegation worked wonders, not only in regard to productivity but equally to alignment, engagement, commitment, loyalty and, above all, in fostering extreme ownership of projects, targets and results.

Over the next twelve years (1982–1995), my career advanced in a new, very different direction. I was mandated to plan and execute an organisation-wide process-reengineering and automation programme, covering initially the budget lifecycle of the organisation and, subsequently, all of its core and most of its support processes. At the beginning of this period, I became acquainted, entirely by chance, with Professor Andrew Kakabadse. Soon afterwards, I attended one of his early leadership development workshops, underwent a battery of his assessment for development tests, and was surprised to hear his verdict. To be frank, at the time, I believed his predictions were unrealistically positive and ambitious but, unbelievably (to me), he proved to be absolutely right.

Managing the process-reengineering and automation programme, I headed the building of various enterprise business architectures – following James Martin's Information Engineering philosophy and methodology – and acquired a deep comprehension of the organisation's core, support and staff processes and data, as well as of all technical infrastructures and systems. I continued developing my management and leadership capabilities, attending courses at Ashbridge, and Cranfield School of Management.

Heading the information management division and information systems development teams, I further honed, on the job, my management and leadership competence and competency. Implementing the reengineered and automated processes, I acquired broad experience in effecting radical change across the organisation from end to end. During this time, I applied various state-of-the-art management and leadership approaches and prepared myself for significant business reengineering, attending Michael Hammer's business (process) reengineering seminars in the USA.

Having been promoted to assistant general manager (the equivalent of executive vice president), in 1996 I developed and headed, during the next year, the execution of a fully fledged business reengineering programme, which transformed the slow-moving state-owned organisation into a lean, agile and innovative enterprise. During implementation, I was promoted (in 1998) to CEO, a post in which I served for nine years, successfully employing the latest management and leadership activities, methods and techniques, elevating the organisation to unprecedented productivity, profitability and innovation levels for Cyprus and beyond.

During my tenure as CEO, and afterwards, I continued to meet periodically with Professors Andrew and Nada Kakabadse to discuss management and leadership issues and their latest research findings, comparing these to my own empirical findings, while following the most recent literature on these subjects.

Since my early retirement from Cyprus Telecoms in 2007, I have consulted with a few of the most forward-looking local and international private and public organisations and served as a non-executive director on a number of boards. In 2014, I was joined in my consulting work by Koralia, my daughter, a graduate civil and environmental engineer who, by that time, had served for sixteen years with the consulting group of the Cyprus branch of one of the big four accounting firms and consulted with a couple of hundred local and international organisations of various sizes on all kinds of business issues.

Over our long careers, Koralia and I had come to two significant conclusions. First, there is an urgent need for holistic and cohesive development of the organisational, management and leadership competence and competency of executives at all levels, from the aspiring young graduate who has just been recruited as a junior executive, to the upcoming, mid-level and even the seasoned executive. Second, there is a wide gap in the specialised executive development literature and a lack of services that could have helped meet that need.

That's why we decided to write the definitive guide to *Executive Excellence* you have in your hands, which aims at bridging that gap. We hope you will find it useful.

Nicos Timotheou, Cyprus

* * *

Hi, I'm Koralia. In my personal life, I am a mother of three daughters and an adventure-seeker. I am also a lifelong learner who aspires to grow a little bit more every single day. Professionally, I am an intuitive life coach also practising hypno-empowerment. Eighteen years in management consulting have taught me that no matter how hard the external consultant tries to achieve a result for you, all efforts will fail if you do not play your part. Every achievement requires commitment, and commitment begins at the top. The people at the top need to manage and lead. For that, they need tools – this is what we are hoping to provide you with.

My brightest days have been those when my clients have turned to say, 'Thank you. We needed this. What you did for us has helped. We will take it from here.' My most profound disappointments have included seeing people demoralised merely because they had not been given direction, attention, feedback or gratitude for their work. Being a manager and a leader is a role that is assigned to us in the narrative of our life. We either play it well, or moderately, or we can even be terrible at it. We don't have to accept this assignment. Not everybody will. If we do, we need to honour the role, the script and the rest of the cast. We have to put our soul into it. Otherwise, it will be lifeless.

When you are the manager and leader, people will turn to you for almost everything. Please, remember that you are there for them as much as they are there for you. If we want to make our organisations and our societies better, we must focus on our executives – our managers and leaders – invest in their development so that they can, in turn, lift the entire organisation, its people, its products, its services and its processes. We must empower our leaders to cultivate sustainable and nurturing cultures. Culture is key and it is built on example. In this effort, we are here for you, as best as we can. We want to help make you, the leaders of today and tomorrow, extraordinary; skilled and sharp, resilient and agile, but most of all respectful. Respectful to your staff, your bosses, your customers, your communities. And more eager to learn.

In this book, we have compiled and condensed everything we have learnt in our lives about organisational, management and leadership excellence, everything that could possibly benefit you in your role as an executive. Working through our book may, at times, prove overwhelming and tiring. It is not supposed to be a bedtime reading. It is intended as a guide and if you use it as such, it will support you down your management and leadership path, and past many common pitfalls. We believe in you, your abilities and your will.

Best of luck, and enjoy your business class flight as a successful executive.

Koralia Timotheou, Cyprus

GET TO IT!

In 2008, our consultancy firm, NAN Strategic Change Consultants Ltd, was born.

We are a boutique consultancy firm providing advice and support to executives and organisations wishing to grow beyond their boundary lines and well into the new fast-changing business era.

The widespread international economic crisis, coupled with the global crisis in ethics and values, is increasingly driving business people to escape from today's well-worn business models. Many executives have finally begun to revert to management and leadership styles that not only value customers but also empower and inspire their employees, support their local and global communities every day (rather than once a year), treat their competitors fairly and respectfully, and align their business goals with those of their suppliers, partners and sellers in both directions.

In today's highly competitive environment, which is characterised by chaoplexity and glocalisation, only enterprises with leadership that creates value for all stakeholders succeed and achieve sustainability.

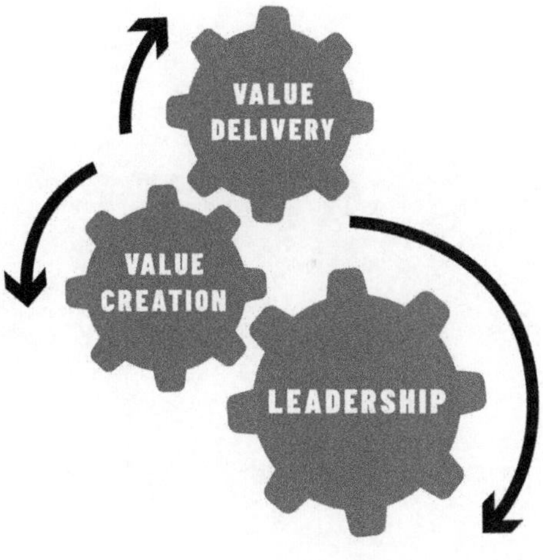

This is the business world that we believe in. This is what we are determined to help our clients achieve. Their success, and your success, in creating and delivering value is our success and pride.

From strengthening your executive – leadership and management – capability and helping you improve your organisational culture, to refining your processes and inspiring your people to increase their productivity; from improving your relationship with your customers, to fostering commitment; from formulating your business values, to formulating KPIs and setting your operational and strategic targets; from measuring your performance, to introducing performance-based employee payment schemes.

We and our extensive partner network are at your disposal, ready to advise and support you and sail together on the journey to executive and organisational excellence in creating and delivering value.

As a first step, we propose organising a residential half-day seminar on executive development for one of your executive teams, at which we will present the gist of our *Executive Excellence* guide or a three- to five-day fully fledged seminar-workshop.

Please, do not hesitate to drop us a line to discuss your mission, vision, needs, or your concerns or to organise a seminar/workshop.

Nicos and Koralia

koralia.timotheou@strategic-change-consultants.com

nicos.timotheou@strategic-change-consultants.com

www.strategic-change-consultants.com

BIBLIOGRAPHY

The following bibliography is arranged by chapter, with the most significant works in bold.

Chapter One – The Executive's World

Brady B. and Brady T. (2000) *Rules of the Game – Business: A Player's Guide.* Harlow: Pearson Education Limited.

Christensen C. (1997) *The Innovator's Dilemma: When New Technologies Cause Great Firms to Fail.* Boston, MA: Harvard Business School Press.

Fairholm, M. and Fairholm G. (2009) *Understanding Leadership Perspectives: Theoretical and Practical Approaches.* Cham, Switzerland: Springer.

Griffin D. and Stacey R. (2005) *Complexity and the Experience of Leading Organisations.* London: Routledge.

Harnish V. (2014) *Scaling Up: How a Few Companies Make It... and Why the Rest Don't.* Asburn, VA: Gazelles, Inc.

Kakabadse A. (2015) *The Success Formula: How Smart Leaders Deliver Outstanding Value.* London: Bloomsbury Information.

Kakabadse A. and Kakabadse N. (2001) *The Geopolitics of Governance.* Basingstoke: Palgrave MacMillan.

Krause D. (1995) *Sun Tzu: The Art of War for Executives.* London: Nicholas Breadley Publishing.

Logan D., King J. and Fischer-Wright H. (2008) *Tribal Leadership: Leveraging Natural Groups to Build a Thriving Organization.* New York, NY: HarperCollins Publishers.

Martin J. (2006) *The Meaning of the 21st Century: A Vital Blueprint for Ensuring Our Future.* New York, NY: Riverhead Books.

Rampersad H. and Hussain S. (2014) *Authentic Governance: Aligning Personal Governance with Corporate Governance.* Cham, Switzerland: Springer International Publishing.

Roberts J. (2004) *The Modern Firm: Organisational Design for Performance and Growth.* Oxford: Oxford University Press.

Thaler R. H. and Sunstein C. R. (2008) *Nudge: Improving Decisions About Health, Wealth, and Happiness.* London: Yale University Press.

Ulrich D. and Smallwood N. (2003) *Why the Bottom Line Isn't! How to Build Value Through People and Organization.* Hoboken, NJ: John Wiley & Sons.

Zaffron S. and Logan D. (2009) *The Three Laws of Performance: Rewriting the Future of Your Organization and Your Life.* San Francisco, CA: Jossey-Bass.

Chapter Two – The Business Model

Gassmann O., Frankenberger K. and Csik M. (2014) *The Business Model Navigator.* Harlow: Pearson Education Limited.

Koestler A. (1976) *The Ghost in the Machine.* New York, NY: Random House.

Massy W. F. (2016) *Reengineering the University: How to be Mission Centered, Market Smart and Margin Conscious.* Baltimore, MD: Johns Hopkins University Press.

Osterwalder A. and Pigneur Y. (2010) *Business Model Generation.* Hoboken, NJ: John Wiley & Sons Inc.

Tennet J. and Friend G. (2010) *Guide to Business Modelling.* London: The Economist in association with Profile Books Ltd.

Chapter Three – Organisational Architectures And Process Management

Freund J. and Rueker B. (2014) *Real-Life BPMN.* Berlin: Camunda.

Hammer M. (1996) *Beyond Reengineering.* New York, NY: HarperBusiness.

Jeston J. and Nelis J. (2014) *Business Process Management.* New York, NY: Routledge.

Martin, J. (1995) *The Great Transition: Using the Seven Disciplines of Enterprise Engineering to Align People, Technology, and Strategy.* New York, NY: Amacom.

Martin J. (1989) *Information Engineering: A Trilogy.* Englewood, NJ: Prentice Hall.

Petrie, C. J., Jr (Editor) (1992) *Enterprise Integration Modelling: Proceedings of the First International Conference.* Cambridge, MA: The MIT Press.

Smith H. and Fingar P. (2003) *Business Process Management: The Third Wave.* Tampa, FL: Meghan-Kiffer Press.

The Business Process Management Group (2005) *In Search of Business Excellence.* Tampa, FL: Meghan-Kiffer Press.

Whittle R. and Myrick C. (2005) *Enterprise Business Architecture: The Formal Link between Strategy and Results.* Boca Raton, FL: Auberbach Publications.

Chapter Four – Generic Business Subprocesses

Babich P. (2015) *Hoshin Handbook: Chart the Course for Your Organization.* Poway, CA: Total Quality Engineering Inc.

Cokins G. (2004) *Performance Management: Finding the Missing Pieces (to Close the Intelligence Gap).* Hoboken, NJ: John Wiley & Sons.

Evans V. (2013) *Key Strategy Tools: The 80+ Tools for Every Manager to Build a Winning Strategy.* Harlow: Pearson Education Ltd.

Liker J. K. and Convis G. L. (2012) *The TOYOTA Way to Lean Leadership: Achieving and Sustaining Excellence Through Leadership Development.* New York, NY: McGraw-Hill.

Papaioannou J. (2007) *Project Management: Survival of the Fittest.* Nicosia: Kosmos Business Systems Ltd.

Walsh C. (2008) *Key Management Ratios: The 100+ Ratios Every Manager Needs to Know.* Harlow: Pearson Education Ltd.

Chapter Five – Managing The Organisation In Executing Its Mission And Vision

Dolence, M. G. (1997) *Working Toward Strategic Change: A Step-by-Step Guide to the Planning Process.* San Francisco, CA: Jossey-Bass.

Drucker P. (1969) *The Practice of Management*. London: Heinemann.

Kakabadse A. and Kakabadse N. (2008) *Leading the Board*. Basingstoke: Palgrave.

Kaplan R. and Norton D. (2006) *Alignment: Using the Balanced Scorecard to Create Corporate Synergies*. Boston, MA: Harvard Business School Press.

Kim C. and Mauborgne R. (2015) *Blue Ocean Strategy, Expanded Edition: How to Create Uncontested Market Space and Make the Competition Irrelevant*. Boston, MA: Harvard Business Review Press.

Leinwand, P. (2016) *Strategy That Works: How Winning Companies Close the Strategy-to-Execution Gap*. Boston, MA: Harvard Business Review Press.

Mintzberg H. (2004) *Managers Not MBAs: A Hard Look at the Soft Side of Managing and Management Development*. San Francisco, CA: Berrett-Koehler Publishers, Inc.

Nolan R. and Croson D. (1995) *Creative Destruction: A Six-Stage Process for Transforming the Organization*. Boston, MA: Harvard Business School Press.

Recardo R. and Totehri T. (2014) *Strategic Planning Unleashed: An Applied Methodology and Toolkit*. Minneapolis, MN: Ruis Publishing.

Rowntree D. (1989) *The Manager's Book of Checklists*. Aldershot: Gower Publishing Company Ltd.

Chapter Six – Leading The Organisation In Creating And Delivering Value

Belbin M. (1996) *How to Build Successful Teams* (CD-ROM). Oxford: Butterworth-Heinemann.

Belbin M. (2000) *Beyond the Team*. Oxford: Butterworth-Heinemann.

Dourado P. and Blackburn P. (2005) *Seven Secrets of Inspired Leaders: How to Achieve the Extraordinary... by the Leaders Who Have Been There and Done It*. Chichester: Capstone Publishing Ltd.

Edmonds C. (2014) *The Culture Engine: A Framework for Driving Results, Inspiring Your Employees, and Transforming Your Workplace*. Hoboken, NJ: John Wiley & Sons.

Evans V. (2013) *FT Essential Guide to Developing a Business Strategy: How to Use Strategic Planning to Start Up or Grow Your Business*. Harlow: Pearson Education Ltd.

Evans V. (2013) *The FT Essential Guide to Writing a Business Plan*. Harlow: Pearson Education Ltd.

Horgan J. (1996) *The End of Science: Facing the Limits of Knowledge in the Twilight of the Scientific Age*. New York, NY: Basic Books.

Kakabadse A. (2015) *The Success Formula: How Smart Leaders Deliver Outstanding Value*. London: Bloomsbury Information.

Kakabadse A. and Kakabadse N. (1999) *Essence of Leadership*. Andover: Cengage Learning EMEA.

Kotter J. (1999) *John Kotter on What Leaders Really Do*. Boston, MA: Harvard Business Review Press.

Logan D., King J. and Fischer-Wright H. (2008) *Tribal Leadership: Leveraging Natural Groups to Build a Thriving Organization*. New York, NY: HarperCollins Publishers.

Richman R. (2014) *The Culture Blueprint*. Creative Commons License: Culture Hackers.

Tsoukas H. and Mylonopoulos N. et al (2004) *Organizations as Knowledge Systems: Knowledge, Learning and Dynamic Capabilities.* Basingstoke: Palgrave.

Ulrich D., Zenger J. and Smallwood N. (1999) *Results-based Leadership.* Boston, MA: Harvard Business School Press.

Chapter Seven – The Executive: Manager Or Leader?

Daverne G. (2017) *Secrets From the Podium: True Musical Happenings.* Kindle Editions.

Mauceri J. (2018) *Maestros and Their Music: The Art and Alchemy of Conducting.* New York, NY: Knopf Publishing Group.

Chapter Eight – The Successful Executive's Competencies And Competences

Allenbaugh, E. (2002) *Deliberate Success: Realise Your Vision with Purpose, Passion, and Performance.* Newburyport, MA : Career Press Inc.

Benton D. (1999) *Secrets of a CEO Coach: Your Personal Training Guide to Thinking Like a Leader and Acting Like a CEO.* New York, NY: McGraw-Hill.

Bodaken B. and Fritz R. (2006) *The Managerial Moment of Truth: The Essential Step in Helping People Improve Performance.* New York, NY: Free Press.

Carucci R. and Hansen E. (2014) *Rising to Power: The Journey of Exceptional Executives.* Austin, TX: Green Leaf Book Group Press.

Donkin R. (2001) *Blood, Sweat and Tears: The Evolution of Work.* London: Texere Publishing Ltd.

Gestner L. (2003) *Who Says Elephants Can't Dance?* London: HarperCollinsPublishers.

Harvard Business Review (2017) *Harvard Business Review Manager's Handbook: The 17 Skills Leaders Need to Stand Out.* Boston, MA: Harvard Business Review Press.

Herman C. (2017) *Become a Leader: How to Transition from Manager to Leader.* Boston, MA: Harvard Business Review Press.

Horstman M. (2016) *The Effective Manager.* Hoboken, NJ: John Wiley & Sons.

Mariama-Arthur K. (2018) *Poised for Excellence: Fundamental Principles of Effective Leadership in the Boardroom and Beyond.* Basingstoke: Palgrave MacMillan.

Meir L. (2017) *How to Improve Your Leadership and Management Skills: Effective Strategies for Business Managers.* CreateSpace Independent Publishing Platform.

Osborne C. (2008, 2015) *Leadership.* London: Penguin Random House.

Rampersad H. and Hussain S. (2014) *Authentic Governance: Aligning Personal Governance with Corporate Governance.* Cham, Switzerland: Springer International Publishing.

Starr J. (2016) *The Coaching Manual: The Definitive Guide to the Process, Principles and Skills of Personal Coaching.* Harlow: Pearson Education Ltd.

Starr J. (2014) *The Mentoring Manual: Your Step by Step Guide to Being a Better Mentor.* Harlow: Pearson Education Ltd.

Tate W. (2003) *The Organisational Leadership Audit.* Cambridge: Cambridge Strategy Publications Ltd.

Thomas M. (2006) *The Complete CEO: The Executive's Guide to Consistent Peak Performance. Chichester: Capstone Publishing Ltd.*

Tocquigny R. and Butcher A. (2012) *When Core Values are Strategic: How the Basic Values of Procter & Gamble Transformed Leadership at Fortune 500 Companies.* Upper Saddle River, NJ: FT Press.

Tsoukas H. et al. (2004) *Managing the Future: Strategic Foresight in the Knowledge Economy.* Oxford: Blackwell Publishing Ltd.

Van Velsor E., McCauley C. D. and Ruderman M. N. (Editors) (2010) *Handbook of Leadership Development.* San Francisco, CA: Jossey-Bass.

Welsh J. (2011) *Straight from the Gut.* London: Headline Book Publishing.

Willink J. (2017) *Discipline Equals Freedom: Field Manual.* New York, NY: St. Martin's Press.

Willink J. (2017) *Extreme Ownership: How U.S. Navy SEALs Lead and Win.* New York, NY: St. Martin's Press.

Zenger J. H. and Folkman J. R. (2009) *The Extraordinary Leader: Turning Good Managers into Extraordinary Leaders.* New York, NY: McGraw-Hill.

Epilogue

Kruger J. and Dunning D. (1999) 'Unskilled and Unaware of It: How Difficulties in Recognizing One's Own Incompetence Lead to Inflated Self-Assessments'. *Journal of Personality and Social Psychology,* 77(6), 1121–1134.

Schein E. with DeLisi P., Kampas P., and Sonduck M. (2003) *DEC is Dead, Long Live DEC: The Lasting Legacy of Digital Equipment Corporation.* San Francisco, CA: Berrett-Koehler Publishers, Inc.

INDEX

In the following index, significant references are shown in bold. Furthermore, terms appearing more than nine times in the book are shown in bold with page numbers for only the most significant references.

A

B

C

I

K

L

M

ACKNOWLEDGEMENTS

We acknowledge with sincere gratitude the input and insights of all those who devoted their valuable time to exchanging, over many years, views, opinions and ideas with us, or who have reviewed our manuscript and fed back to us useful comments, suggestions and or praise:

- Prof Andrew Kakabadse, Professor of Governance and Strategic Leadership, Henley Business School, UK, and Emeritus Professor, Cranfield School of Management, UK
- Prof CL Max Nikias, President Emeritus, University of Southern California, USA
- Constantinos Petrides, Minister of the Interior, Republic of Cyprus
- Dr Michael Sarris, Former World Bank Department Director, Former Finance Minister
- Nicos Peristianis, PhD, Founding President, University of Nicosia
- Prof George Boustras, Dean of the School of Business Administration, European University, Nicosia
- Demetris Georgiades, Chairman of the Fiscal Council of the Republic of Cyprus
- Dimis Michaelides, consultant, author, speaker and workshop leader on leadership, creativity and innovation
- Michael Spanos, Green Dot Cyprus Chairman, acclaimed CEO, sought-after non-executive director and experienced consultant
- Antonios Spanos, EFQM Excellence Ambassador, EU-approved management and CSR Expert
- Nikos Angelopoulos, Group CIO, MTN, Johannesburg, South Africa
- Dr Christos Georgiades, MD, PhD, FSIR, FCIRSE, Associate Professor of Radiology & Surgery, Director of Interventional Oncology, Vascular & Interventional Radiology, Johns Hopkins University, USA
- Prof Nada Kakabadse, Professor of Policy, Governance and Ethics at Henley Business School, UK
- Odysseas Michaelides, PhD, Auditor General, Republic of Cyprus
- Angelos Gregoriades, Chairman, KPMG (Cyprus) Ltd
- Stavros Ioannou, CEO, Grant Thornton, Cyprus
- Christoforos Christodoulides, Director of Administration and Finance, Open University of Cyprus

- Dr Paris Cleanthous, Director of MBA and MPSM Programmes, Associate Professor of Marketing and Strategy, CIIM
- Yianna Thalassinou, Director of Musica Mundana Music School, Cyprus Music Schools Organisation President, conductor of young and adult choirs

Our deepest gratitude is owed to the hundreds of our colleagues, associates and customers who made possible the creation and delivery of value during our diverse careers, and who helped us develop our competences and competencies; and to our teachers, trainers, coaches and mentors, in Greece, the UK, Cyprus, Germany, the USA and Japan. They are so many that we cannot possibly mention them all by name.

A warm thank you also to all those who made this book possible, and especially Rethink Press Managing Editor, Lucy McCarraher, Managing Publisher, Joe Gregory, Project Manager, Kathleen Steeden, our editor, Abigail Woodford, our designer, Nelly Murariu, and our cover designer, Katie Bell.

Nicos and Koralia Timotheou

THE AUTHORS

Nicos Timotheou is a freelance consultant offering his services in the areas of leadership, enterprise business architectures, business reengineering and reorganisation, process management and automation, electronic communications management, strategic planning and analysis, and business excellence. He has worked for thirty-five years at Cyprus Telecoms (the incumbent state-owned telecoms operator of the Republic of Cyprus), ten of which as Manager of its Information Management Division and nine as its CEO. He has been instrumental in reengineering, automating and reforming the organisation by successfully practising what is exposed and recommended in this book. Since 2007, he has been consulting private and governmental organisations at the top executive and board of directors levels.

Koralia Timotheou is a freelance consultant offering her services in the areas of enterprise business architectures, process management, strategic planning and analysis, and business excellence. Previously, she worked for sixteen years as a consultant with one of the big four auditing firms, consulting more than one hundred local and international organisations on a wide spectrum of subjects, ranging from quality management to business continuity and anti-money laundering.

Recognising that the soul of every organisation is its people, Koralia is now assisting individuals in uncovering their best selves. To this end, she has recently enriched her career and now offers services as an Intuitive Life Coach and Rapid Transformation Facilitator.

More information can be found at:
www.strategic-change-consultants.com

THE AUTHORS